COUNSEL AND STRATEGY
IN MIDDLE ENGLISH
ROMANCE

This book considers Middle English romance from a new historical perspective, by examining its development, audience, and ethos against a background of thirteenth- and fourteenth-century royal–baronial conflict, which was largely precipitated by the reluctance of Henry III, Edward II, and Richard II to acknowledge the lords of the realm as the monarch's 'natural counsellors'. Friction between Plantagenet kings and dissident barons contributed to the development of parliament as a representative body and to the prominence of the 'problem of counsel' as a topos in learned and popular literature of the period. Rule by counsel, an ideal which informs medieval English government at every level – from royal, baronial, and manorial councils to parliament itself – is, it is argued, central to the ethos of Middle English romance; and the shire knights, the most influential members of the parliamentary 'commons', constitute the core of its socially diverse audience.

Sage advice, as supplied by a variety of 'counsellor' figures, provides the tactics for success in the hero's quest. The procedural formula of 'counsel and strategy' is tested against a number of romances: *Ywain and Gawain*, *Havelok*, *Gamelyn*, *Athelston*, a selection of nine romances from the Auchinleck manuscript, and *Sir Gawain and the Green Knight*. Some of these narratives, such as *Athelston* and *Beves of Hamtoun*, actively engage with the 'problem of counsel' and promote wholesome counsel as a strategy against tyranny. *Guy of Warwick*, on the other hand, explores the relationship between counsel and prowess, and *Floris and Blauncheflur* and *Kyng Alisaunder* focus on the planning and execution of a wide range of military and 'social' strategy. In *Sir Gawain and the Green Knight* the hero's rejection of divine guidance in favour of worldly counsel and strategy leads to his humiliation and failure.

GERALDINE BARNES is a Senior Lecturer in English Language and Early English Literature at the University of Sydney.

COUNSEL AND STRATEGY
IN MIDDLE ENGLISH
ROMANCE

Geraldine Barnes

D. S. BREWER

First published 1993 by D. S. Brewer, Cambridge

D. S. Brewer is an imprint of Boydell & Brewer Ltd
PO Box 9, Woodbridge, Suffolk IP12 3DF, UK
and of Boydell & Brewer Inc.
PO Box 41026, Rochester, NY 14604, USA

ISBN 0 85991 362 7

British Library Cataloguing-in-Publication Data
Barnes, Geraldine
 Counsel and Strategy in Middle English Romance
 I. Title
 820.9001
 ISBN 0–85991–362–7

 Library of Congress Cataloging-in-Publication Data
Barnes, Geraldine.
 Counsel and strategy in Middle English romance / Geraldine Barnes.
  p.   cm.
 Includes bibliographical references (p.   ) and index.
 ISBN 0–85991–362–7 (acid-free paper)
  1. English poetry – Middle English, 1100–1500 – History and
criticism. 2. Romances, English – History and criticism.
 3. Politics and literature – England. 4. Counseling in literature.
 5. Strategy in literature.
 PR321.B36 1993
 821′.030901 – dc20   92–43903

The paper used in this publication meets the minimum requirements
of American National Standard for Information Sciences –
Permanence of Paper for Printed Library Materials, ANSI Z39.48–1984

Printed in Great Britain by
St Edmundsbury Press Ltd, Bury St Edmunds, Suffolk

Contents

FOR
ROBERT D. BARNES
AND IN MEMORY OF
JEAN M. BARNES

Acknowledgments

For her wise counsel over many years, strategic aim with a life belt, and constructively critical readings of the first and final drafts of this book, I owe an inestimable debt to my friend and colleague, Diane Speed. For his largely unsought counsel, unflagging impatience, and unsurpassed *gyn* in the mouse crisis of 1991, I am grateful to my friend and spouse, Peter Wilson. The stimulating comments of the anonymous reader for Boydell & Brewer inspired some major revisions, for which a period of study leave from the University of Sydney provided time and opportunity. Sonya Jensen, Annette Krausmann, Judy Quinn, and Diane Speed have been generous with their computer expertise; Peter Wilson with his prowess in computer packing and transportation throughout the southwestern United States. A grant from the University of Sydney, shared with Diane Speed and Betsy Taylor, made possible the expert research assistance of Florence Percival in the latter stages of compositon.

Preface

The Fool-Trickster has received its fair share of social and literary attention over the last fifty years; its less flamboyant *alter ego*, the Wise Counsellor, has, on the other hand, attracted little notice.[1] Wise Counsellors nevertheless play crucial parts as shapers of policy and guides to ethics in medieval epic, romance, and overtly didactic narrative. The two *personae* are not, moreover, mutually exclusive: sometimes, in figures such as Merlin, prophet, magician, and sage of Arthurian legend; Njál, moral and legal counsellor, and deviser of elaborate tricks, in the Icelandic *Njáls saga*; and the less celebrated prophetic fool in Chrétien's *Li Contes del Graal*,[2] Fool-Trickster and Wise Counsellor are one and the same.

In literature and in history, the counsellor's office may be political, paedagogical, or moral: to interpret or expatiate upon religious, judicial, and intellectual authority, to offer practical advice, to devise strategy, or to advise against unwise or ill-considered action. Expertise in counsel is often the reward of advanced years: the topos of *sapientia et fortitudo* – the wisdom of maturity and the vigour of youth – is a motif which permeates classical and medieval epic.[3] In the vast amount of secular 'counsel' literature produced in the Middle Ages (mirrors of princes, chivalric manuals, courtesy books, and the like) the counsellor's authority is often vested in the age and experience of figures like the hermit in Ramón Llull's *Libre del orde de cavayleria* and the fathers in the Old Norwegian *Konungs Skuggsjá* and Middle English *Book of the Knight of La Tour Landry*.

---

1 On the former, see Enid Welsford, *The Fool. His Social and Literary History* (1935; rpr. New York, 1961); William Willeford, *The Fool and His Scepter: A Study in Clowns and Jesters and Their Audience* (Evanston, Ill. , 1969); Paul V.A. Williams, *The Fool and the Trickster. Studies in honour of Enid Welsford* (Cambridge and Totowa, N.J., 1979); Sandra Billington, *A Social History of the Fool* (Brighton and New York, 1984). See also Philippe Ménard, 'Les fous dans société médiévale. Le témoignage de la littérature au XIIe et au XIIIe siècle,' *Romania* 98 (1977), 433–59; Penelope B.R. Doob, *Nebuchadnezzar's Children. Conventions of Madness in Middle English Literature* (New Haven and London, 1974). For a recent discussion of the role of the wise man, especially as poet, in oral societies, see Morton W. Bloomfield and Charles W. Dunn, *The Role of the Poet in Early Societies* (Cambridge, 1989), pp. 110–12, 117–18.

2 Who predicts Perceval's greatness. See Alfons Hilka, ed., *Der Percevalroman (Li Contes del graal)* (Halle, 1932), ll. 1058–62.

3 See Ernst Robert Curtius, trans. Willard R. Trask, *European Literature and the Latin Middle Ages* (New York and Evanston, 1963), pp. 170–77.

The hero's education – chivalric, moral, and, sometimes, scholarly – is a recurrent motif in medieval European romance.[4]

The ruler's need for wise counsel is a theme in Old English heroic and didactic literature: in *Beowulf*, the hero mourns Æscere as, among other things, a wise counsellor;[5] pre- and post-conquest works on statesmanship written in England, such as Ælfric's *De XII abusivis* (late tenth century) and John of Salisbury's *Policraticus* (1156–59) emphasize the ruler's obligation to seek and heed wise counsel.[6] 'Counsel' also plays a pivotal role in medieval English government. Throughout the Anglo-Saxon, Anglo-Norman, and Plantagenet periods, the counselling of lord by vassal or retainer, and king by *witan* ('wise ones'), magnates, or parliament is both privilege and obligation, serving as a bulwark against tyranny and insurance against weak leadership.

Anglo-Saxon kings had the counsel of the *witan*, 'a fluid, expandable and mainly aristocratic assembly of bishops and abbots, earls and thegns'.[7] In the Norman period, the principle of *consilium et auxilium* governed the bond between lord and vassal.[8] The vassal was expected to give his lord honest counsel; the lord was dependent on such consultation to establish the extent of the support on which he could count in any undertaking:

> . . . the taking and giving of counsel was essential to the stability and hence the strength of a great lordship. If, for example, a lord were contemplating defiance of his own superior he would need to know how far his vassals would support him, for he was powerless without their armed service. . . . So what happened in practice was that before

4 See Madeleine Pelner Cosman, *The Education of the Hero in Arthurian Romance* (Chapel Hill, 1966).

5 'min runwita ond min rædbora' (Fr. Klaeber, ed., *Beowulf and The Fight at Finnsburg*, 3rd edn. (Boston, 1950), l. 1325.

6 'Impossibile enim est ut salubriter disponat principatum qui non agitur consilio sapientum' (Clemens C.I. Webb, ed., *Ioannis Saresberiensis Episcopi Carnotensis Policratici* [London, 1909; rpr. Frankfurt am Main, 1965], I, V:6, p. 549, ll. 15–17). ('For it is impossible to administer princely power wholesomely if the prince does not act on the counsel of wise men.' John Dickinson, trans., *The Statesman's Book of John of Salisbury* [New York, 1963], p. 85).

7 R. Allen Brown, *The Normans and the Norman Conquest* (Woodbridge, 1962; 2nd edn., 1985), p. 56. See further, Tryggvi J. Oleson, *The Witenagemot in the Reign of Edward the Confessor. A Study in the Constitutional History of Eleventh-Century England* (London, 1955).

8 'Consilium is cited side by side with *auxilium* by Fulbert of Chartres as one of the services due from a vassal to his lord. The vassal was bound to assist his lord by his advice, and since this advice was a form of service it implied an obligation on the vassal to attend his lord when the latter summoned him' (F. L. Ganshof, *Feudalism*, trans. Philip Grierson [London, New York, and Toronto, 1952], pp. 83–84).

making a decision or judgement the lord took counsel with his vassals as to what he should do.[9]

Consilium is frequently cited in medieval English sources as the necessary basis of the royal-baronial relationship.[10] The *Leges Henrici Primi*, for example, declare that Henry I (1100–35) has been crowned 'communi consilio et assensu Baronum regni Anglie'.[11] Nevertheless, the matter of royal counsel was an often contentious issue between king and barons in the thirteenth and fourteenth centuries. Among the early Plantagenet kings, relations between Edward I (1272–1307) and Edward III (1327–77) with the magnates who considered themselves the king's 'natural counsellors' were relatively harmonious, Henry III's (1216–72) acrimonious, and, in the cases of Edward II (1307–27) and Richard II (1377–99), ended in deposition.

The monarch's obligation to seek the 'counsel and consent' of the wider community of the realm as well, particularly in matters of finance, is the principle of the national assemblies or 'parliaments' instituted in the latter part of the thirteenth century. In the late fourteenth and early fifteenth century, the notion that a king should heed the advice of all his subjects becomes a repeated theme in the poetry of complaint, while the 'problem of counsel' is a major issue in the literature of late fifteenth-century social comment.[12]

The following discussion of a selection of that amorphous collection of Middle English 'popular' verse narratives, whose heroes range from members of the Round Table to scions of the rural gentry, and which are known, for want of a better appellation, as Middle English 'romance', focusses on *Ywain and Gawain*, *Havelok*, *Athelston*, *Gamelyn*, a number of works in National Library of Scotland Advocates' MS 19.2.1 (the Auchinleck manuscript), and *Sir Gawain and the Green Knight*. What, apart from an unsatisfactory generic label, do these diverse narratives have in common? The answer tendered in the following chapters is the *modus operandi* of 'counsel and strategy'.

The process of counsel often has independent thematic significance in Middle English romance, as a means of measuring royal and knightly

---

9 W.L. Warren, *The Governance of Norman and Angevin England 1066–1272* (Stanford, 1987), p. 14.

10 See, for example, *Bracton de Legibus et Consuetudinibus Angliæ*, ed. George E. Woodbine; *Bracton on the Laws and Customs of England*, trans. Samuel E. Thorne, 4 vols. (New Haven, 1922; rpr. Cambridge, Mass., 1968–77), II, 19, 21, 305.

11 L.J. Downer, *Leges Henrici Primi, edited with translation and commentary* (Oxford, 1972), p. 80.

12 See Arthur B. Ferguson, 'The Problem of Counsel in *Mum and the Sothsegger*,' *Studies in the Renaissance* 2 (1955), 67–83 (substantially rpr. in *idem, The Articulate Citizen and the English Renaissance* [Durham, N.C., 1965], pp. 75–90).

competence (see chs. 2–3). It also serves to formulate strategies which aid the hero in his quest (ch. 4). 'Strategy' may be a question of policy or military tactics, or, especially in narratives deriving in whole or in part from the Matter of Araby,[13] like *Beves of Hamtoun*, *Floris and Blauncheflur*, and *The Seven Sages of Rome* entail elaborate schemes and plots. In *Sir Tristrem* and *Sir Gawain and the Green Knight*, on the other hand, the Matter of Britain supplies a native tradition of wizardry, trickery, and cunning in the exploits of figures such as Merlin, Morgan le Fay, and Tristan.

'Counsel' (ME *counseil, red*) and 'strategy' (ME *red; gyn*) are elements in many of the French and Anglo-Norman narratives translated and adapted by the composers of Middle English romance. The 'epic' councils of war and policy-making in French *chansons de geste* reappear, for example, in English 'Charlemagne romances' such as *Otuel*, and also in *Beves of Hamtoun* and *Guy of Warwick*, adaptations of the Anglo-Norman 'ancestral romances', *Boeve de Haumtone* and *Gui de Warewic*. Merlin plays a pivotal role as adviser to four kings of Britain in *Of Arthour and of Merlin*, which derives from the French prose *Merlin*.

The argument of this study is that 'counsel and strategy' assumes a distinctively 'English' countenance in the romances, composed in the period *ca.* 1260–1400, which are considered in the following chapters. Methodologically, the approach is broadly 'historical', in that the ethos and audience of Middle English romance are located within the framework of government and administration in the late thirteenth and the fourteenth century, with particular reference to the role of lesser gentry and burgesses in parliament and local government. The prominence given to the process of consultation in Middle English romance is, it will be argued, a reflection of the feudal tradition of *consilium et auxilium* as well as a more topical reminder of the royal-baronial conflicts of the thirteenth and fourteenth centuries, which accelerated the emergence of the 'middle ground' of society as a political force.

As a procedural formula in Middle English romance, 'counsel and strategy' has a variety of applications: it may refer to the devising of military or political strategy; to the planning of strategy in the cause of love; or to the formulation of a stratagem to outwit an opponent or trap an enemy. After some consideration of the historical context, ethos, and audience of medieval romance in English (ch. 1), the starting point for analysis of individual works (chs. 2–5) will be the mechanism and medium of counsel and strategy: the consultative dialogue.

---

[13] The term coined by Dorothee Metlitzki in *The Matter of Araby in Medieval England* (New Haven and London, 1977).

CHAPTER ONE

'Working by Counsel' in Plantagenet England

The context, ethos, and audience of Middle English Romance

Councils, assemblies, parliaments

William Marshall, Earl of Pembroke, regent for the first part of the minority of Henry III, and possible exemplar for the fictional Guy of Warwick,[1] is, as Ronald Butt puts it, 'in many respects the epitome of the medieval ideal of chivalry,' not simply because of his loyalty and military accomplishments, but because his faithful service to Henry II, Richard I, and John was grounded in 'disinterested and candid advice'.[2] 'Work all things by counsel' may be a medieval literary commonplace,[3] but 'counsel' is also a principle, if not always a clearly defined institution, of feudal custom and constitutional rule in medieval England.

William the Conqueror's council, the *consilium* or *curia regis*,[4] which set the pattern for royal councils in the twelfth, thirteenth, and fourteenth centuries, was the 'feudalized' counterpart of gatherings of the *witan* in the Anglo-Saxon period.[5] Its capacities were executive, judicial, and legislative; its composition, depending on the circumstances, might include those of lesser rank as well as the tenants-in-chief. As Baldwin explains:

> . . . the medieval king's council . . . was intended to be a comprehensive body including 'of every estate some'. The king's councillors, with great differences of rank and employment . . . were retained largely for

---

1 M. Dominica Legge, *Anglo-Norman Literature and Its Background* (Oxford, 1963), p. 170.
2 Ronald Butt, *A History of Parliament. The Middle Ages* (London, 1989), p. 66.
3 See Curt F. Bühler, 'Wirk Alle Thyng By Conseil,' *Speculum* 24 (1949), 410–12.
4 The functions of the *consilium* and the *curia* were differentiated at a later period, *consilium* denoting the council in its advisory capacity, *curia* its status as a judicial body. See James Fosdick Baldwin, *The King's Council in England During the Middle Ages* (Oxford, 1913), p. 15 and ch. 3.
5 R. Allen Brown, *The Normans and the Norman Conquest*, pp. 211–12,

their individual services, some for law cases, some for diplomatic work, some to serve on commissions, and others for political counsel.[6]

In addition to convening sessions of 'general' or 'great' royal councils, English kings had been accustomed from Norman times to consult with a smaller 'kitchen cabinet' of confidants.[7]

The hierarchy of advisory bodies extended from the royal *consilium* to those of barons and knights. By the middle of the thirteenth century, most nobles and knights conducted their affairs with the aid of some form of council. Although, in the absence of written record, little is known of the workings of baronial councils, their core component was probably 'other peers, knights, esquires, and gentlemen'. By the four-teenth century they included men of professional expertise, such as lawyers and 'higher servants of yeoman stock'.[8] 'Even quite a modestly endowed gentleman,' remarks Maurice Keen, 'would have regular ad-visers whom he would describe as being "of counsel with him".'[9] The largest of these medieval English conciliar bodies were extensions of the king's 'great' councils,[10] the assemblies known as 'parliaments'.

Parliament, it has been said, is 'a new name for an old habit: the practice of kings to surround themselves from time to time with their great subjects in order to discuss and decide about important public matters'.[11] The term 'parliament' is used somewhat loosely in chancery records of the reign of Henry III to refer to special sessions of the royal council, such as that of 1237;[12] however, after the 'Provisions of Oxford' (1258), which required that three *parlemenz* be held a year, with twelve *prodes homes* chosen from *le commun* ('the commons') in addition to the king's counsellors,[13] 'parliament' normally refers to assemblies with rep-resentation from the ranks of the non-noble.

The thirteenth century brings the formal entry of the gentry[14] and

---

6 *The King's Council*, pp. 112–13.
7 Baldwin, *The King's Council*, pp. 10–12 (on the distinctions between 'general' and more private forms of royal councils and the problems they pose for modern his-torians, see pp. 105–06).
8 Kate Mertes, *The English Noble Household 1250–1600* (Oxford, 1988), pp. 128, 129 (for a discussion of baronial councils, see pp. 126–31). See also N. Denholm-Young, *Seignor-ial Administration in England* (London, 1937; rpr.1963), pp. 25–31.
9 Maurice Keen, *English Society in the Later Middle Ages, 1348–1500* (London, 1990), p. 174.
10 'Any assemblage of the estates . . . which was not of sufficient formality to be con-sidered a parliament continued to be known as a great council' (Baldwin, *The King's Council*, p. 106).
11 Edward Miller, *The Origins of Parliament* (London, 1960), p. 12.
12 See Butt, *A History of Parliament*, pp. 77–80.
13 R.E. Treharne, ed. I.J. Sanders, *Documents of the Baronial Movement of Reform and Rebellion 1258–1267* (Oxford, 1973), p. 110.
14 The term 'gentry' here and throughout this discussion refers to that 'economically

mercantile class into the affairs of the realm by way of increased respon-
siblities in local administration, parliaments, and other deliberative assemblies. The emergence of the shires and boroughs as a visible
component of English government was, to some extent, directly precipitated by the royal-baronial conflicts of the reigns of John, Henry III, and
Edward II, in which both sides found them a useful source of support.
John had summoned four *discretos homines* from every shire to a meeting,
which may or may not have taken place, to discuss the state of the
realm[15] as early as 1213. When Henry III assumed responsibility for
government in 1227, four knights from several shires were summoned to
an assembly, whose business, 'although not distinctly declared, is more
of the character of *political deliberation* than anything that has hitherto
been laid before them.'[16] The writ of summons to Henry's parliament of
1254 required representation by two knights from every shire to give
consent to financial supply for his campaign in Gascony.[17] During the
baronial reform movement later in Henry's reign, Simon de Montfort,
Earl of Leicester, along with the Earl of Gloucester, and Bishop of
Worcester, summoned three knights from every shire to an assembly at
St Albans in 1261.[18] Knights and, for the first time, borough representatives, were summoned in the king's name to Simon de Montfort's
parliament of January 20, 1265, to consider 'matters concerning our
realm, which we do not wish to settle without your counsel'.[19]

Parliaments were held at regular intervals during the reign of Edward
I, who, in a writ of 1295, declares that: 'It is the custom of the realm of
England . . . that in all things touching the state of the same realm there
should be asked the counsel of all whom the matter concerns.'[20] Edward

diverse class of landholders lying between the free peasantry and the magnates,
which was characterized by the dominant role it played in local justice, administration, and politics and which was frequently bound together through intermarriage, tenure and service' (S.L. Waugh, 'The Profits of Violence: The Minor Gentry in
the Rebellion of 1321–1322 in Gloucestershire and Herefordshire,' *Speculum* 52 [1977],
844).

15 'ad loquendum nobiscum de negotiis regni nostri' (William Stubbs, *Select Charters
and Other Illustrations of English Constitutional History* [7th edn., Oxford, 1890], p. 287).

16 Stubbs, *Select Charters*, p. 357.

17 Stubbs, *Select Charters*, pp. 375–77. On the parliament of 1254 and its significance as a
representative body, see Butt, *A History of Parliament*, pp. 93–95.

18 Treharne, *Documents of the Baronial Movement*, p. 247. On this period see *idem, The
Baronial Plan of Reform, 1258–1263* (Manchester, 1932; rpr. with additional material,
1971).

19 Treharne, *Documents of the Baronial Movement*, p. 301.

20 B. Wilkinson, *Studies in the Constitutional History of the Thirteenth and Fourteenth Centuries* (Manchester 1937; 2nd edn. 1952), p. 22 (citing William Stubbs, *The Constitutional History of England* [5th edn., Oxford, 1891], II, 159: 'consuetudo est regni
Angliae quod in negotiis tangentibus statum ejusdem regni requiratur consilium
omnium quos res tangit'). On Edward I's council and parliaments, see Michael
Prestwich, *Edward I*, ch. 17.

(and his successors) duly consulted wool merchants on the question of supply, the height of mercantile political power coinciding with the commencement of the Hundred Years' War.[21] Knights and burgesses, the latter 'usually merchants or craftsmen of the richer sort . . . a kind of citizens' aristocracy, controlling the borough court and the market,'[22] were present at Edward's first parliament in April, 1275. They were frequently summoned in the latter part of his reign, although called to only few assemblies between 1275 and 1290. Parliamentary writs of summons 1290 and 1294 formally summoned knights and burgesses 'ad consulendum et consentiendum'.[23]

From around the beginning of the reign of Edward III, the presence at national parliaments of knights and burgesses, as representatives of the commons, came to be regarded as essential. Although they had played no active role in the parliament of 1311, at which Edward II was forced to accept the 'New Ordinances' intended to re-establish the conciliar authority of the barons, knights were probably 'consulted on certain general grievances and points of detail'.[24] Knights and burgesses were summoned to all parliaments after 1325, where their numbers were substantial. Parliamentary writs of summons required the presence of two knights from every shire, two burgesses from every borough, and two citizens from every city. Records of attendance from 1290–1397 show an average of about 70 knights and 60 burgesses per parliament, re-election being frequent but by no means customary.[25] The number of 'chivalers et esquiers et citisayns et burgeis' listed by the writer of the *Anonimalle Chronicle* in his account of the 'Good Parliament' of 1376 is 280.[26]

Contemporary records do not define the exact meaning of 'counsel' in the context of medieval parliaments or the conciliar function of the repre-

---

21 See Sylvia Thrupp, *The Merchant Class of Medieval London [1300–1500]* (Chicago, 1948), p. 53. On the role of London merchants in municipal government and their representation in fourteenth-century parliaments, see Thrupp, *The Merchant Class*, pp. 53–102.

22 Butt, *A History of Parliament*, p. 123.

23 Stubbs, *Select Charters*, pp. 478, 481.

24 Butt, *A History of Parliament*, p. 189.

25 For details of shire and borough representation in the reigns of Edward I and Edward II, see J.G. Edwards, 'The Personnel of the Commons in Parliament under Edward I and Edward II,' in *Essays in Medieval History presented to Thomas Frederick Tout*, ed. A.G. Little and F.M. Powicke (Manchester, 1925), pp. 197–214 (rpr. in *Historical Studies of the English Parliament, Volume I: Origins to 1399*, ed. E.B. Fryde and Edward Miller [Cambridge, 1970], pp. 150–67); K.L. Wood-Legh, 'The Knights' Attendance in the Parliaments of Edward III,' *English Historical Review* 47 (1932), 398–413; N.B. Lewis, 'Re-election to Parliament in the Reign of Richard II,' *English Historical Review* 48 (1933), 364–94; May McKisack, *The Parliamentary Representation of the English Boroughs During the Middle Ages* (Oxford, 1932; rpr. 1962).

26 *The Anonimalle Chronicle, 1331–1381*, ed. V.H. Galbraith (London, 1927; rpr. 1970), p. 80.

sentatives of the commons. Wilkinson, however, delineates the crucial distinction between the advisory capacities of parliament and the king's council: 'Both represented a form of advice; but a very different form. In parliament the king wanted agreement rather than counsel . . . In his council he merely wanted discussion with those who were near enough or informed enough to supply his immediate need.'[27]

What medieval kings undoubtedly had in mind for parliamentary knights and burgesses by way of 'counsel and consent' was agreement to grants of money.[28] The question of taxation did, however, actively involve the joint participation of the commons and lords in a form of consultation, recorded in parliaments from Edward III's time, called *entrecommuner* ('to intercommunicate', 'to consult'), in which a group of between twenty-four and thirty knights and burgesses would consult with a committee of barons.[29] The consent of the commons was not necessarily a foregone conclusion. The macaronic poem, *Against the king's taxes*, probably addressed to Edward III and composed against the background of financial crisis (1337–40) preceding the Hundred Years' War, asserts the right of *la commune* (l. 7) to have its counsel heeded.[30]

By the end of the thirteenth century, the feudal tradition of *consilium* was established, in principle and, ideally, in practice, as the basis for the relationship between governing and governed at both the personal and nascent institutional levels. Royal, baronial, and manorial councils, national assemblies and parliaments operated, however imperfectly, on the principle of 'counsel' sought and given. As an ideal of kingly rule, however, 'work all things by counsel' was one frequently honoured in the breach by the early Plantagenets.

The 'problem of counsel' (1189–1399)

Although the duty and privilege of counsel between ruler and nobles was a long-established tradition of Anglo-Saxon and Norman government, the king's obligation to heed the advice of his magnates was a consistently contentious issue in the relationship between crown and baronage throughout the thirteenth and fourteenth centuries. 'It was,' says Dicey, 'only a weak or tyrannical king – a John or a Richard II – who

27 *Studies in the Constitutional History of the Thirteenth and Fourteenth Centuries*, pp. 135–36.
28 On Edward III's relationship with parliament, see Scott L. Waugh, *England in the reign of Edward III* (Cambridge, 1991), chs. 12 and 13.
29 On this custom, see Butt, *A History of Parliament*, pp. 266–67.
30 See Isabel S.T. Aspin, *Anglo-Norman Political Songs* (Oxford, 1953), pp. 105–15.

neglected to ask counsel; for the ruler who acted without the advice of his great men distinctly outraged the moral feeling of his day.'[31] Time and again, particularly in the reigns of Henry III, Edward II, and Richard II, literary and historical records charge the king with heeding bad or unsuitable counsel. Opinion amongst the barons as to their role in royal government was 'polarized between those who thought the purpose was to ensure that an untrustworthy king had sound counsel and should be restrained from foolish acts, and those who thought that the realm would be better governed through a baronial politburo.'[32]

The history of Æthelred the 'Unready' (983–1016) is probably the best known case in English history of bankrupt royal counsel. The failure of the men of Wessex against the Danes is attributed by the *Anglo-Saxon Chronicle* (*sub anno* 1011) to the king's poor policies (*urædes*),[33] but Æthelred's famous epithet *unred* is of post-conquest origin. He is so named for the first time in the early thirteenth-century *Leges Anglorum*, as 'Ethelredus Unrad', and later in that century, in the historical poem *Le Livere de Reis de Engleterre*.[34] To a manuscript page containing abridgements of stories from the *Disciplina Clericalis* by Petrus Alfonsi, a mid-thirteenth-century scribe has added two verses on 'Ailredus rex', beginning: 'Wanne king is radles.'[35] Such references are indicative of an increasingly articulated consciousness in English writing of the king's duty to solicit and to take note of good counsel. Æthelred's deficiency of counsel is even more strongly condemned, on the grounds of his ill-considered choice of advisers, in the mid-fifteenth-century chronicle of Thomas Rudbourne, where he is said to have been given the epithet *unredi*, 'since he chose to take counsel with his perfidious betrayers, who flatteringly deceived him, rather than with the leading and loyal men of his kingdom.'[36]

Baronial counsel had been a significant factor in the running of the kingdom during a period extending from Richard I's absence from England for most of his reign, for the early part of his by John, and during the minority of Henry III. Richard's justiciar, the Norman-born William Longchamp, Bishop of Ely, was dismissed for disregarding the tradition

31 Albert Venn Dicey, *The Privy Council. The Arnold Prize Essay 1860* (London and New York, 1887), p. 5.
32 W.L. Warren, *The Governance of Norman and Angevin England*, p. 228.
33 Charles Plummer (on the basis of an edition by John Earle), ed., *Two of the Saxon Chronicles* (Oxford, 1892; reissued 1952, with a bibliographical note by Dorothy Whitelock; rpr. 1972), I, 141.
34 See Simon Keynes, 'The declining reputation of King Æthelred the Unready,' in David Hill, ed., *Ethelred the Unready: Papers from the Millenary Conference* (Oxford, 1976), p. 240.
35 Keynes, 'The declining reputation,' p. 227.
36 Cited and translated by Keynes, 'The declining reputation,' p. 241.

of baronial counsel, whereas his successor, the Englishman, Walter of Coutances, Archbishop of Rouen, made a more successful start by announcing his intention to act 'by the counsel of the barons of the exchequer'.[37] The barons strongly opposed the administrative 'reforms' inaugurated on behalf of Henry III by the treasurer, Peter des Rivaux, which led to their exclusion from their self-appointed role of 'natural counsellors' to the king. Later in Henry's reign, baronial plans for the reform of government and administration, which required the restoration of their conciliar status, led to prolonged unrest between 1258 and 1267, an outbreak of rebellion in 1263 ending with the victory of Simon de Montfort over the king at the battle of Lewes in the following year.

The failure of the reign of Edward II ultimately lies in the bad counsel, tendered with the motive of self-aggrandizement and wilfully heeded by the infatuated king, of the Gascon knight, Piers Gaveston, probably the least qualified and the most powerful counsellor in medieval English history. Edward was formally charged with accepting the unsuitable counsel of his favourite ('By his counsel he withdraws the king from the counsel of his realm and puts discord between the king and his people')[38] in a declaration of 1308, and, in a petition presented to Parliament two years later, the barons charged Edward with, among other things, accepting evil counsel.[39] Article 20 of the New Ordinances cites, among other charges, the malign counsel of Gaveston.[40]

Edward's entire reign was blighted by his susceptibility to men like Gaveston and Hugh Despenser, the younger, whose counsel, unlike that of William Marshall's in the reign of his grandfather, was anything but disinterested. The king disregarded the New Ordinances, and his failure to heed the strategic advice of the Earl of Gloucester at the Battle of Bannockburn (1314) was probably a major factor in the English defeat.[41] Eventually, Edward's persistent acceptance of bad counsel and rejection of good played a large part in his deposition.[42] Petitions from the

---

37 'per consilium baronum scaccari' (Baldwin, *The King's Council*, p. 9 [citing Roger of Hovedon, Chronica, 4 vols. (London, 1868–71), III, 141]).

38 *English Historical Documents (EHD) III, 1189–1327*, ed. Harry Rothwell (London, 1974), Item 98: 'Articles against Gavaston presented by the earl of Lincoln to the King, March to April 1308,' p. 526. Doubts about the authenticity of this document are raised by H.G. Richardson and G.O. Sayles in *The Governance of Medieval England. The Conquest to Magna Carta* (Edinburgh, 1963), pp. 15–16.

39 See Butt, *A History of Parliament*, p. 184; J.R. Maddicott, *Thomas of Lancaster 1307–1322. A Study in the Reign of Edward II* (Oxford, 1970), p. 111.

40 *EHD III*, Item 100: 'The New Ordinances, 1311,' p. 532.

41 Butt, *A History of Parliament*, p. 197.

42 On Edward II's relationship with his barons and on the events leading to his deposition, see James Conway Davies, *The Baronial Opposition to Edward II, its Character and Policy. A Study in Administrative History* (Cambridge, 1918); Natalie Fryde, *The Tyranny and Fall of Edward II 1321–1326* (Cambridge, 1979); J.R. Maddicott, *Thomas of*

commons presented at the Westminster Epiphany-Candlemas parliament of 1327, the first of his successor, Edward III, refer to the 'faux consails' and treasonable 'malueise consail' of the Despensers, and others, and make a plea for 'bones gentz et couenables et sages entour le roi de li bien consailer'.[43] A proclamation issued after the successful coup against Isabella and Mortimer at Nottingham in October, 1330, reassures the shires of the intention of Edward III to rule with justice and baronial counsel.[44]

Parliamentary records from the reign of Richard II contain repeated pleas that the king surround himself with wise men and heed the advice of his barons. At the parliament of October 1386, which impeached Richard's chancellor, Michael de la Pole, for various alleged acts of malfeasance and nonfeasance, the lords and commons threatened the king with deposition in the manner of Edward II, if he continued to disregard his rightful counsellors, and delivered the following grim pronouncement on the constitutional consequences:

> It is permitted by another ancient law – and one put into practice not long ago – that if the king by malignant counsel or foolish contumacy or contempt or wanton will or for any other improper reason, should alienate himself from his people, and should be unwilling to be governed and guided by the laws and statutes and laudable ordinances with the wholesome counsel of the lords and magnates of the realm, but rashly in his insane counsels exercise his own peculiar desire, then it is lawful for them, with the common consent of the people of the realm to pluck down the king from his royal throne . . .[45]

Rule by a policy which, Butt suggests, might be called 'consultative absolutism',[46] whereby Richard attempted to exert his authority over parliament towards the end of his reign, contributed to the grim

---

Lancaster; J.R.S. Phillips, *Aymer de Valence, Earl of Pembroke 1307–1324. Baronial Politics in the Reign of Edward II* (Oxford, 1972); J.S. Hamilton, *Piers Gaveston, Earl of Cornwall 1307–1312. Politics and Patronage in the Reign of Edward II* (Detroit and London, 1988).

[43] *Rotuli Parliamentorum Anglie Hactenus Inediti MCCLXXIX–MCCCLXXII*, ed. H.G. Richardson and George Sayles (London, 1935), pp. 117, 118, 121.

[44] 'Et voloms que totes Gentz sachent que, desore enavant, nous voloms governer nostre People solonc Droiture & Reson, sicome appent a nostre Roiale Dignite, & que les Bosoignes, que nous touchent, & l'estat de nostre Roialme, soient mesnez par commun Conseil des Grantz de nostre Roialme, & nemi en autre manere.' *Foedera, Conventiones, Literæ, et cujuscunque generis acta publia, inter reges Angliæ*, ed. Thomas Rymer, 3rd edn. (The Hague, 1739), II, 51–52.

[45] *EHD IV*, ed. A.R. Myers (London, 1969), Item 60: 'The impeachment of Michael de la Pole and the appointment of the Commission of Reform, 1386,' p. 151. See Butt, *A History of Parliament*, pp. 389–92.

[46] *A History of Parliament*, p. 442. See further, Richard H. Jones, *The Royal Policy of Richard II: Absolutism in the Later Middle Ages* (Oxford, 1968).

fulfilment of these words with the king's forced abdication and imprisonment in September, 1399, and his death in suspicious circumstances shortly thereafter.

The 'problem of counsel' is articulated in thirteenth- and fourteenth-century complaint poetry, which criticizes Edward II and Richard II explicitly, and Henry III and Edward III implicitly, for being *unrede* in various ways. Some macaronic verses, openly critical of Edward II for breaking the New Ordinances,[47] pointedly precede *The Sayings of the Four Philosophers*, Item 20 in the Auchinleck manuscript (ca. 1330–40), in which a king seeks the advice of wise men. *Against the king's taxes* (ca. 1340) gives no names but accuses a 'maveis consiler' (l. 37) of wickedly advising the young king, (presumably Edward III) to tax the poor to excess. The Latin poem written shortly after the battle of Lewes speaks of the real enemies of the unnamed Henry III as duplicitous counsellors, who flatter him and wreak havoc on the kingdom,[48] and advocates counsel by the *communitas regni* (l. 765), the ideal counsellors being those who have the good of the community at heart (ll. 765–94).

The subject of *Richard the Redeless* (ca. 1399), the first part ('Fragment R') of the complaint poem, *Mum and the Sothsegger*,[49] is Richard II's alleged failure of counsel. This work, which echoes, more specifically, many of the sentiments of the poem inspired by the battle of Lewes, is a product of what Arthur B. Ferguson calls 'articulate citizenship'.[50] Its author, he suggests, was 'probably a member of the lesser gentry, perhaps one who had actually served in parliament as a knight of the shire'.[51]

The poem attributes Richard's mistakes to appointment of advisers who, instead of offering him wise counsel, encourage him to neglect the common weal for his own pleasure. The poet invokes the topos of 'the king's ignorance'[52] to plead for direct, verbal, extra-parliamentary access to the king by the lower orders of society, claiming it as his right to offer

47 Ed. Rossell Hope Robbins, in *Historical Poems of the XIVth and XVth Centuries* (New York, 1959), ll. 1–16.
48 Thomas Wright, ed. and trans., 'The Battle of Lewes,' in *The Political Songs of England, from the reign of John to that of Edward II* (London, 1839; rpr. Hildesheim, 1968), ll. 548–85.
49 On this division of the poem, and for all references, see Mabel Day and Robert Steele, ed., *Mum and the Sothsegger* EETS 199 (London, 1936), ix–xix.
50 *The Articulate Citizen and the English Renaissance* (Durham, N.C., 1965), p. 80.
51 'The Problem of Counsel in *Mum and the Sothsegger*,' *Studies in the Renaissance* 2 (1955), 67 (cf. Janet Coleman: 'He sounds like one of the lesser landed gentry who was acquainted with the Parliaments of the 1390s' [*English Literature in History 1350–1400. Medieval Readers and Writers* (London, 1981), p. 119]).
52 On this subject, see Dan Embree, 'The King's Ignorance: A Topos for Evil Times,' *Medium Ævum* 54 (1985), 121–26.

counsel to his liege, the king: 'So rithffully be reson my rede shuld also,/ For to conceill, and I cou3the my kyng and þe lordis' (*Prologus*, ll. 48–49).[53] He condemns magnates, corrupt courtiers, advisers, and officials, all of whom keep the king in ignorance of the machinations of his administrators and the wretchedness of the lower orders of society, and castigates some parliamentary knights (perhaps his former fellow representatives) for a litany of failings which have since achieved the status of cliché in the literature of parliamentary complaint: corruption, rashness, laziness, somnolence, and stupidity (IV. ll. 53–73).[54]

Variously engaged in a discourse of counsel in works which are not always explicitly or topically 'political' are the major Ricardian poets: Langland, Gower, Chaucer, and the *Gawain*-poet.[55] As poetry which Anne Middleton defines as 'public', that is, concerned with serving and speaking for the 'common good',[56] *Piers Plowman* offers a definition of ideal kingship in which the ruler's principal advisers are Reason, 'Kynde Wytt', and Conscience.[57] Gower directly addresses the issue of royal counsel in *Vox Clamantis*,[58] and the 'counsel topos' is also voiced, with kingly and more general application, in dialogue between the Confessor and the Lover and in the stories of his *Confessio Amantis*,[59] which the poet

---

[53] Cf. *Mum and the Sothsegger* (Fragment 'M'): 'And þerefore my cunseil (þough þe king knowe hit/ And alle þe lordz of þis londe, right lite is my charge)/ Ys to be oone with trouthe . . .' (ll. 193–95).

[54] T.F.T. Plucknett's survey of the records of corruption and assault on the part of the representatives from Bedfordshire in the period 1327–37 suggests that not all shire knights were models of conduct. Plucknett notes, however, that: 'It is not necessary to stress the number of seeming crooks and bandits who were elected, for it must be remembered that their generation was one of fierce faction and sometimes of civil war, which will explain most of the assaults, homicides, and house-breakings . . . . As for financial probity, it must likewise be remembered that handling or collecting public funds was a difficult task which often placed the official between the upper and nether millstone' ('Parliament,' in Fryde and Miller, ed., *Historical Studies of the English Parliament, Volume I*, p. 216; rpr. from *The English Government at Work, 1327–1336*, ed. J.F. Willard and W.A. Morris, I [Cambridge, Mass., 1940], 82–128).

[55] So termed by J.A. Burrow in *Ricardian Poetry* (London, 1971).

[56] See Anne Middleton, 'The Idea of Public Poetry in the Reign of Richard II,' *Speculum* 53 (1978), 94–114.

[57] See Anna P. Baldwin, *The Theme of Government in Piers Plowman* (Cambridge, 1981), *passim*.

[58] 'Est quid rex, nisi consilium fuerit sibi sanum?/ Sunt quid consilia, rex nisi credat ea?' (G.C. Macaulay, *The Complete Works of John Gower* [Oxford, 1899–1902; republ. Grosse Pointe, Mich., 1968], IV, Lib.VI, ll. 530–31): 'Of what use is a king, unless he has sound counsel? And of what use is counsel, unless the king trusts it?' (Eric W. Stockton, trans., *The Major Latin Works of John Gower: The Voice of One Crying and the Tripartite Chronicle* [Seattle, 1962], p. 231).

[59] For example: 'For conseil passeth alle thing/ To him which thenkth to ben a king' (III, Lib. VIII, ll. 2109–10), says Confessor to Amans; in the story of Athemas and Demephon, in which these two kings are persuaded by the wise counsel of Nestor to

dedicated first to Richard II and later to Henry, Duke of Lancaster.[60] Chaucer's *Tale of Melibee* is, among other things, a general treatise on counsel and counsellors, possibly directed at Richard;[61] and, within the framework of chivalric romance, the *Gawain*-poet makes a more oblique contribution to the Ricardian 'discourse of counsel' in *Sir Gawain and the Green Knight.*[62]

Apart from the testimony of parliament and poetry, there is ample other fourteenth-century evidence – collective, individual, and socially broad based – of a perceived need for kings to take wise counsel from sources considered appropriate in the eyes of their subjects. In the course of her discussion of *Richard the Redeless*, whose author associates himself with Bristol (l. 2), Janet Coleman points to the opposition of the burgesses of that city to Richard II's financial demands, and comments: 'Doubtless, urban officials as well as country landowners felt they were the appropriately informed citizens to counsel the king, at least in conjunction with the customary counsel of the nobility.'[63] Coleman cites two specific occasions on which individual citizens expressed a desire, or took it upon themselves so to do, to offer counsel to Edward III. The first is a speech on behalf of the commons by Peter de la Mare, knight of the shire for Herefordshire and steward of the Earl of March, to the 'Good Parliament' (1376), in response to the king's request for financial aid towards the war with France. The removal of self-interested, financially corrupt counsellors was stipulated as a prerequisite to supply of the desired funds, and a number of royal ministers were impeached. The second is a dream, recounted in Walsingham's *Chronicon Angliæ*, by Thomas Hoo, knight of the shire for Bedfordshire at the same parliament, which is attributed to his thoughts of 'how or by what means the

---

abstain from vengeance on their mutinous vassals, their rule is restored without bloodshed, 'al thurgh conseil which was good' (II, Lib. III, l. 1855.

60 On Gower, see, for example, John H. Fisher, *John Gower, Moral Philosopher and Friend of Chaucer* (London, 1965); Coleman, *Medieval Readers and Writers*, pp. 126–56; Ferguson, *The Articulate Citizen*, pp. 42–75 (on Gower and Langland).

61 Lee Patterson suggests that, as a companion piece for the tale of the childlike Sir Thopas, *Melibee* is intended as a *miroir de prince* for Richard II (' "What Man Artow?" Authorial Self-Definition in *The Tale of Sir Thopas* and *The Tale of Melibee*,' *Studies in the Age of Chaucer* 11 [1989], 117–75). Lynn Staley Johnson argues that *Melibee* was directly aimed at Richard II and 'explores the responsibility of a ruler for the bad advice he receives and takes' ('Inverse Counsel: Contexts for the *Melibee*,' *Studies in Philology* 87 [1990], p. 150). See also Leonard Michael Koff, *Chaucer and the Art of Storytelling* (Berkeley and Los Angeles, 1988), pp. 91–99; Richard Firth Green, *Poets and Princepleasers. Literature and the English Court in the Late Middle Ages* (Toronto, Buffalo, London, 1980), pp. 143, 166.

62 See Chapter 5, below.

63 *Medieval Readers and Writers*, p. 45.

king could be restored to a more correct life and to employ sounder counsel.'[64]

Following his leading role at the Good Parliament, which resulted in his imprisonment, without due process of law, in Nottingham Castle until shortly after the death of Edward III, Peter de la Mare became, according to his biographer, 'a popular hero, and verses were composed extolling his attitude and audacious eloquence.'[65] He received a hero's welcome from the citizens of London on his release and a royal pardon from the new king, Richard II, at whose first parliament, in 1377, he was re-elected Speaker for the commons.[66]

Less celebrated, but no less significant, were the actions of Henry of Keighley, knight of the shire for Lancashire at Edward I's Lincoln parliament of 1301, who challenged royal policy on behalf of the Arch-bishop of Canterbury and, as a result, spent some time as a prisoner in the Tower of London.[67] Another fourteenth-century 'articulate citizen' who was prepared to make a public statement of his views on royal counsel was John Bedwynd, sheriff of Cornwall, who was charged at the exchequer in 1313 by Edward II's money-lender, Anthony Pessagno, for having stated, at the county court at Lostwithiel, that the king had evil counsellors.[68] The non-noble had developed a public voice in the affairs of state by the fourteenth century, and, as *Mum and the Sothsegger* de-mands of members of parliament,[69] and as demonstrated by men like John Bedwynd, Peter de la Mare, and Henry of Keighley, they were prepared to exercise it.

---

[64] *Medieval Readers and Writers*, p. 45 (citing George Holmes, *The Good Parliament* [Ox-ford, 1975], pp. 100–03 and the *Anonimalle Chronicle*, ed. Galbraith, pp. 80–82, in the case of Peter de la Mare; and Holmes, *The Good Parliament*, p. 136, and the *Chronicon Angliæ*, ed. E.M. Thompson [London, 1874], p. 70 ['qualiter videlicet vel quibus mediis rex ad correctiorem vitam reduci posset et consilio perfrui saniori'], in Thomas Hoo's).

[65] J.S. Roskell, *Parliament and Politics in Late Medieval England*, II (London, 1981), 7. See also Butt, *A History of Parliament*, pp. 341–52.

[66] On de la Mare's career as Speaker, see Roskell, *Parliament and Politics*, II, 1–14 (rpr. from *Nottingham Medieval Studies* 2 [1958], 24–37).

[67] On this incident, see Butt, *A History of Parliament*, pp. 164–65.

[68] Davies, *The Baronial Opposition to Edward II*, p. 329 ('dicebat dominun Regem malos habuisse consiliaros et male consultum fuisse . . .' App. No. 19, p. 553).

[69] For a discussion of this point in *Mum and the Sothsegger*, see Helen M. Cam, 'The relation of English Members of Parliament to their constituencies in the Fourteenth Century: a neglected text,' in *eadem*, *Liberties & Communities in Medieval England* (London, 1963), pp. 223–35.

The ethos of Middle English romance

Unlike classical French chivalric romance, the ethos of Middle English romance is not the idealized self-image of an insecure aristocracy, its authority challenged from above by an ambitious monarchy and from below by an emerging *bourgeoisie*,[70] but the principles of constitutional government. The ideal state in Middle English romance is the longed for utopia of contemporary complaint poetry: a community of benevolent rule, peace, and justice, extending to all classes of society. Its corruption and loss are mourned by the composers of complaint; its establishment and defence celebrated in romance. In both romance and complaint, 'working by counsel' is an ideal of conduct, and the model ruler is wise in judgment and heedful of good advice. But whereas complaint focusses on negative exemplars, the heroes of romance attain exemplary status, and tyrannical rulers are reformed or overthrown.

The positioning of the complaint poem, *The Simonie* (or *Poem on the Evil Times of Edward II*), in the Auchinleck manuscript offers a codicological instance of this 'reverse affinity' between romance and complaint. *The Simonie* (Item 44), which employs some of the lexis and conventions of romance ('Hii sholde ben also hende as any levedi in londe,/ And for to speke alle vilanie nel nu no kniht wonde/ for shame,' ll. 261–63)[71] to articulate an ideal of crusading knighthood while simultaneously deploring its current debasement, appears in the company of *Richard Coer de Lion* (Item 43) and *Horn Childe and Maiden Rimnild* (Item 41)[72] in what may be an intentional 'indirect comparison . . . between a glorious past and a very recent miserable decline.'[73] Among romances themselves, *The Tale of Gamelyn* has a distinct echo of complaint in its condemnation of gluttonous, godless clerics and corrupt sheriffs,[74] as, less obviously, do *Athelston* and *Beves of Hamtoun*, in their depiction of wrongs caused the misuse of authority.

Wise counsel, sometimes as substitute for, and regularly as stimulus to, the exercise of prowess in just causes, serves the hero and his allies as

---

70 See Erich Köhler, *L'aventure chevaleresque. Idéal et réalité dans le roman courtois. Études sur la forme des plus anciens poèmes d'Arthur et du Graal*, translated from the German by Eliane Kaufholz (Paris, 1974).

71 Ed. Thomas Wright, in *The Political Songs of England*.

72 Item 42, *Alphabetical Praise of Women*, is a 'filler' (see Derek Pearsall and I.C. Cunningham, introd., *The Auchinleck Manuscript* [London, 1979], p. ix).

73 John Finlayson, 'Richard, Coer de Lyon: Romance, History or Something in Between?,' *Studies in Philology* 87 (1990), 163.

74 Richard Kaeuper comments: 'If not a part of this *genre*, the tales of Robin Hood and Gamelyn are close adjuncts' (*War, Justice, and Public Order. England and France in the Later Middle Ages* [Oxford, 1988], p. 336).

a means to counter tyranny and to resolve conflict. In *Athelston*, *Beves of Hamtoun*, and *The Seven Sages of Rome*, the ruler's barons demand their right to exercise the feudal privilege of *consilium* as a check to royal arbitrariness and injustice. The ability to give and to recognize good counsel is the mark of a good king, like the hero of *Havelok*, and its converse a weak or tyrannical one, such as Costentine (*Of Arthour and of Merlin*), Athelston (*Athelston*), and the emperor in *The Seven Sages*. To be without counsel is to be helpless, to be an incapable knight or ruler, like the hapless Costentine or the disorganized lone knight-errant, Sir Thopas, hero of Chaucer's parodic *Tale of Sir Thopas*.[75] On the other hand, to refuse or to ignore counsel from one's vassals, in the manner of King Athelston in *Athelston* and Duke Morgan in *Sir Tristrem*, is the hallmark of the tyrant, and the giving of bad or false counsel by, for example, Godrich in *Havelok* and Wymound in *Athelston*, is a standard mark of villainy.[76]

In many romances, the ideal society is illustrated by the confrontation of contrasting and opposing kingdoms, one a force for good and the other for evil: for example, England as opposed to the Saracen world in *Guy of Warwick*; Orfeo's England and Fairyland in *Sir Orfeo*; Athelwold's England and Godrich's in *Havelok*; the ideal 'forest' kingdom of the outlaws in *Gamelyn* versus the corrupt machine in control of the shire. All the 'negative' kingdoms are unsuccessful in their confrontation with the 'positive' because they lack, in various ways, the harmony and well-being which prevail in the ideal society governed by a benevolent ruler guided by wise counsel.

Whereas the heroes of Chrétien's *romans courtois* usually confront dilemmas of conflicting loyalties between love and chivalry, with which they grapple in internal debate, the insular hero is more likely to be offered a clear choice at certain critical stages of his quest: to accept or reject some form of counsel. A willingness to accept or simply to express

---

75 Who, for example, is caught without his armour (ll. 818–19) when he finds himself face to face with a giant instead of an 'elf-queen' on his quest for love. The following *Tale of Melibee* in Fragment VII of the *Canterbury Tales*, with which 'Chaucer the pilgrim' continues his interrupted story-telling session when his fictional audience can bear no more of *Sir Thopas*, provides in abundance the counsel lacking in its companion piece. (Chaucer references are to F.N. Robinson, *The Works of Geoffrey Chaucer*, 2nd edn. [London, 1957]).

76 William Ian Miller offers an interesting analogy in the thirteenth-century Icelandic 'family' sagas (*Íslendingasögur*), where the consultative function of kin parallels that of vassals, royal councillors, and parliament: 'Uncounseled deeds were considered reckless deeds. Those who acted repeatedly without taking counsel, either with kin or chieftain, were judged harshly by the sagas . . . . Mutual consultation was perceived as a duty and breaches of it were enforced with informal sanctions, mostly by a cooling in relations, but at times by actual repudiation' (*Bloodtaking and Peacemaking. Feud, Law, and Society in Saga Iceland* [Chicago and London, 1990], pp. 164–65.

a need for wholesome counsel is often a sign that the hero is on the road to success; and his demonstrated ability to recognize bad counsel, or to give wise counsel himself, is a further indication of maturity. To disregard good advice, as Guy, for example, does at the beginning of *Guy of Warwick*, is to court disaster.

Counsellors come in a variety of breeds. Guy is advised by his foster-father, Heraud, in *Guy of Warwick*, and Beves by his uncle, Saber, in *Beves of Hamtoun*. Aristotle is credited with Alisaunder's success in *Kyng Alisaunder*. Often, however, it is not a knight's peers or superiors who serve as his counsellors, but squires, servants, and women: Adam the Spencer in *Gamelyn*, Goldeboru in *Havelok*, a squire and a chambermaid in *Sir Degrevant*, and Lunet, lady-in-waiting in *Ywain and Gawain*. The counsellor *par excellence* of Middle English romance is Merlin: magician, trickster, strategist, engineer, and practical and moral adviser to King Arthur.

The hero of Middle English romance operates within clearly defined spheres of counselling resources: parental, feudal, and divine. Throughout his life he is bonded by blood, love, and loyalty to a network of friends, family, and lord, who provide him with counsel, strategy, and, when possible, armed support. The knight who maintains his *trawþe* with God has the advantage of heavenly counsel and guidance as well. Often companions who constitute 'a symbolic family',[77] like the tutor-counsellors Heraud in *Guy of Warwick* and Saber in *Beves of Hamtoun*, join him on his quest. When, for example, Havelok travels to Denmark to reclaim his birthright, he is accompanied by his wife and three foster-brothers.

More often than not, the quest in Middle English romance is precipitated by the hero's deprivation of something which is rightfully his and which defines his position in society: Orfeo's queen in *Sir Orfeo*; Floris's future queen in *Floris and Blauncheflur*; and the birthrights of Havelok in *Havelok*, Beves in *Beves of Hamtoun*, and Gamelyn in *The Tale of Gamelyn*. The natural enemy of the insular hero, the usurper-tyrant, is the natural enemy of society. Treason and tyranny prove to be serious threats not only to the hero but to the kingdom as a whole in a number of romances: the security of England depends on the defeat of tyranny in *Havelok*, *Beves*, and *Athelston*. Whether for birthright or beloved, the quest may result in temporary and involuntary exile, but it never entails complete social alienation.[78] Restoration of title and lands may be achieved in part

---

77 Lee C. Ramsey, *Chivalric Romances. Popular Literature in Medieval England* (Bloomington, Ind., 1983), p. 61.

78 As John Ganim comments of Horn and Havelok: 'The hero of early English romance is kept from his rightful reward, but he is never caught in a contradictory ethical situation and is always surrounded by images of community' (*Style and Consciousness*

by force of arms, but success ultimately depends on the mechanisms which society provides: feudal custom and the law.[79] By being enforced in locations both associated with thirteenth- and fourteenth-century parliaments and identified with specific geographical detail in *Havelok* (Lincoln), *Athelston* and the last section of *Beves* (both London), the validity of that custom and law gains extra-textual reinforcement

The 'socialization' of the insular hero is also marked by the limited portrayal of his inner life; his private world and emotions are of little interest; the emphasis is on his interaction with the givers of counsel and implementation of their strategies. The essentially anti-social force of 'courtly' love, which competes with the feudal obligations of chivalry for the hero's allegiance in chivalric romance, has no place in the ideal world of Middle English romance. Women may be ignored altogether, as in *Gamelyn*, or explicitly blamed by the heroes themselves for instances of knightly misconduct in *Guy of Warwick* and *Sir Gawain and the Green Knight*, or reduced to a subordinate role, as in *Ywain and Gawain*. *Sir Orfeo*, on the other hand, celebrates the socially sanctioned institution of married love. In *Havelok*, Goldeboru's role as political strategist supersedes that of wife and lover. When Havelok does address her in the terms of love lyric in his account of the dream which he has had on their wedding night ('And, Goldeborw, Y gaf þe./ Deus! lemman, hwat may þis be?,' ll. 1311–12),[80] it is to offer her his *visio* of political power.[81] It is Denmark, not Goldeboru, that Havelok embraces in his dream.

The socially disruptive phenomenon of passion may also be 'contained' by other means: by, for example, comedy in *Floris and Blauncheflur*, where the fact that the lovers happen to be children makes their affair a matter of sentimentality rather than sexuality, and by 'socialization' in *Sir Tristrem* and *Ywain and Gawain*. Susan Crane draws attention to the very different conceptions of love in *Sir Tristrem* and Thomas of England's *Tristan*: whereas the erotic obsession of Tristan and Isolde isolates them from society in Thomas's poem, in *Sir Tristrem* Tristrem's dog also has some of the love potion and, possibly, Brengwain as well. Similarly, Lunet and the lion join Ywain and Alundyne to live out their

---

in *Middle English Narrative* [Princeton, 1983], p. 52). *Robert of Sicily* might be considered an exception, but, although they include this poem in their collection of Middle English romances, French and Hale remark that it is: 'Strictly speaking . . . a pious legend' (Walter Hoyt French and Charles Brockway Hale, *Middle English Metrical Romances* [New York, 1930; reissued 1964], II, 933). (On the difficulties of classifying this narrative, see Margaret Bradstock, 'Roberd of Cisyle and the Amalgamation of Forms,' *Parergon*, n.s. 5 [1987], 103–16).

[79] See Susan Crane, *Insular Romance. Politics, Faith, and Culture in Anglo-Norman and Middle English Literature* (Berkeley, Los Angeles, London, 1986), esp. chs. 1 and 2.

[80] *Havelok* references are to the edition by Diane Speed in *Medieval English Romances*, 2 vols. (Sydney, 1989).

[81] As John Ganim points out in *Style and Consciousness*, p. 33.

days in 'joy and blis' (l. 4024) at the conclusion of the English version of Chrétien's *Yvain, Ywain and Gawain*. Crane also cites the case of Horn, who gives rings in love and friendship in *King Horn*, whereas his Anglo-Norman counterpart in the *Romance of Horn* confines ring-giving to the beloved.[82] The isolating passion of French and, sometimes, Anglo-Norman romance is often thus transformed in Middle English into affec-tionate alliances. The most impor,tant bonds are not with wives and lovers but with sworn brothers and tutor-counsellors who serve both as mentors and guardians.

Middle English romance is, in fact, distinctly negative in its attitude to passionate love. Gawain's invocation of the *blasme des femmes* tradition[83] at the end of *Sir Gawain and the Green Knight* may seem out of place in this 'courtly' romance, but it has its antecedents in the antifeminist views expressed by Guy of Warwick and Beves of Hampton. Alisaunder, too, is reluctantly ensnared by Candace in *Kyng Alisaunder*. There is even an occasional element of overt brutality, if not downright sadism, in the treatment of Josian in *Beves* and the queen in *Athelston*, and the threats of physical violence towards Heurodis in *Sir Orfeo*.[84]

On the other hand, the stratagems which play a large part in many Middle English romances provide an undercurrent of humour which tempers those misogynist tendencies and makes for narratives which offer more in the way of entertainment than unrelieved heroism and knightly striving. The pivotal role of *gyn* gives works as diverse as *King Horn, Floris and Blauncheflur, Athelston, Richard Coer de Lion, The King of Tars, Sir Orfeo*, and *Sir Gawain and the Green Knight* a common pattern of strategy and counter-strategy, with considerable comic potential.

The ideological underpinning of Middle English romance is suffi-ciently resilient to sustain a robust undercurrent of humour. Instead of Chrétien's subtle and sustained irony, which is based on discrepancies between the theory and practice of chivalry,[85] there are episodes of cruder comedy inspired, in the main, by trickery of various kinds: for example, the 'exchange of blows' bargain in *Sir Cleges*; the Punch-and-Judy violence of the first part of *Gamelyn*; the outwittings in *Floris and*

---

82 *Insular Romance*, pp. 193–94.

83 See Mary Dove, 'Gawain and the *Blasme des femmes* tradition,' *Medium Ævum* 41 (1972), 20–26.

84 Lee Ramsey considers that *Guy, Beves*, and *Ipomedon* 'display an ill-hidden resent-ment toward the heroines by deliberately and unnecessarily tormenting them in various ways' (*Chivalric Romances*, p. 59). On elements of misogyny and their func-tion in Anglo-Norman romance, see Judith Weiss, 'The wooing woman in Anglo-Norman romance,' in *Romance in Medieval England*, ed. Maldwyn Mills, Jennifer Fellows, Carol Meale (Cambridge, 1991), pp. 149–61.

85 See, for example, the studies by D.H. Green, *Irony in Medieval Romance* (Cambridge, 1979); Norris J. Lacy, *The Craft of Chrétien de Troyes. An Essay in Narrative Art* (Leiden, 1980).

Blauncheflur; the 'king in disguise' motif of *Rauf Coilȝear*, the grotesqueries of *Richard Coer de Lion*; and the wooings, which teeter on the farcical in both cases and encompass adultery in the latter, of Beves by Josian and, with more delicacy, of Gawain by Lady de Hautdesert.[86] Occasionally, in such scenes of trickery within confined spaces, Middle English romance approaches the *fabliau* mode.[87]

There is also enclosure of a chronological kind. The heroes of Chrétien's narratives neither procreate nor die; their stories, focussing on a crisis in their chivalric careers, begin and end in the present.[88] The pattern of insular romance, on the other hand, tends to be biographically complete, often beginning with the hero's childhood and ending with some reference to his death, and, sometimes, descendants. The heroes and heroines of *Beves of Hamtoun*, *Havelok*, *King Horn*, and *Guy of Warwick* live out their exemplary lives and, especially in the cases of Guy and Beves, make admirably pious ends. Even the lives of Chrétien's forever young Arthurian knights become finite in *Ywain and Gawain*, whose conclusion tells us that Ywain, Alundyne, Lunet, and the lion lived happily, 'Until þat ded haves dreven þam down' (l. 4026); and, although they make no reference to the death or later life of the hero, the events of *Sir Gawain and the Green Knight* are played out within the cycle of the seasons and the context of world history. The effect of their mortality and occasional brushes with the absurd is to reinforce the accessibility of the heroes of Middle English romance as role models. Another, particularly in the cases of *Guy of Warwick*, *Beves of Hamtoun*, and *Gamelyn*, is to convey the impression of a process of maturation, from youthful ignorance to an understanding of the ideals of chivalry.

Whereas complaint literature idealizes the heeding of good advice as a political virtue, romance makes it the basis of a code of chivalry in which wise counsel regulates prowess, channels it to constructive ends, and constitutes the medium for devising successful strategy. The principle of policy- and decision-making by consultation, one officially, if not always willingly, espoused by thirteenth- and fourteenth-century English monarchs, is integral to the ethos of Middle English romance, where to 'work

---

86 On the comic elements of Josiane's wooing in *Boeve de Haumtone* and their similarities to that of Lady de Hautdesert, see Weiss, 'The wooing woman,' pp. 149, 152–53.

87 Ganim remarks in his study of *King Horn* and *Havelok* that the worlds of these early Middle English romances are enclosed ones, and the heroes' journeys geographically perfunctory. The most important scenes in *Horn* and *Havelok* take place 'in towers, in bedrooms, in cottages, in dining halls' (*Style and Consciousness*, p. 49). The same could also be said for *Floris and Blauncheflur*, *Sir Gawain and the Green Knight*, *Sir Cleges*, and *Rauf Coilȝear*.

88 The exceptions are *Li Contes del Graal*, which has a brief account of Perceval's family history (Hilka, *Der Percevalroman*, ll. 412–88), and *Cligès*, which is to some extent a parody of the Tristan legend, and where the adventures of Cligès are preceded by the story of his father, Alexandre.

by counsel' extends beyond proverbial commonplace, and the 'problem of counsel', a fully articulated issue in the literature of fifteenth- and sixteenth-century political and social commentary,[89] is an underlying discourse.

Reception and audience

The circumstances in which thirteenth- and fourteenth-century Middle English romance was either read, recited, or sung[90] probably ranged from essentially 'private' readings, either silent,[91] like that of Chaucer's insomniac narrator in *The Book of the Duchess* (ll. 47–61), or aloud, to performances by professional *disours* at large, public gatherings. P.R. Coss canvasses the possibility that the reception of Middle English romance was, as M. Dominica Legge suggested of Anglo-Norman literature,[92] a small-group activity, better suited to chamber than to hall, the difference being that, for Middle English romance, the venue was more likely to have been the household of a country gentlemen than of a nobleman.[93] Derek Pearsall points to the likelihood of a volume like the Auchinleck manuscript being used both for private reading and recitation to small groups, formal and informal.[94]

---

[89] See Arthur B. Ferguson, *The Articulate Citizen, passim.*

[90] On the oral presentation of Middle English romance see, for example, Ruth Crosby, 'Oral delivery in the Middle Ages,' *Speculum* 11 (1936), 88–110; Albert C Baugh, 'Improvisation in the Middle English Romance,' *Proceedings of the American Philosophical Society* 103 (1959), 418–54; *idem*, 'The Middle English Romance. Some Questions of Creation, Presentation, and Preservation,' *Speculum* 42 (1967), 1–31; J.A.W. Bennett, ed. Douglas Gray, *Middle English Literature* (Oxford, 1986), pp. 123–25.

[91] On the expansion of silent reading in the fourteenth and fifteenth centuries, see Paul Saenger, 'Silent Reading: Its Impact on Late Medieval Script and Society,' *Viator* 13 (1982), 391–414.

[92] *Anglo-Norman Literature and Its Background*, pp. 3, 42–43

[93] 'Aspects of Cultural Diffusion in Medieval England: The Early Romances, Local Society and Robin Hood,' *Past and Present* 108 (1985), 43–46.

[94] 'Middle English Romance and its Audiences,' in *Historical and Editorial Studies in Medieval and Early Modern English for Johan Gerritsen*, ed. Mary-Jo Arn and Hanneke Wirtjes, with Hans Jensen (Groningen, 1985), p. 42. One manuscript which directly associates the gentry with the transmission of romance in the mid-fifteenth century (and therefore goes beyond the scope of the present study) is MS Lincoln 91 (the Thornton manuscript), which was almost certainly copied by Robert Thornton (d. 1465), lord of the manor of East Newton in North Yorkshire (see D.S. Brewer and A.E.B. Owen, introd., *The Thornton Manuscript (Lincoln Cathedral MS.91)* [London, 1975], p. viii). For interesting recent discussions of the compilation of fifteenth-century manuscripts containing Middle English romances, see John J. Thompson, 'Collecting Middle English romances and some related book-production activities in the later Middle Ages,' in *Romance in Medieval England*, ed. Mills, Fellows, and Meale,

Among a number of interesting possibilities which Coss raises for the dissemination of romance among the rural gentry in the thirteenth century is the passing around of unbound 'booklets', produced locally, for copying, possibly by chaplains and chantry priests in their households.[95] The provenance of the Auchinleck manuscript, the largest repository of early Middle English verse romances, which total eighteen of its forty-four items,[96] remains unclear. Laura Hibbard's 'London bookshop' theory, that the Auchinleck was a commercial, collaborative effort, produced on a bespoke basis and intended for a wealthy merchant,[97] has been modified in recent years: Derek Pearsall argues that the volume was probably fascicular in origin, an independent collection of booklets, subsequently bound for a particular customer of the merchant class;[98] Timothy Shonk agrees with A.I. Doyle's view that the work may have been intended for an audience of wealthy Londoners with court connections.[99] A more specific proposal by Laura Hibbard, which has found less support than the 'London bookshop', is that the manuscript was, at some time, in the possession of Geoffrey Chaucer.[100] As a counter to Pearsall's argument that the Auchinleck manuscript was intended for 'the coffee-table, or mid-fourteenth-century equivalent thereof, of an aspiring

---

pp. 17–38; and, in the same volume, Lynne S. Blanchfield's 'The romances in MS Ashmole 61: an idiosyncratic scribe' (pp. 65–87).

[95] 'Aspects of Cultural Diffusion,' pp. 56–63.

[96] *The King of Tars* (Item 2); *Amis and Amiloun* (Item 11); *Sir Degare* (Item 17); *The Seven Sages of Rome* (Item 18); *Floris and Blauncheflur* (Item 19); *Guy of Warwick* (Items 22 and 23); *Reinbrun* (Item 24); *Beves of Hamtoun* (Item 25); *Of Arthour and of Merlin* (Item 26); *Lay le freine* (Item 30); *Roland and Vernagu* (Item 31); *Otuel* (Item 32); *Kyng Alisaunder* (Item 33); *Sir Tristrem* (Item 37); *Sir Orfeo* (Item 38); *Horn Childe and Maiden Rimnild* (Item 41); *Richard Coer de Lion* (Item 43). With the exception of *Floris and Blauncheflur* and *Sir Tristrem* (probably both late thirteenth century), the date of composition of all these romances is the early fourteenth century, with *Of Arthour and of Merlin, Guy of Warwick* and *Beves of Hampton* probably the earliest (*ca.* 1300).

[97] See 'The Auchinleck Manuscript and a Possible London Bookshop of 1330–1340,' *Publications of the Modern Language Association* 57 (1942), 595–627.

[98] *The Auchinleck Manuscript*, pp. viii–ix.

[99] 'Those Londoners who lent large sums of money to the king for his wars, though not "courtiers", must have been called to court, and cannot have been unacquainted with French, or with Anglo-Norman literature, but they and their families, and equally some at court, could have welcomed or commissioned the Auchinleck enterprise' (A.I. Doyle, 'English Books in and out of Court from Edward III to Henry VII', in *English Court Culture in the Later Middle Ages*, ed. V.J. Scattergood and J.W. Sherborne [London, 1983], p. 165); Timothy A. Shonk, 'A Study of the Auchinleck Manuscript: Bookmen and Bookmaking in the Early Fourteenth Century,' *Speculum* 60 (1985), 90.

[100] See 'Chaucer and the Auchinleck Manuscript: *Thopas* and *Guy of Warwick*,' in *Essays and Studies in Honor of Carleton Brown* [New York, 1940], pp. 111–28; *eadem*, 'Chaucer and the Breton Lays of the Auchinleck Manuscript,' *Studies in Philology* 38 [1941], 14–33).

member of the London merchant élite,'[101] Coss raises the possibility of a provincial buyer from among the gentry, perhaps visiting London on judicial or parliamentary business.[102]

He also touches, implicitly, on the likelihood of parliament and county courts as occasions for the publication of romance:

> On the wider scene there was opportunity enough for social intercourse outside of court and retinue. In this context one naturally thinks first of parliament and of the hundred and county courts . . . As J.R. Maddicott writes, "Parliament was a social gathering, a season for conviviality, display, the exchange of news and the doing of business."[103]

The convivial side of parliament is attested by a surviving instruction to the chamberlain of London to obtain 'one hundred tuns of wine' for the king's cellar in preparation for the parliament of May, 1265.[104] This parliament , as it happened, never met, but 10,032 gallons of ale were consumed at the Lincoln parliament of 1301.[105] Four London merchants who attended the 1388 Cambridge parliament 'rented and furnished a house there, hired a staff of household servants, and bought so much wine that they should have been able to entertain handsomely.'[106] Sessions could last for several weeks, attracting, in addition to the magnates and representatives of the commons themselves, large numbers of attendants and other interested parties, who brought custom for the local inns and taverns of London.[107]

The alehouse setting of the opening lines of *Havelok* ('At þe biginning of ure tale/ Fil me a cuppe of ful god ale,' ll. 13–14) is formulaic,[108] but parliaments might well have provided occasion for congregation in recreational circumstances conducive to the publication of romance. This is not to argue in favour of the return of the beer-swilling minstrel, entertaining the peasantry with a recitation of *Havelok* in the tavern or market-

---

[101] 'Middle English Romance and its Audiences,' p. 42.

[102] 'Aspects of Cultural Diffusion,' p. 64.

[103] 'Aspects of Cultural Diffusion,' p. 47 (citing J.R. Maddicott, 'Parliament and the Constituencies', 1272–1277,' in R.G. Davies and J.H. Denton, ed., *The English Parliament in the Middle Ages* [Manchester, 1981] p. 79).

[104] Butt, *A History of Parliament*, p. 112.

[105] Michael Prestwich, *Edward I*, p. 444.

[106] Thrupp, *The Merchant Class*, p. 58 (citing McKisack, *The Parliamentary Representation of the English Boroughs*, pp. 82–86).

[107] See Keen, *English Society*, pp. 112–14.

[108] On such formulaic internal references to audiences see Carol Fewster (*Traditionality and Genre in Middle English Romance* [Cambridge, 1987], pp. 22–28), who concludes that: 'Ultimately the references to transmission – whether it is oral presentation or source book – are part of the fictions themselves, for the references' historical accuracy is superseded in importance by their own function as fictional devices creating a sense of poetic status' (p. 28).

place,[109] but rather for the possibility of a more sophisticated audience of imbibers. Festive public occasions, such as the scenario which Rosamund Allen posits for the first recitation of *King Horn* – a London banquet 'to celebrate the appointment of a sheriff or alderman'[110] – may also have provided hospitable contexts for romance presentation.

Preserved in a manuscript dating from around 1300,[111] *Havelok* is an early romance with multiple parliamentary associations. The poem, which exhibits a familiarity with the geography of Lincoln, and whose central episode is a parliament held in there,[112] has been linked with the parliaments held in that city in 1226 and 1284, as well as with the well-victualled assembly of 1301.[113] David Staines, for example, suggests a direct compositional connection with the festivities accompanying the parliament of 1284.[114] The coincidence of the marriage of Edward I's

---

[109] The market-place minstrel is suggested by Karl Brunner with reference to the *Havelok* manuscript ('Middle English Metrical Romances and Their Audiences,' in *Studies in Medieval Literature in Honor of Albert Croll Baugh*, ed. MacEdward Leach [Philadelphia, 1961], p. 223). For a corrective to this view, see Dieter Mehl, *The Middle English Metrical Romances of the Thirteenth and Fourteenth Centuries* (London, 1968), pp. 7–13, and 166–67: 'It can safely be assumed that "a cuppe of ful god ale" . . . was available not only in the market-place or a tavern, but in any bourgeois household throughout the country.' The part which professional minstrels may have played in the composition and transmission of Middle English romance has become a controversial issue. For some recent discussions, see William A. Quinn and Audley S. Hall, *Jongleur. A Modified Theory of Oral Improvisation and Its Effects on the Performance and Transmission of Middle English Romance* (Washington, D.C., 1982); Michael Chesnutt, 'Minstrel Reciters and the Enigma of the Middle English Romance,' *Culture and History* 2 (1987), 48–67; Murray McGillivray, *Memorization in the Transmission of the Middle English Romances* (New York and London, 1990); Andrew Taylor, 'The Myth of the Minstrel Manuscript,' *Speculum* 66 [1991], 53–60. For an historical study of individual minstrels and their known role in the transmission of poetry in England, see John Southworth, *The English Medieval Minstrel* (Woodbridge and Wolfeboro, N.H., 1989), esp. ch. 7: 'Sir Orfeo: Later Harpers and the English Romances' (pp. 87–100).

[110] 'The Date and Provenance of *King Horn*: Some Interim Reassessments,' in *Medieval English Studies Presented to George Kane*, ed. Edward Donald Kennedy, Ronald Waldron, Joseph S. Wittig (Cambridge, 1985), p. 125.

[111] The sole complete text of *Havelok*, Laud Misc. 108, has been dated from between 1290 and 1325, *ca.* 1300 being the usually accepted date (see Rosamund Allen, ed., *King Horn: An Edition Based on Cambridge University Library MS Gg.4,27 (2)* [New York, 1984], pp. 8, 102–03; G.V. Smithers, ed., *Hauelok* [Oxford, 1987], p. xvi; Diane Speed, *Medieval English Romances*, 2nd edn. [Sydney, 1989], I, 30). The date of composition is more difficult to establish. Speed concludes that 'the period 1189–1295 cannot be ruled out' (*Medieval English Romances*, I, 31); Smithers inclines to the end of this period. For surveys of scholarship on the subject, see Smithers, *Hauelok*, pp. lxiv–lxxiii; Speed, *Medieval English Romances*, I, pp. 30–32.

[112] And whose linguistic features type it as 'English of Lincolnshire' (G.V. Smithers, *Havelok*, p. lxxxix).

[113] For a summary of views, see Speed, *Medieval English Romances*, I, 31.

[114] It may, he suggests, 'have originated as part of the festivities in Lincoln at the time of the 1284 parliament' ('*Havelok the Dane*,' p. 623, n. 42).

daughter, Joan, to the Earl of Gloucester with a parliament in 1290[115] may have its fictional, and deliberately travestied, counterpart in the celebration of the marriage of Havelok and Goldeboru at Godrich's Lincoln assembly. The account of the athletic competition (ll. 1000–59) between the men accompanying those summoned to the *parlement* (ll. 1107, 1179) in *Havelok* may be a genuine reflection of the recreational activities of large retinues in attendance upon parliament's more affluent members.[116]

As Diane Speed expresses it: 'In terms of occasion, *Havelok* provides an entertainment promoting the self-esteem of Lincoln and Grimsby.'[117] If, as seems likely, *Havelok* does commemorate one of the early Lincoln parliaments, it is also conceivable that its recitation may have provided *sentence* and *solas* for later parliaments held there, such as those of 1301 and 1315. *Havelok* may also have associations with the Shrewsbury parliament of Michaelmas, 1283, held shortly before the Lincoln assembly of February, 1284. Representatives from both Lincoln and Grimsby were summoned to Shrewsbury by Edward I after the Welsh rebellion of 1282–83 for the dual purpose of celebrating his victory and dealing with the Welsh prince, Dafydd ap Gruffydd, who, judged as a traitor, suffered a judicial slaughter similar in some details to the sentences pronounced upon the *Havelok* villains, Godrich and Godard.[118] Dafydd's death may have made a particular impression on the Lincoln representatives, presumably present at the parliament as witnesses,[119] not only because of its savagery, but because, unlike the men of London, York, and Winchester, who squabbled over the distribution of the dismembered body, they refused any part of the gory trophy and were obliged to buy their way out of the king's displeasure with a substantial fine.[120]

Lincoln's record of thirteenth- and early fourteenth-century parliamentary service is substantial. It is one of twenty-two cities represented at each of the seven parliaments for which there is something approaching full documentation in the reign of Edward I. Six Lincoln representatives were also summoned to an assembly not officially designated as a 'parliament' in 1268.[121] The specific associations between *Havelok* and these parliaments may be debatable, but the various links

---

[115] See Miller, *The Origins of Parliament*, pp. 13–14.
[116] On the retinues accompanying magnates to parliament, see Butt, *A History of Parliament*, pp. 246–47, 264; Keen, *English Society*, pp. 112–14.
[117] *Medieval English Romances*, I, 36.
[118] Staines suggests that: 'The manner of David's execution may have served as a basis for the treatment of Godrich' ('*Havelok the Dane*', p. 620).
[119] Prestwich, *Edward I*, p. 202.
[120] Prestwich, *Edward I*, p. 203. Neither Godrich nor Godard is quartered in *Havelok*.
[121] McKisack, *The Parliamentary Representation of the English Boroughs*, pp. 2–3.

between *Havelok*, Lincoln, and the parliaments of Edward I are too numerous to be discounted.

Other Middle English romances may have topical allusions, either to particular parliaments and events of political notoriety or to more humdrum disputes and litigation. An incident in December, 1263, in which a London mob, incited by supporters of Henry III, barred the gates against Simon de Montfort may have been the stimulus for the London street battle towards the end of *Beves of Hamtoun*.[122] Some details of the central episode of *Athelston* recall the parliamentary crisis of 1340–41, in which the major players were John Stratford, Archbishop of Canterbury, and Edward III.[123] At a humbler level, *The Tale of Gamelyn* exhibits a detailed knowledge of fourteenth-century law, court procedure, and petitions reflecting the grievances of the rural gentry, which, Richard Kaeuper suggests, appeals to an audience of 'minor landowners, lesser knights and retainers – those who might at most hobnob with the prior of a nearby religious house and know the sheriff, but whose horizons are essentially local.'[124]

By the latter half of the thirteenth century, the gentry as a whole, and the knights of the shire in particular, exercised considerable control over local government. Contemporary evidence suggests that both shire knights, those 'work-horses of thirteenth-century government',[125] and burgesses were positively overburdened with administrative responsibilities. The 'Provisions of Oxford' required that a panel of four knights in every shire 'hear all complaints of any trespasses and injuries whatsoever, done to any persons whatsover by sheriffs, bailiffs, or any other persons'.[126] By this time, notes Helen Cam, 'the thirteenth-century shire is the field of the gentry, the knights, the squierarchy. The magnates have ceased to attend it, probably well before 1259; but, though the knights or gentlemen will undoubtedly take the lead in country doings, they will be working with freemen of ungentle blood, yeomen, *valetti*, who may represent the shire at parliaments if knights are not available.'[127] The boroughs also required their parliamentary representatives to further petitions and report on proceedings,[128] and the election of those

---

122 As suggested by Judith Weiss ('The Major Interpolations in *Sir Beues of Hamtoun*,' *Medium Ævum* 48 [1979], 74).
123 See further, chapter 2, below.
124 'An Historian's Reading of *The Tale of Gamelyn*,' *Medium Ævum* 52 (1983), 53.
125 J.C. Holt, 'The Prehistory of Parliament,' in Davies and Denton, *The English Parliament in the Middle Ages*, p. 28.
126 Treharne, *Documents of the Baronial Movement*, p. 99.
127 'The Theory and Practice of Representation in Medieval England,' in Fryde and Miller, ed., *Historical Studies of the English Parliament, Volume I*, p. 274 (substantially rpr. from *History* 1 [1953], 11–26).
128 On the parliamentary duties of burgesses, see McKisack, *The Parliamentary Representation of the English Boroughs*, pp. 131–45.

parliamentary representatives required not mere nomination but the consultation and assent of the community.[129] Attendance at the shire (county) courts, which were held approximately once a month, and where public opinion was formulated and communicated to parliament and government will made known by proclamation, often numbered in the hundreds in the fourteenth century.[130] The burden of local administration extended beyond the gentry to men engaged on an *ad hoc* basis for a specific task, such that, by 1300, it ranged 'from the friends of kings and members of the nobility to the remotest township constables'.[131]

The simultaneous emergence in the latter part of the thirteenth century of the 'middle ground' of society as a political force, the issuing of a proclamation to the shires by Henry III (in October, 1258) declaring support for his baronial counsellors (*rædesmen*) in English as well as the customary Latin and French,[132] and the appearance of romance in English[133] is suggestive of more than mere coincidence. With its heroes who prosper and win renown through wise counsel and service to the community, and who favour fellowship over passion, thirteenth- and fourteenth-century Middle English romance invites an audience of 'men of public affairs' – and their domestic and social circles. Opinion may differ as to its precise makeup, but that audience is likely to have been drawn from this socially heterogeneous estate of 'public servants', many of whom were familiar with French in the contexts of parliament,[134] the law, and commerce, but whose mother tongue was English.

This proposed audience excludes the lowest orders of society and, to go by the evidence of French romances known to have been in the

---

[129] J.R. Maddicott, 'Parliament and the Constituencies 1272–1377,' in Davies and Denton, ed., *The English Parliament in the Middle Ages*, p. 72. On the process of election, see Butt, *A History of Parliament*, pp. 255–58.

[130] See J.R. Maddicott, 'The County Community and the Making of Public Opinion in Fourteenth-Century England,' *Transactions of the Royal Historical Society*, 5th Series 28 (1978), 27–43.

[131] Helen M. Jewell, 'The cultural interests and achievements of the secular personnel of the local administration,' in *Profession, Vocation, and Culture*, ed. Cecil H. Clough (Liverpool, 1982), p. 131.

[132] The English version is available in Fernand Mossé, trans. James A. Walker, *A Handbook of Middle English* (Baltimore, 1952; rpr. 1961), pp. 187–89. See also Treharne, *Documents of the Baronial Movement*, pp. 116–17.

[133] The earliest extant romances are *King Horn* and *Floris and Blauncheflur*. *King Horn* has often been dated at *ca.* 1225, but a date of 1250 or 1270 is more probable, given the current dating of Cambridge University Library MS Gg.4.27(2) to 1300. See Rosamund Allen, *King Horn*, pp. 3, 101, 113–14; *eadem*, 'The Date and Provenance of *King Horn*,' pp. 99–125. F.C. de Vries puts *Floris and Blauncheflur*, which is found with *Horn* in the Cambridge manuscript, at *ca.* 1250 (*Floris and Blauncheflur: a Middle English Romance edited with introduction, notes and glossary* [Groningen, 1966], pp. 1–6, 50–51), although, as in the case of *Horn*, a date later in the thirteenth century is perhaps more likely.

[134] Parliament was opened for the first time in English in 1363.

possession of Richard II and his circle,[135] the royal court and some members of the nobility, but not necessarily the barons at large, for whom Anglo-Norman romance had been composed in earlier generations, although aristocratic tastes are more likely to have run to *Sir Gawain and the Green Knight* and *Ywain and Gawain* than to *Gamelyn*.[136] Its core, however, is what Noël Denholm-Young calls the 'parliamentary gentry', who, owing to a scarcity of knights by the fourteenth century, comprised not only 'belted knights' but also franklins and esquires.[137] The category of 'knight' at the parliaments of Edward III included 'anything from members of noble or knightly families, duly dubbed, to prosperous freemen without knightly forbears.'[138]

Divisions of the social hierarchy were not, in any case, clearly drawn. In the absence of an aristocratic English class defined by birth, on the French model, distinctions between barons and knights were largely on the basis of wealth, some knightly families approaching the lower baronial ranks in affluence, others being of much more modest means. Marriages between gentry and merchants were not uncommon, and, although they remained the dominant force amongst the commons in medieval parliaments, knights had no real exclusivity as a socio-political group after borough and city representatives joined them there.

Coss is inclined to exclude the mercantile class in his discussion of the origins of Middle English romance, which he places in the provinces, amongst the rural gentry.[139] In her discussion of the date and provenance of *King Horn*, however, Rosamund Allen notes the possibly coincidental prominence of the Horn family in the London guild of fishmongers in the thirteenth and fourteenth centuries.[140] Sylvia Thrupp's study of gentry-merchant relations from 1300–1500 points to integration – social,

---

135 See Edith Rickert, 'King Richard II's Books,' *The Library* (*Transactions of the Bibliographical Society*) 13 (1932–33), 144–47; V.J. Scattergood, 'Literary Culture at the Court of Richard II,' in *English Court Culture in the Later Middle Ages*, ed. Scattergood and Sherborne, pp. 29–43.

136 Citing the aristocratic bent of *Sir Gawain and the Green Knight*, Derek Pearsall draws attention to the wide range and probable differences in the composition of metropolitan and rural romance audiences ('Middle English Romance and its Audiences,' p. 43).

137 N. Denholm-Young, *The Country Gentry in the Fourteenth Century* (Oxford, 1969), p. 15. For the example of the highly successful career of Simon Pakeman, who falls into the 'non-gentry' category but represented Leicestershire at parliaments in 1334, 1346, 1348, and 1365, see G.G. Astill, 'Social Advancement through Seignorial Service? The case of Simon Pakeman,' *Transactions of the Leicestershire Archaeological and Historical Society* 54 (1978–79), 14–25. Many parliamentary burgesses may actually have been shire knights (see May McKisack, *The Parliamentary Representation of the English Boroughs*, pp. 100–101).

138 Butt, *A History of Parliament*, p. 254.

139 'Aspects of Cultural Diffusion,' pp. 40–41.

140 'The Date and Provenance of *King Horn*,' pp. 124–25.

economic, and cultural – rather than separatism from the beginning of this period, leading to a joint occupation of the 'middle ground' of society.[141] French being the language of commerce, the merchants of London might well, as Coss suggests, have enjoyed the French songs of the organization known as the *Pui*[142] in a professional context, but their tastes could also have run to English romance in another.[143] A hypothetical analogy could be drawn with the gentry: using French in public life but English for pleasure. The evidence of the allusions to Horn, Guy, and Beves in *Sir Thopas*[144] suggests that Chaucer and his wide circle were as familiar with romance in English as with more sophisticated narrative.

In summary, the production and audience of romance in English might have developed along the following lines: Middle English romance originated among the rural gentry in the second half of the thirteenth century; its audience and stimulus to production grew towards the end of that century as a result of the increasing common interests of gentry and merchants, making the purchaser of the Auchinleck manuscript as likely to have been Coss's gentleman from the provinces as Pearsall's London merchant; by the mid-fourteenth century, the audience for romance in English included the nobility, especially in the provinces, as anti-French sentiment accelerated the reinstatement of English as the language of culture among the upper classes.

Perfectly, although hardly typically, representative of this proposed audience is Chaucer himself: fringe dweller in royal circles, soldier, diplomat, vintner's son, civil servant, knight of the shire for Kent in 1386, and author and self-styled narrator of the failed romance of *Sir Thopas*, which makes specific reference to the heroes of three (*Horn Childe, Beves of Hamtoun, Guy of Warwick*) preserved in the Auchinleck manuscript.

This postulated audience of 'public servants' differs from the audience of French chivalric romance in its social diversity and experience of power; for, unlike the aristocratic consumers of *romans courtois*, whose position was firmly fixed in the feudal hierarchy, the administrators of

---

[141] For a detailed discussion, see Thrupp, *The Merchant Class*, pp. 247–87.

[142] 'Aspects of Cultural Diffusion,' pp. 40–41. The *Pui* existed in London in the thirteenth and fourteenth century; its membership was both English and foreign (see further, J.H. Fisher [*John Gower*, pp. 78–83], who suggests that Gower may have written his balades for it).

[143] If, as seems likely, *King Horn* was written in the London area, Rosamund Allen proposes that: 'its first audience must have consisted of London citizens, probably the merchants of the City, familiar with Anglo-Norman for business purposes and perhaps engaged in some official business with court dignitaries, but less interested in the socially and culturally prestigious Anglo-Norman literature' ('The Date and Provenance of *King Horn*,' p. 121).

[144] 'Men speken of romances of prys,/ Of Horn child and of Ypotys,/ Of Beves and sir Gy' (ll. 897–99).

fourteenth-century England exercised a range of constitutional authority, from royal councils to county courts. Through various forms of the conciliar process, this socially diverse group was commonly engaged, at different levels of the body politic, in an occupation which actively engaged the interest of the composers of Middle English romance: the exercise and regulation of power and authority.[145]

[145] In arguing that these 'public servants' shared a common ideology of power, I am essentially in agreement, although from a different perspective, with the view recently expressed by John Simons: 'that the court, the aristocracy and the gentry both urban and rural had a common relationship to the power to rule produced by the feudal economy and that, therefore, they may be considered as constituting a class in the most fundamental sense . . . just as they had a more-or-less common purpose as rulers, so they shared a culture which presented to them idealized pictures of that power' ('Northern *Octavian* and the question of class,' in *Romance in Medieval England*, p. 107).

CHAPTER TWO

The Custom of Counsel in Middle English Romance

Ywain and Gawain, Havelok, Gamelyn, Athelston

From the viewpoint of social history, the conciliar process in Middle English romance reflects Norman feudal tradition and nascent English institutions. Within the context of fourteenth-century English literature, the romance ideal of 'working by counsel' touches on the concern for the common good which finds expression in the 'public' poetry of the Ricardian period and the literature of complaint.

The immediate literary models for consultative dialogue in insular romance are, however, to be found elsewhere: in Old French *chansons de geste*, where lord and vassals publicly debate questions of military and diplomatic strategy,[1] and where private counsel on the subject of warfare is also sometimes supplied by women.[2] These patterns of 'epic' counsel are repeated and extended in insular romance: in public assemblies and formal councils of war, judgment, and policy, and in scenes of private consultation between lord and vassal, husband and wife, tutor and pupil, fellow knights, and less typical combinations of counsellor and counselled. Whereas public counsel tends to be a response to crisis, private consultation, often as the medium for conspiracy, may set the crisis in motion. In *Havelok, Gamelyn*, and *Athelston*, and, to a lesser extent, in *Ywain and Gawain*, the conciliar process itself is subjected to scrutiny.

'Counsel' comes under two lexical headings in Middle English romance: *red* (OE *ræd*) and the loan-word *counseil* (OFr *consoil*). The *Middle English Dictionary* gives 'advice' (1a) as the primary definition of *red*, but its semantic field extends to 'decision' (2a); 'judgment' (2b); 'course of

---

[1] On the 'epic council' see R. Howard Bloch, *Medieval French Literature and Law* (Berkeley, Los Angeles, London, 1977), pp. 104–07.

[2] See Micheline de Combarieu du Grès, *L'idéal humain et l'expérience moral chez les héros des chansons de geste, des origines à 1250*, 2 vols. (Paris, 1979), I, 396–99; Penny Gold, *The Lady and the Virgin. Image, Attitude, and Experience in Twelfth-Century France* (Chicago and London, 1985), pp. 6–18. Women also play a 'goading' consultative role in the *Íslendingasögur* (see, for example, Miller, *Bloodtaking and Peacemaking*, pp. 212–14).

action', 'plan', (3a); 'assistance' (4a); 'remedy' (4b); 'consultation', (5a); 'wisdom' (6a). *Counseil* has a similar range, which includes 'council' (1a); 'the act of discussing or conferring' (2); 'a body of advisers to a ruler' (3a); 'advice' (5a); 'decision', 'plan', 'scheme' (6a); 'judgment', 'wisdom' (9).

As 'advice', *red* and *counseil* have a variety of application – moral, political, legal, strategic, and paedogogical – in Middle English romance. *Red* also frequently appears in the sense of 'remedy', and *counseil* as 'confidence' or 'secret'.[3] Private scenes of consultation often concern the giving or exchange of such confidential *counseil*,[4] but when counsel as 'private conferring' has to do with evil plotting, the term is *counseil* rather than *red*. In *Athelston*, for instance, Wymound represents his slander of Egeland to the king as *counseil* (l. 122);[5] in *Beves of Hamtoun*, Beves's mother calls her messenger to *consaile* (l. 71) to plot the murder of her husband; in *Guy of Warwick*, a steward, who has been plotting against the hero, is killed in the very act of conspiratorial *counseyl* (l. 4377).

The characteristics which John Ganim attributes to the crucial scenes of the early romances of *King Horn* and *Havelok* – direct speech in the service of 'revelation, discovery, information, and communication'[6] – hold true for Middle English romance in general. *Floris and Blancheflur*, for example, which radically abbreviates its French source, *Floire et Blanchefleur*, completely excises an internal debate in the hero's mind between *Savoir* and *Amours*, but focusses in some detail on scenes of direct speech devoted to the seeking of counsel in the cause of strategy.[7] Verbal communication is itself of central significance in the apparently sourceless romances of *Athelston* and *Sir Gawain and the Green Knight*.

Attempted resolution by consultation sets *chansons de geste* and insular romance apart from French chivalric romance, where problem solving is largely a matter of internal debate.[8] There is no Merlin figure in the

---

3   *Middle English Dictionary* (*MED*), ed. Hans Kurath, *et al.* (Ann Arbor, 1956-), s.v. *red; counseil.*

4   The metonymical sense of *counseil* as 'love affair' is largely the province of French romance. For a discussion of *counseil* in this context, see Leigh A. Arrathoon, 'Jacques de Vitry, the Tale of Calogrenant, *La Chastelaine de Vergi*, and the Genres of Medieval Narrative Fiction,' in Arrathoon, ed., *The Craft of Fiction. Essays in Medieval Poetics* [Rochester, Mich., 1989], pp. 333–36.

5   References are to A.McI. Trounce, ed., *Athelston. A Middle English Romance*, EETS 224 (London, 1951).

6   'History and Consciousness in Middle English Romance,' *The Literary Review* 23 (1979–80), 493.

7   See chapter 4, below.

8   See Bloch, *Medieval French Literature and Law*, pp. 164–66, 189–90; Eugene Vance, *From Topic to Tale* (Minneapolis, 1987), pp. 23–25. Charles Muscatine's article, 'The Emergence of Psychological Allegory in the Old French Romance,' *Publications of the Modern Language Association* 68 (1953), 1160–82, is seminal.

narratives of Chrétien de Troyes, where, unlike Beowulf or Charlemagne, Arthur himself is rarely a giver and never a seeker of counsel, and women, such as Lunete in Chrétien's *Yvain*, are restricted to devising strategies in love.[9] Drawing on his inner resources for counsel and guidance, the hero of the *roman courtois* tends to be an introverted and isolated figure.[10] Lacking the counselling resources of tutor, father, or lord, he must ask himself, 'what shall I do?'[11]

Instead of cerebral consideration of the nature of the problem, Middle English romance gives us verbal discussion of its solution. The deliberative process normally takes the form of question-and-answer discussion, short exchanges of dialogue replacing the lengthy internal monologues of chivalric romance. When monologue does appear, it tends to be declarative rather than interrogative.[12] Even in a work as reminiscent, in some respects, of Chrétien's narratives as *Sir Gawain and the Green Knight*, we are not made privy to Gawain's inner turmoil from a first-person viewpoint. The procedural model in thirteenth- and fourteenth-century English romance is therefore not first-person debate but second-person resolution. In the first of several monologues in the opening, 'courtly' section of *Guy of Warwick*, the hero asks himself, 'Allas, wreche, what may y do?' (l. 307),[13] but, customarily, heroes – and villains,

9 Their objective, as Penny Gold notes, being 'the personal goal of the reunion of the estranged lovers rather than a social goal of defense of Christendom, king, or family' (*The Lady and the Virgin*, pp. 23–24).

10 In *Li Contes del Graal* Perceval has the benefit of the advice of, but is not accompanied on his travels by, a series of chivalric instructors.

11 Bloch makes the following distinction between the epic *concilium* and the internal debate of 'courtly' romance: 'Instead of the recurrent questions debated before the epic council . . . the chivalric hero or heroine asks himself, like Enide, "Wretch, what shall I do?", like Soredamors, "Mad that I am, what shall I do?", or like Lancelot, "God, what shall I do?" (*Erec* v. 3715 ['A li meïsmes s'an consoille'], *Cligés* v. 889 ['Fole, qu'ai je a feire'], *Lancelot* v. 1097 ['Dex, que porrai ge feire?']). And though the issues and responses differ in each case, the fact remains that the individual and not the assembled community, bears the sole responsibility of choice' (*Medieval French Literature and Law*, p. 233). (Bloch's Chrétien references are to Mario Roques, ed., *Erec et Enide* [Paris, 1963]; André Micha, ed., *Cligés* [Paris, 1957]; Mario Roques, ed., *Le Chevalier de la charrete* [Paris, 1958]).

12 Ganim comments that: 'Oddly, the characters of early Middle English romance . . . lack introspection, perhaps because . . . they are meant to embody synthesis and not internal conflict' ('History and Consciousness,' p. 493; cf. *Style and Consciousness*, p. 51). There an example of what Susan Crane refers to as 'vestigial monologue' in *Sir Tristrem*, where Tristan's internal debate on whether or not to marry Isolt of Britanny, a passage of some 365 lines in Thomas's *Tristan* (Bartina Wind, ed., *Les fragments du Roman de Tristan, poème du XIIe siècle* [Paris and Geneva, 1960], Fragment Sneyd, ll. 1–364) is distilled into one stanza in the English poem (*Insular Romance*, p. 190).

13 References are to Julius Zupitza, ed., *The Romance of Guy of Warwick, edited from the Auchinleck MS. in the Advocates' Library, Edinburgh and from MS.107 in Caius College, Cambridge*, EETS, e.s. 42, 49, 59 (London, 1883, 1887, 1891; rpr. as one volume, 1966).

too – solicit counsel (*counseil, red*) from individual or collective interlocutors or to appeal to them for a specific course of action (*red*). Instead of 'what shall I do?,' the characters of Middle English romance are more likely to ask: 'Wat shal me to rede?'[14]

Dialogue is the linguistic mark of the 'socialization' of the heroes of Middle English romance, but the importance of direct speech goes beyond the mechanics of consultation. As the instrument of counsel, the spoken word may also be the means of resolving conflict and, as statement of intent or pledge of *trawpe* ('fidelity') to a verbal contract, serve as the measure and test of knightly integrity. In *King Horn*, at least half of which is in direct speech, the hero's honesty is underlined by the congruence of his words and deeds.[15] In *Ywain and Gawain* and *Sir Gawain and the Green Knight*, on the other hand, a knight's word proves not to be his bond; and *Athelston* demonstrates the negative power of speech as slander.[16]

Three of the four narratives under consideration in this chapter – *Havelok*, *Athelston*, and *Gamelyn* – illustrate the consequences of bad counsel at royal, baronial, and knightly levels. *Havelok* and *Athelston* focus on problems of royal counsel, the duties of kingship, and the well-being of the nation, while *Gamelyn*, which shares some similarities of plot with *Havelok*, relates an instance of ill-considered counsel leading to the abuse of power at the shire level. In *Ywain and Gawain* benign manipulation, through private counsel, of a ruler and her council of barons brings about her marriage in the first place and reconciliation with her spouse after a period of estrangement.

---

[14] E.g. *Havelok*, ll. 118, 693; *Guy of Warwick*, ll. 1902–03, 2485; *Beves of Hamtoun* (ed. Eugen Kölbing, *EETS*, e.s. 46, 47, 48 [London, 1885, 1886, 1894]), l. 2912; *Floris and Blauncheflur*, (ed. F.C. de Vries [Groningen, 1966]), Egerton MS l. 64; *Gamelyn* (ed. W.W. Skeat [Oxford, 1893]), l. 429; *Otuel* (ed. Sidney J.H. Herrtage, *EETS*, e.s. 39 [London, 1882], ll. 657, 1517).

[15] 'Horn's honest deeds are repeatedly shown to confirm his honest words, his honest words and deeds project honest intentions and desires' (Anne Scott, 'Plans, Predictions, and Promises: Traditional Story Techniques and the Configuration of Word and Deed in *King Horn*,' in Derek Brewer, ed., *Studies in Medieval English Romances: Some New Approaches* [Cambridge, 1988], pp. 49–50). Similarly, Mary Hynes-Berry demonstrates that the focus of interest in *King Horn* is 'not in why or in the details of how something is done, but in the fact that heroes do what they say they will do' ('Cohesion in *King Horn* and *Sir Orfeo*,' *Speculum* 50 (1975), 654). Carol Fewster demonstrates how, at the end of the period of composition of Middle English verse romance, *The Squyr of Low Degre* (*ca.* 1450) uses direct speech for a very different purpose: to articulate the pronounced generic self-consciousness of that narrative in long speeches by two characters who assume the role of narrator and take over the composition of the romance (*Traditionality and Genre*, pp. 139–47).

[16] 'the betrayer works "þorwz wurd" [through speech] (87), his falseness renders even language untrustworthy, so that truth becomes accessible only through direct appeal to God' (Crane, *Insular Romance*, p. 126).

Ywain and Gawain

The emphasis on direct speech over internal monologue in *Ywain and Gawain* (*ca.* 1325–50),[17] an often close adaptation of Chrétien's *Yvain*, is a significant factor in transforming the English narrative from an unresolved, or only superficially resolved, case of the 'courtly dilemma',[18] to the straightforward story of a knight who breaks his word, acknowledges his fault, and seeks reconciliation through the offices of a third party.

Speech, as print tends to be today, is acknowledged as an authenticating, although often abused, narrative medium in the prologue to the English romance. It is not the condemnation by Chrétien's narrator of the contemporary deterioration in love service (*Yvain* [Y], ll. 18–28)[19] which concerns the narrator of *Ywain and Gawain* (YG) so much as the decline in standards of reporting, caused by the abuse of oral authority, which misrepresents fiction as fact:

> For trowth and luf es al bylaft;
> Men uses now anoþer craft.
> With worde men makes it trew and stabil,
> Bot in þaire faith is noght bot fabil;
> With þe mowth men makes it hale,
> Bot trew trowth es nane in þe tale.   (ll. 35–40)

After a conventional opening ('listens a lytel stownde,' l. 6), suggestive but not necessarily indicative of oral presentation, in the next forty-five lines of *Ywain and Gawain* verbs (*carped, tald*), phrases (*with worde, went the worde*), and formulaic expressions concerning speaking and telling (*als says the buke, the soth to say*) dominate the references to story-telling and the dissemination of facts. Whereas *Yvain* tends to confine itself to unmodified verbs of speaking and replying, tone or manner of speaking is also frequently qualified in *Ywain and Gawain*: for example, when Yvain merely speaks (Y l. 631), Ywain does so *ful hendly* (l. 496); Guinevere speaks *with milde mode* (l. 483), and Kay *smertly* (ll. 117, 466) and *ful tite* (l. 105).

---

17 All references are to Albert B. Friedman and Norman T. Harrington, ed., *Ywain and Gawain*, EETS 254 (London, New York, Toronto, 1964). On the dating of the poem, see pp. lvi–lviii. The sole copy is preserved in Cotton Galba E. ix.

18 I am subscribing here to Tony Hunt's illuminating reading of *Yvain* in 'Beginnings, Middles, and Ends: Some Interpretative Problems in Chrétien's *Yvain* and its Medieval Adaptations,' in Leigh A. Arrathoon, ed., *The Craft of Fiction. Essays in Medieval Poetics* (Rochester, Mich., 1984), pp. 83–117.

19 References are to T.B.W. Reid, *Chrestien de Troyes: Yvain (Le Chevalier au lion). The critical text of Wendelin Foerster with introduction, notes and glossary* (Manchester, 1942).

33

Ywain and Gawain is filled with images of the process of speech and oral reporting, a stylistic feature underlined by the formulaic reinforcement of references to speech and narrative by phrases like *with mowth* and *with tong*:

> *With þe mowth* men makes it hale' (l. 39)
> He answerd me mildeli *with mowth* (l. 172)
> *Of tong* sho was trew and renable' (l. 209).
> No reson forto speke *with mowth* (l. 276)
> It es no lifand man *with mowth*,
> þat half hir cumforth tel kowth (ll. 1381–2)
> no man *with tong* may tell (l. 1427)
> Al if he [the lion] myght noght speke *with mowth* (l. 2006)

The term *word* exercises its full semantic range, denoting not only speech (ll. 100–101, 128, 467, 700, etc.) and its physical production ('And kene *wordes* out gan he cast,' l. 408), but reputation (ll. 46,1574) and the proclamation of royal intent: 'The kynges *word* might noght be hid' (l. 529). In an utterance unparalleled in *Yvain*, Ywain admonishes his lion in the middle of his duel with Alundyne's seneschal to remove himself from the fray: 'Als *with wordes* did his main/ Forto chastis hys lyowne' (ll. 2624–25). Discord within Arthur's court in the opening scene of the narrative is entirely the result of Kay's verbal abuse, which is emphasized not by Chrétien's general reference to his maliciousness ('. . . qui mout fu ranposneus,/ Fel et poignanz et afiteus,' ll. 69–70) but by a specific, if formulaic, reference to the agent of that spite, his tongue: 'he was of his tong a skalde' (l. 69).

A non-verbal response in *Yvain* becomes spoken on at least one occasion in *Ywain and Gawain*.[20] The scornful gesture with which Salados, the Knight of the Fountain, dismisses Colgrevance (Fr. Calogrenant) after winning their skirmish, is expressed in negative verbal terms in the English narrative ('A worde to me wald he noght say,' l. 429), whereas in *Yvain*, Esclados signifies his contempt by denying him a further glance: 'Qu'onques puis ne me regarda' (l. 543). And while Yvain is left wordless

---

[20] Although the exemplar of *Yvain* used by the English adaptor does not appear to duplicate any of the extant manuscripts of *Yvain*, correspondences between *Ywain and Gawain* and Foerster's edition of BN f.fr. 1433 and BN f.fr. 794 are sufficiently consistent to justify French-English comparisons. On the relationship of *YG* to the French manuscripts and for a detailed comparison of the two narratives, see Friedman and Harrington, *Ywain and Gawain*, pp. xvi–xxxiv. See also Mehl, *The Middle English Romances*, pp. 180–85; W.R.J. Barron, *English Medieval Romance* (London and New York, 1987), pp. 160–63; Keith Busby, 'Chrétien de Troyes English'd,' *Neophilologus* 71 (1987), 596–613.

at the accusation of faithlessness by Laudine's messenger (Y ll. 2774–75),[21] Ywain utters a brief speech of remorse (YG ll. 1644–48). Short passages of reported speech in Yvain frequently become direct, often complete in a single couplet, and attributed to minor characters in the English version. The brief speech (YG ll. 1959–62) by a lady, who offers herself and her lands as the Ywain's reward after he has saved from a predatory count, is, for example, expressed only indirectly in the French (Y ll. 3317–19; 3330–35). The English author adds that, despite the force of her pleading, Ywain is unmoved: 'Bot al hir speche avayles noght' (l. 1964).[22] In one instance dialogue is preferred over collective speech: the chorus of approval for the hero by the occupants of a besieged castle in Yvain (Y ll. 3196–242) becomes a conversation between the lady of the castle and her lady-in-waiting (YG ll. 1892–908).

Internal monologue in Yvain is either greatly reduced, reported indirectly, or omitted altogether. Pondering characters are reported as being, simply, 'in stody' (YG ll. 909, 972–73). Monologues of some 130 lines (Y ll. 1355–405; 1428–506), in which first the narrator and then Ywain contemplate the latter's paradoxical bond of love and enmity with Laudine, the lady whom he has just widowed in order to avenge the defeat of his kinsman and fellow knight of the Round Table, Colgrevance, are reduced to a total of twenty-five (YG ll. 871–78; 891–908). On the other hand, whereas Ywain and Gawain prunes Laudine's imaginary internal debate with Yvain (Y ll. 1757–72) during a night-long tançon (Y l. 1735) to a spare five lines on the subject of her relationship with Lunet (YG ll. 1028–32), the substance of Laudine's parlemanz (Y l. 1878) with Lunete the following morning, in which the latter counsels her on the necessity of, and the

---

21 Eugene Vance makes an interesting comment on the significance of Yvain's muteness here: 'Since speech is one of the most obvious differentiae of human beings as species, it should come as no surprise that the first property that Yvain loses when Lunette demands the return of the ring that Laudine had given him at their wedding is, precisely, his faculty of speech' (From Topic to Tale, p. 66).

22 For other examples, see YG ll. 527–8: 'Swith,' he sayd, 'wendes with me,/ Who so wil þat wonder se' and Y ll. 671–72: 'Et dit que avuec lui iront/ Tuit cil, qui aler i 'voldront'; YG ll. 1713–14: 'A naked [man] me think I se;/ Wit I wil what it may be' and Y ll. 2890–93: 'Et une lor dame avuec eles . . . Vers l'ome nu, que eles voient,/ Cort et desant l'une des trois'; YG ll. 1943–44: 'He said, 'Madame, have þi presoun/ And hald him here in þi baundoun' and Y ll. 3302–03: 'Mes sire Yvains par la main tient/ Son prisonier, si li presante'; YG ll. 1959–70, Y ll. 3315–35; YG ll. 2217–18: 'Þai said, "Syr, withowten dowt,/ Þat best byhoves þe leve þarout" ', and Y ll. 3791–92: 'Si li dïent, que, se lui plest,/ Son lion a la porte lest'; YG ll. 2339–40: 'Þai said, "He es of grete renowne,/ For with hym dwels þe lyoun"',' and Y ll. 4009–10: 'Et mout cuident, qu'il soit prodon,/ Por la conpaignie au lion'; YG ll. 2381–2: '3owre sons bringes he him byforn,/ Wel nere naked als þai war born', and Y l. 4095: 'Et il n'avoient pas vestu.' For similar, more extended comparisons, see YG 1723–30, Y ll. 2909–12; YG 1763–68, Y ll. 2967–73; YG ll. 1792–96; Y ll. 3020–22; YG ll. 1841–54, Y ll. 3092–112; YG ll. 2397–404, Y ll. 4113–29; YG ll. 2517–22, Y ll. 4332–36; YG ll. 2688–98; Y ll. 4640–50; YG ll. 3352–56, Y ll. 5800–04; YG ll. 3373–78, Y ll. 5824–31.

appropriate strategy for, obtaining the consent of her court to marriage with her husband's slayer (Y ll. 1795–877), is recounted at length (YG ll. 1040–96). Similarly, the long dialogue between Yvain and Lunete (Y ll. 978–1025), in which the latter pledges her assistance to him, appears in *Ywain and Gawain* in virtually line-for-line detail (YG ll. 701–46).

The romantic alliance between Yvain/Ywain and Laudine/Alundyne is the central relationship of Chrétien's *Yvain* and its Middle English adaptation, but the English author's reduction of the love component makes the story's several 'counselling' alliances – between Lunete and Yvain, Lunete and Laudine, Gauvain and Yvain, Laudine and her barons, and Arthur and his subjects – more prominent. The most important counsellor in *Ywain and Gawain* is Lunet, strategist and go-between for Ywain and Alundyne, who is specifically elevated from the position of Laudine's 'mestre et sa garde' (Y l. 1593) or 'maidservant and her keeper' to that of her '. . . maystres,/ Her keper and hir cownsaylere' (YG ll. 936–37).

Lunet's counsel to and on behalf of Ywain ranges from the offer of life-saving, practical advice ('If þou wil my kownsail leve,/ Þou sal find na man þe to greve,' ll. 735–36), when he finds himself trapped inside Alundyne's castle after mortally wounding her husband, Salados, to formulating a strategy for winning her love and, eventually, effecting the reconciliation of the couple after a period of estrangement. Lunet's relationship with Alundyne, who needs a new husband to defend her lands and magic spring, is more complicated: combining the roles of trickster-counsellor, she successfully presents amatory strategy for Ywain as political strategy for her mistress. Her manipulation, by means of her privileged role as Alundyne's counsellor and confidante, of the latter's council of barons, who are characterized in both French and English as cowardly and ineffectual (Y ll. 1628–35; YG ll. 1083–84), eclipses the emotional turmoil of Yvain and Laudine to become the focus of narrative interest in *Ywain and Gawain*. The role of Alundyne's barons in the matter of her remarriage is reduced merely to giving *assent* (YG ll. 1182, 1188, 1229) to that which has previously been decided between Lunet and Alundyne in private consultation.

Lunete proves to be a brilliant counsellor and strategist in matters of love in *Yvain*, but Gauvain fails miserably. When Arthur and his court visit the newlyweds, Yvain becomes the object of an exhortatory speech by Gauvain (Y ll. 2484–538) on the dangers of idleness and uxoriousness. The sub-text of this oration is, in Tony Hunt's view, a 'farrago of *raisonnements* and *non-sequiturs* . . . a burlesque of Ovidian and Courtly Love doctrines for purely selfish purposes,'[23] which ultimately leads to the loss

[23] Hunt, 'Beginnings, Middles, and Ends,' pp. 92–96.

of Yvain's happiness. In both French and English, Gauvain's urging leads the hero to request a twelve-month furlough from marriage in order to return to the tournament circuit, with a promise to do everything in his power to return at the end of that term (YG ll. 1515–24). Preoccupied with the pursuit of renown, he fails to do so. Laudine/Alundyne denounces and renounces him; and, after a temporary bout of insanity brought on by grief and remorse, the hero embarks on a series of adventures in which he saves the life of a lion, who becomes his companion and epithet, selflessly rendering assistance to ladies in distress, and winning a reputation for matchless prowess in good causes.

The corresponding and much shorter speech by Gawain in *Ywain and Gawain* (ll. 1455–78) lacks any suggestion of humbug. Gawain simply warns Ywain against sloth for the sake of his chivalric reputation and marital happiness.[24] The logic of his counsel here:

> Þat knyght es nothing to set by,
> Þat leves al his chevalry
> And ligges bekeand in his bed
> When he haves a lady wed   (ll. 1457–60)

is illustrated later in the poem, when Ywain echoes it to indicate that he knows exactly what the proper response by a knight to a plea from a distressed damsel should be:

> He said, 'Þat knyght þat idil lies
> Oft siþes winnes ful litel pries.
> Forþi mi rede sal sone be tane'   (ll. 2923–25)

Although Yvain's words in the corresponding scene in Yvain are similar:

> ... de reposer
> Ne se puet nus hon aloser,
> Ne je ne reposerai mie,
> Ainz vos siurai, ma douce amie!'   (ll. 5095–98)

they lack the pointed parallel with Gauvain's earlier counsel.

When, during the course of his adventures in *Yvain*, the hero, unrecognized, encounters Lunete, now awaiting execution for 'treason' and lamenting her own lack of *consoil* (Y 3676, 3681, 3694), she tells him that she is the victim of the envy of Laudine's wicked ('Uns fel, uns lerre, uns desleaus,' l. 3668) steward. Bitter about Laudine's well justified inclina-

---

24 Hunt comments that Gawain's words to Ywain 'seem designed to enhance his chivalry' ('Beginnings, Middles, and Ends,' p. 101)

tion to put her trust in Lunete rather than in him ('Por ce, que ma dame creoit/ Moi plus, que lui de maint afeire,' ll. 3670–71), the steward has, she says, seized the opportunity to settle the score when Yvain fails to return by the due date, and had her convicted for initiating an ill-advised marriage. In *Ywain and Gawain*, on the other hand, the implication is that Lunet has been condemned by all of Alundyne's barons for being her preferred counsellor. She is the victim of their collective envy for her privileged position as counsellor-confidante rather than of the individual spite of the steward:

> Sir, þai say þat my lady
> Lufed me moste specially,
> And wroght al efter my rede;
> Þarefore þai hate me to þe ded.
> Þe steward says þat done have I
> Grete tresone unto my lady   (ll. 2159–64)

Although Friedman and Harrington consider Lunet's account here to be somewhat confused, because of its lack of reference to the cause of the steward's hostility,[25] the English author may have deliberately substituted the motif of the jealous counsellor for that of the wicked steward, the initial description of Lunet as Alundyne's *cownsaylere* providing an implicit motive for the collective enmity of Alundyne's baronial council.

Having vindicated Lunet in judicial combat, Ywain remedies another problem of 'counsel', that of the *redeless* king. In the penultimate of the adventures which follow his estrangement from Alundyne, he liberates a kingdom from the consequences of its youthful ruler's lack of *red*. *Yvain* refers to the folly of this king of the *Isle as Puceles* in capitulating to the demand for payment of an annual ransom of maidens to two demons as, simply, 'the best he could do' ('S'an delivra au miauz qu'il pot,' l. 5280), but in *Ywain and Gawain*, it is said to be the best course of action which the king of 'Maydenland' can manage: 'he kouth no better rede' (l. 3030). The expression is a formula, variations of which occur elsewhere in *Ywain and Gawain* (e.g. l. 2376) and in other Middle English romances, and its appearance may simply be illustrative of a difference in French and English idiom. Nevertheless, in this particular instance, 'kouth no better rede' may have thematic significance in its explicit association of kingly failure and poverty of *red*. In overcoming, with the aid of his lion, a temporary failure of red on his own account when hard-pressed in

---

[25] 'Chrétien takes some pains to tell how and why Lunete finds herself in her predicament, but E [*Ywain and Gawain*] (2159–66) foreshortens this background to the point of distortion, leaving the motive for the steward's enmity obscure and arbitrary' (*Ywain and Gawain*, p. xxix).

combat with the demons ('Þarof cowth Ywayn no rede,' l. 3235), Ywain simultaneously becomes the remedy for the woes of the people of Maydenland and the embodiment of the *red* of which their king is bereft.

There are clear parallels between the last two episodes of *Ywain and Gawain*, in which wise counsel and shrewd strategy are the means of resolving legal and marital conflict. The first concerns two sisters in a dispute over their inheritance, which requires settlement through judicial combat. The younger sister seeks the assistance (*cownsayl*, l. 2758) of a champion from Arthur's court, but the services of Gawain, who has undertaken to act, incognito, for the elder, are unavailable, and, she decides, her only hope is the renowned 'Knight with the Lion', whose reputation has reached the Round Table. Once again, Ywain embodies *counseil* as remedy and acts as the maiden's champion in an inconclusive duel with Gawain in which neither recognizes the other. When the two knights identify themselves after a gruelling contest, their reunion is joyful, prompting Arthur to ask: 'Wha had so sone made saghteling/ Bitwix þam þat had bene so wrath' (ll. 3682–83).

Whereas the English author reduces the narrator's long, speculative monologue on the paradoxical nature of Love and Hate, when Yvain and Gauvain begin their duel (*Y* ll. 6001–105), to four lines (*YG* ll. 3521–24), Arthur's question here faithfully renders his words in *Yvain*:

> Qui si tost a mis antre vos
> Ceste amistié et cest acorde?
> Que tel haïne et tel descorde
> I a hui tote jor eüe! (ll. 6322–25)

Saghteling ('reconciliation'), between knights, siblings, and spouses, is the dominant theme of *Ywain and Gawain* from this point on. The sisters' case is finally resolved when Arthur delivers judgment, thus showing himself to be possessed of the ability conspicuously lacking in the king of Maydenland, and brings their 'grete debate' (l. 3732)[26] to an end. Arthur's ruling is given legal reinforcement by his statement that nothing will persuade him to act other than according to the law of the land (*YG* ll. 3739–40) and, in a rare first-person appearance by the narrator (*YG* ll. 3767–78), is said to have established an English precedent for the laws of inheritance.[27]

When Ywain returns to Alundyne's demesne and demonstrates her vulnerability to attack by raising a storm at the spring, once again she

---

[26] 'A legal controversy, a suit, an action; a dispute submitted to legal arbitration,' *MED*, s.v. *debate* (2).

[27] On the legal aspects of Arthur's judgment here, see Friedman and Harrington, *Ywain and Gawain*, pp. 130–31 (note to ll. 3767–72).

turns to Lunet for advice[28] and learns that, although her best prospect for defence is the Knight with the Lion, his turbulent private life has put his chivalric career in abeyance. Lunete represents the knight as the passive object of his lady's ire in *Yvain* (*Y* ll. 6606–07) and elicits a formal oath from Laudine that she will strive to assist him in assuaging the lady's enmity (*Y* ll. 6611–12), to be reconciled with her (*Y* 6620–21; l. 6735), to regain her love (*Y* ll. 6648–49) and *grace* (*Y* l. 6656), and to win her pardon (*Y* l. 6735). A slight but significant change of emphasis in *Ywain and Gawain* alters the issue to one of reconciliation between warring parties, rather than of the restoration of his lady's good graces to a distraught lover. Lunet speaks of the renowned knight as being actively 'at debate' (*YG* l. 3890), that is, 'quarrelling' with his lady, in an explicit reminder of the litigious sisters in the previous episode. She therefore asks Alundyne to pledge to do all that she can to reconcile the couple:

> To mak him and hys lady saght   (l. 3898)

> To saghtel þe knyght with þe liown
> And his lady of grete renowne   (ll. 3917–18)

and Alundye pledges her *trawpe* (*YG* l. 3902) so to do. When Lunete's stratagem and the Knight with the Lion's true identity are revealed, Laudine, enraged, states that it is only considerations of the wickedness of perjury which compel her to reconciliation with Yvain (*Y* ll. 6759–76). On the other hand, in *Ywain and Gawain* Alundyne states her intention to keep *trawpe* with Lunet ('Þat I have said, I sal fulfill,' l. 3992), and, in response to Lunet's repeated pleas for *saghteling* (ll. 3952, 3974), without further ado, she 'asented saghtelinȝ to mak' (l. 4005).

Tony Hunt's analysis of *Yvain* reveals its (deliberate) failure to resolve the 'courtly dilemma' through the lack of substantive connection between Yvain's triumphs of prowess after his estrangement from Laudine and his stated desire for reconciliation, or a convincing display of love renewed at the conclusion of the narrative.[29] Lunete's tactic provides a bandaid, but not a cure, for the conflict between love and prowess. By contrast, sidestepping the ethical (and pseudo-ethical) problems of

---

[28] The importance of Lunet's counsel in these closing stages of the narrative is under-lined by the occurrence of the term *kownsail* (or *kownsaylere*) four times (*YG* ll. 3867, 3870, 3872, 3881), and of *rede* once (*YG* l. 3866) in the course of the seventeen-line (*YG* ll. 3867–3883) discussion by Lunet and Alundyne on her best means of defence against this assault. The corresponding passage in *Yvain*, which is more than twice as long (*Y* ll. 6556–601), has only four references to *conseil* (or the verb *conseillier*).

[29] 'The ideology of knightly love service according to which the man's chivalric acts are inspired by love of a lady and in turn intensify her devotion to him is completely belied here and the bottom knocked out of courtly romance' ('Beginnings, Middles, and Ends,' pp. 102–04).

'courtly' love, this 'no-frills' English re-telling of *Yvain* throws into relief the motif, embedded in the infrastructure of Chrétien's narrative, of conflict and accord. The concluding rapprochement between Ywain and Alundyne is the culmination of a process which begins with the *saghteling* of Ywain and Gawain; and the unresolved 'courtly dilemma' of *Yvain* becomes, instead, a story of broken *trawpe*,[30] rehabilitation, and reconciliation, achieved through *red* as both 'counsel' and 'remedy'.

Havelok

The proper exercise of *red*, as 'counsel' and 'remedy', has wider implication in *Havelok*, where the fortunes of both England and Denmark are at stake. *Red* controls the narrative on a threefold level: rhetorically, as the component of numerous formulas seeking or stating a course of action,[31] procedurally, as the basis for action, and ethically, as moral yardstick.

Havelok is perhaps the most broadly 'political' of all the Middle English romances[32] in its overt concern with royal power and responsibility. The story deals with the recovery of their birthrights by Havelok and Goldeboru, heirs to the kingdoms of Denmark and England respectively and reluctantly united in marriage midway through the narrative, but its scope goes well beyond the 'loss and restoration' theme to a concern with the exercise of political power, focussed on the rights and duties of the royal office. *Havelok* propounds an ideal of kingship whose essential virtues are justice, mercy, piety, and the taking of wise counsel.[33]

The poem begins and ends with scenes of good kings seeking counsel: Athelwold of England and Birkabein of Denmark call deathbed councils to appoint regents for their respective heirs, the English princess

---

30 On the subject of *trawpe* in *Ywain and Gawain*, see Penelope Doob, *Nebuchadnezzar's Children*, pp. 140–43; Gayle K. Hamilton, 'The Breaking of the Troth in *Ywain and Gawain*', *Mediaevalia* 2 (1976), 111–35; Tony Hunt, 'Beginnings, Middles, and Ends,' pp. 90–92, 110.

31 For example, 'wat shal me to rede?' (ll. 118, 694); 'Grim ne coupe no god red' (l. 827); 'Wile I taken non oper red' (l. 518); 'so God me rede' (ll. 688, 2719); 'What wile ye, frend, heroffe rede?' (l. 2405).

32 See the readings by Judith Weiss ('Structure and Characterisation in *Havelok the Dane*', *Speculum* 44 [1969], 247–57); David Staines ('*Havelok the Dane*: A Thirteenth-Century Handbook for Princes,' *Speculum* 51 [1976], 601–23); and Sheila Delany and Vahan Ishkanian ('Theocratic and Contractual Kingship in *Havelok the Dane*', *Zeitschrift für Anglistik und Amerikanistik* 22 [1974], 290–302).

33 In '*Havelok the Dane*,' Staines, who proposes Edward I as a possible model for the hero himself, demonstrates similarities between the kingly ideal advanced in *Havelok* and that in John of Salisbury's *Policraticus*, Bracton's *De Legibus et Consuetudinis Angliae*, and the poem on the battle of Lewes.

Goldeboru, and Havelok, prince of Denmark, at the beginning; at the end, Havelok seeks the advice and sanction of his subjects in the judgments of the villains, Godard and Godrich. As Judith Weiss observes: 'This consultation, the mark of constitutional monarchy, is emphasised by the writer, and is one of his most striking additions to the Havelok story.'[34]

The significant narrative turns of *Havelok* all depend on some form of *red*. The story begins with an invocation by Athelwold to Christ ('Loverd, wat shal me to rede?,' l. 118), the divine guide and counsellor ('þat all can wisse and rede,' l. 104), and ends with Havelok's attribution of his triumph to the *red* of his foster-father, Grim the fisherman: 'Sikerlike, þoru his red/ Have ich lived into þis day' (ll. 2690–91). It was, on the other hand, through 'wicke red' (l. 1406), Havelok tells Goldeboru, that he was committed to Godard's care. Although that bad advice, which delivered the kingdom into the hands of a tyrant, is originally given by Birkabein's knights (ll. 366–81), responsibility for it is extended across Danish society when Ubbe declares to the 'Erles, barouns, drenges, theynes,/ Klerkes, knithes, burgeys, sweynes' (ll. 2014–15), whom he summons to do Havelok homage as king, that it was 'bi youre red' (l. 2031) that Godard was appointed the royal guardian.

Athelwold prays to God for guidance, but he also seeks the earthly *red* of his barons on the future of his heir. They recommend Earl Godrich of Cornwall as regent, because he is wise in counsel and deed ('Wis man of red, wis man of dede,' l. 180), advice which pleases the king ('Þe king was payed of þat rede', l. 184). In a parallel scene, Birkabein sends for priests and monks, 'Him forto wisse and to rede' (l. 361). In both cases, although Athelwold's and Birkabein's counsellors are well-intentioned, bad counsel leads to acts of *lèse-majesté*. Good kings though they are, perhaps Birkabein and Athelwold are implicitly at fault for not making provision for the succession while sound in body and mind. In any case, the *Havelok* poet seems to be making a double point here: evil counsel is treason; but earthly kings and counsellors are fallible.

After securing his claim to the Danish throne and defeating Godrich and Godard in battle, Havelok shows himself to be the very antithesis of the tyrant by calling upon representative assemblies to judge the traitors. In the case of Godard, he has Ubbe summon:

> His erles and hise barouns alle,
> Dreng and thein, burgeis and knith,
> And bad he sholden demen him rith   (ll. 2285–87)

---

[34] 'Structure and Characterisation,' p. 250.

and, in Godrich's, he orders a more vaguely constituted assembly: 'Lokes þat ye demen him rith,/ For dom ne spares clerk ne knith' (ll. 2631–32). Before judgment is passed on Godrich, Havelok announces his desire to accept fealty from the English only if it is their wish and counsel: 'Yif ye it wilen and ek rothe' (l. 2636).

Although the judicial assemblies which condemn Godard and Godrich function as parliaments, only one episode in *Havelok*, the assembly which Godrich holds at Lincoln castle, is called a *parlement* (ll. 1007, 1179). Nothing is reported of its deliberations, nor does Godrich seek its counsel about the decision which he makes there to marry Goldeboru to Havelok, who has found employment in the castle as a scullion after famine forces him out of Grim's household. Havelok's display of prowess in a test of strength, initiated by the 'mani chambioun' (l. 1008) accompanying the magnates in attendance at the parliament, inspires the earl with a treasonably literal interpretation (ll. 1078–89) of Athelwold's dying instructions that his daughter wed: 'Þe heste man þat micthe live,/ Þe beste, fayreste, þe strangest ok' (ll. 199–200). Ironically, the *redeless* decision which Godrich makes in the course of this parliament[35] – to complete the degradation of Goldeboru by marrying her to a champion athlete – lays the groundwork for his own downfall and the accession of the rightful heir and her consort.

As in *Ywain and Gawain*, the most important individual counsellor in *Havelok* is a woman. Goldeboru participates in the first significant decision which Havelok makes after their marriage – realizing that their lives are in danger, they jointly decide ('he token anoþer red,' l. 1194) to seek refuge with Grim; unaware that Grim is dead and his *red* (l. 1204) no longer available, the couple are confident that there they will find the means 'Hem forto cloþe and forto fede' (l. 1198) – and, in so doing, joins Havelok in arriving at some answers to the questions, which he posed helplessly some fifty lines earlier, about the need to provide a wife with shelter, sustenance and clothing:

> Hwat sholde ich with wife do?
> I ne may hire fede, ne cloþe, ne sho.
> Wider sholde ich wimman bringe?' (ll. 1138–40)

It is from Goldeboru that Havelok seeks an interpretation of his dream on their wedding night, in which he holds Denmark in his arms and England in his hands. Her divinely inspired (ll. 1264–74) response is to counsel him ('But do nou als Y wile rathe,' l. 1335) to go to Denmark to claim his patrimony, mapping out a plan of action to that end, which he

---

[35] As Judith Weiss notes, in acting without the consultation of his barons here, Godrich 'acts despotically' ('Structure and Characterisation,' p. 250).

unhesitatingly adopts: 'Hwan Havelok herde þat she radde,/ Sone it was day, sone he him cladde' (ll. 1353–54). After his coronation, however, Goldeboru's role as counsellor ends, and Havelok independently asserts his powers of judgment in restoring law, order and rightful rulership to Denmark and England.

Havelok's receptivity to his wife's counsel and strategy signals the beginning of his transition from survivor to leader and ideal ruler. There has already been ample evidence of his physical strength, but now, in a prayer (ll. 1359–84), for the first time he articulates the wrong he has been done and his intention to remedy it. In his account of the details of Godard's treachery to Grim's sons in the scene which follows, Havelok acknowledges, also for the first time, that his disinheritance is the result of that 'wicke red' (l. 1406) given to his father on his deathbed. In his ready acceptance of Goldeboru's good counsel and explicit recognition that his present circumstances are the result of that earlier misguided advice by Birkabein's knights, Havelok exhibits a capacity for good judgment lacking in the other rulers, legitimate and illegitimate, of the narrative.

The hero's most important relationships, private (with Goldeboru and Grim) and public (with the people of England and Denmark), are all based on some form of *red*. Even when the narrative abruptly shifts, after the judgment and execution of Godrich, from political concerns to conventions more commonly associated with 'romance' – rewards for Havelok's helpers, a belated reference to the love between Havelok and Goldeboru, the length of their reign and number of children – the formulation of policy by *red* continues. The ennobling of Grim's daughter, Gunnild, by marriage to the Earl of Chester is brought about through Havelok's exercise of the royal prerogative of *counseil* (the only occurrence of the loan-word in the narrative):

> And þou wile mi conseyl tro,
> Ful wel shal ich with þe do,
> For ich shal yeve þe to wive
> Þe fairest þing þat is o live.   (ll. 2681–84)

Havelok has no identifiable direct source, although it is related to the Anglo-Norman *Lai d'Haveloc* (*ca.* 1200)[36] and to an episode in Gaimar's *Estoire des Engleis* (*ca.* 1135–40), which the English author may or may not have known.[37] The significance of the many references to counsel in

---

[36] See Alexander Bell, ed., *Le Lai d'Haveloc and Gaimar's Haveloc Episode* (Manchester, 1925), pp. 19–28.

[37] On possible sources for the work, other versions of the Havelok story, and the relationship of Havelok to them see G.V Smithers, ed., *Hauelok* (Oxford, 1987), pp. xvi–lvi; Speed, *Medieval English Romances*, I, 29–34.

Havelok is further underlined by their contrasting infrequency in the Havelok episode in the *Estoire des Engleis*, where the term *cunseil* occurs a mere five times,[38] and only twice (ll. 750, 777) in the sense of 'advice', not as taken by Haveloc but, reluctantly, by Edelsi, the counterpart of Godrich.[39]

There are more occurrences of the term in the *Lai d'Haveloc*,[40] but many have negative application to the machinations of Edelsi, in formal council (*asemblement*, l. 284) with all his barons and in private council with his *privez* (l. 307). In both instances, he invites and overrides counsel in the matter of the marriage of Argentille (Goldeboru); but whereas Edelsi treats his counsellors with contempt, Godrich dispenses with even the façade of constitutionality. Argentille is Haveloc's only source of counsel in the *Lai*, but her final piece of advice that he return to England does not appear in *Havelok*, where the hero himself appears to take the initiative (l. 2340ff.)

In Staines's view, the ideal of kingship in *Havelok* is 'delineated from the point of view of the lower classes,'[41] although he does not specifically define 'lower class'. John Halverson considers that the poem 'suggests . . . vaguely a "middle-class" milieu,'[42] his definition of 'middle class' embracing both peasantry and lesser nobility, and his inclination to place *Havelok* at the lower end of this scale.[43] Despite its endorsement of the virtue of manual toil, however, *Havelok*'s viewpoint is not distinctively that of labourers and peasants, but of that broad section of society which, by the late thirteenth century, was to a greater or lesser extent concerned with the administration and regulation of power. *Havelok*'s political dimensions range beyond a portrait of ideal kingship to an ideal of

---

38 *Le Lai d'Haveloc and Gaimar's Haveloc Episode*, ll. 312, 340, 516, 750, 771.

39 Godrich's role as tyrant in *Havelok* is signalled by his failure to take counsel from anyone. On the other hand, as Judith Weiss points out, Edelsi is forced to submit to a certain amount of baronial pressure in the *Lai* ('Structure and Characterisation,' p. 250).

40 'Par le conseil Sigar Estal' (l. 44); 'Altre conseil lur estut prendre' (l. 88); 'Par le conseil de ses tenanz' (of Edelsi's treachery) (l. 226); 'conseillast' (l. 294), 'k'il s'en conseillera' (l. 300), 'il se serra conseillez' (l. 305) (of Edelsi to his *asemblement*); 'Conseil lur quist e demanda' (of Edelsi to his 'privez') (l. 309); 'Co li dïent si conseiller' (of his 'privez' to Edelsi) (l. 315); 'K'il la conseilt e si li die' (Argentille to the hermit whom she consults on the meaning of the flame issuing from Haveloc's mouth) (l. 518); 'Ensemblë unt lur conseil [plan by attackers in Denmark to rape Argentille] pris' (l. 684); 'Argentille li conseilla' (l. 984); 'Quant k'ele li conseillera' (counsel offered by Argentille to Havelok) (l. 990); 'Par le conseil de ses Daneis' (l. 1006); 'Al rei dïent si conseiller' (l. 1079).

41 '*Havelok the Dane*,' p. 602 (cf. pp. 607, 612, 623 [n. 42]).

42 '*Havelok the Dane* and Society,' *Chaucer Review* 6 (1971), 142.

43 '*Havelok the Dane* and Society', p. 150. Mehl suggests 'a middle-class audience . . . There is no indication in the text . . . that illiterate peasants or labourers were the chief listeners' (*The Middle English Romances*, p. 166).

government, where the monarch's power is not absolute: that is, where the king's right to rule might be theocratic, a right of birth, but is successfully exercised only through the fulfilment of his contractual agreements with the community.[44] The basis of that agreement, as advocated in the poem, is the ruler's entitlement to, and respect for, wholesome *red* and *counseil* and the obligation of those who consider themselves his rightful counsellors to provide it.

The Tale of Gamelyn

The appearance of the sourceless *Tale of Gamelyn* (*ca.* 1350–70), usually after the Cook's Prologue, in some twenty-five manuscripts of the *Canterbury Tales*, suggests that Chaucer may have intended, as Thomas Lodge did two centuries later, to rework it. But whereas *Rosalynde* gives *Gamelyn* an aristocratic framework, Chaucer's apparent interest in this 'male Cinderella' story, particularly if he intended it to follow the tales of the Knight, Miller, and Reeve, might well have taken it in a different direction.[45]

In some respects, *The Tale of Gamelyn* reads like a retelling of *Havelok*[46] in a lower register. It begins with a deathbed scene in which a widowed knight, John of Boundes, attempts, in the manner of Athelwold and Birkabein, to make provision for his children, Johan, Ote, and Gamelyn. Just as the dying Athelwold and Birkabein summon magnates (ll. 137–39) and clergy (ll. 358–61) to councils on the future of their children, so John bids his fellow knights to assist him in the just division of his property. Athelwold's and Birkabein's advisers in *Havelok* have every reason to assume that they are offering wise counsel in nominating Godrich and Godard as regents, but when John's 'wise knightes' (l. 17) 'wenten in-to counseil · his londes for to dele' (l. 42), their advice is deliberately, and unwisely, contrary to his wishes. They determine that their neighbour's land will be divided between his two elder sons, Johan

---

44 The argument put forward by Delany and Ishkanian in 'Theocratic and Contractual Kingship' (cf. Crane, *Insular Romance*, p. 49: 'Havelok's mystical signs of flame and glowing cross preserve an older conception of theocratic lordship, while the emphasis on law and the community introduces a newer version of rule based on contractual agreements.')

45 In his edition of *The Tale of Gamelyn, from the Harleian MS. No. 7334*, 2nd revised edn. (Oxford, 1893), the source of all *Gamelyn* references, Skeat nominates the Yeoman as the likely intended teller (pp. xiii–xv).

46 *Gamelyn* is written in the dialect of the Northeast Midlands. Skeat considers it 'highly probable' that its author was familiar with *Havelok* (*The Tale of Gamelyn*, p. xi).

and Ote, until Gamelyn has reached the age of discretion: 'His bretheren might 3eue him lond · whan he good cowde' (l. 48).

The law, in theory, provides a remedy for bad counsel in these circumstances. John disregards the unwelcome advice of his peers and instead makes a verbal will, one which, even though it neglects the custom of primogeniture, is legally valid according to fourteenth-century law,[47] and gives specific bequests of land to all his sons, with the bulk of it reserved for Gamelyn. Although John appeals to his neighbours to acknowledge his action as binding ('And I byseke 3ow, goode men · that lawe conne of londe,/ For Gamelynes loue · that my queste stonde' [ll. 63–64]), by virtue of their legal knowledge and consideration for Gamelyn, at this point, and without further word, they disappear from the narrative. Gamelyn is left defenceless against his rapacious eldest brother, Johan, who, by undisclosed means, quickly tricks him out of his land. Like Havelok and Goldeboru, he is ill-clothed, ill-fed, and ill-treated by the usurper:

> He clothed him and fedde him · yuel and eek wrothe,
> And leet his londes for-fare · and his houses bothe,
> His parkes and his woodes · and dede nothing well
>
> (ll. 73–75).[48]

Gamelyn shares with Havelok great physical strength and a capacity for menial tasks. The latter gets a job as a kitchen hand at Godrich's court in Lincoln, and the former appears to be his brother's cook (ll. 90–92). Both heroes manifest their strength in wrestling matches and in brawls with unconventional weapons, Havelok armed with a door bar and Gamelyn with a pestle, and both are forced into exile among their inferiors – Havelok with Grim and his family, and Gamelyn with an outlaw band – who nevertheless treat them with more courtesy than their peers. Gamelyn, too, is crowned king, not of England or Denmark, but of the outlaws. The real difference between them, however, is that Gamelyn lacks Havelok's nobility of spirit as well as of birth. He remains, for the most part, more brawn than brain, exhibiting a naivety which at times borders on stupidity.

Havelok and *Gamelyn* frequently employ the conventions of chivalric romance in a non-chivalric register. In *Havelok*, when the hero sets forth on his quest (for employment), he is 'armed' with a cloak made from the sail of Grim's ship (ll. 855–61); he proves his mettle in a test of muscle (a

---

[47] See Edgar F. Shannon, Jr. , 'Mediaeval Law in *The Tale of Gamelyn*,' *Speculum* 26 (1951), 458–59.

[48] Cf. *Havelok*: ll. 322–23 ('And þerhinne dede hire fede/ Povrelike in feble wede'), ll. 448–64.

shot-putting contest), rather than of martial skills, and thereby wins a bride. The function of such chivalric conventions in unchivalric contexts in *Havelok* serves to delineate Havelok's humility and innate nobility. In *Gamelyn*, on the other hand, the conventions of chivalric romance are often simply vulgarized. The hero's preferred weapon is brute strength. The feast which follows Gamelyn's prize-winning athletic performance is no ritual celebration of prowess in battle or tournament, but a week-long drinking spree which follows his return home after winning a wrestling match to find himself locked out, whereupon he breaks the porter's back and throws him down a well. Later, Gamelyn and his companion-helper, Adam the spencer, keeper of the household pantry, take to the woods, not on a quest for *aventure*, but in search of refuge after committing various acts of mayhem upon a group of clergy and sheriff's men at a banquet given by the unscrupulous Johan.

The greenwood episode at the centre of the narrative employs chivalric convention for the purpose of social comment. The pointed and sustained contrast between the courteous king of the outlaws and his hospitable fellows on the one hand and, on the other, Johan, his cronies, and the uncharitable abbots, priors, and monks who feast, literally, upon Gamelyn's inheritance, has a strong element of complaint. Motifs from outlaw poetry, such as the Anglo-Norman *Outlaw's Song of Traillebaston* (*ca.* 1305), are prominent in this episode.[49] Outlaw society proves superior in every way to the 'legitimate' world of the shire, where the misuse of power lays waste Gamelyn's property and, when Johan becomes sheriff, corrupts justice as well. [50]

---

[49] R.B. Dobson and J. Taylor comment of *The Outlaw's Song of Traillebaston* that: 'Outlawry itself is assumed to be the outcome of intrigue, false accusations and local oppression rather than of deliberate crime . . . on balance, the outlaw himself is presented as a sympathetic and unjustly persecuted individual' (*Rymes of Robyn Hood. An Introduction to the English Outlaw* [London, 1976], p. 251). See, for example, the following stanzas from the poem:

> Pur ce me tendroi antre bois, suz le jolyf umbray;
> La n'y a fauceté ne nulle male lay,
> En le bois de Belregard, ou vole le jay,
> E chaunte russinole touz jours santz delay. (St. 5)

> Vus qy estes endité, je lou, venez a moy,
> Al vert bois de Belregard, la n'y a nul ploy
> Forque beste savage e jolyf umbroy;
> Car trop est dotouse la commune loy. (St. 14)

(Aspin, *Anglo-Norman Political Songs*, VII).

[50] John Bellamy comments that the position of sheriff is that 'which offered the greatest opportunity for dishonest behaviour and on which contemporaries cast the gravest aspersions', particularly in the matter of the corruption of juries. See *Crime and Public Order in England in the Later Middle Ages* (London, 1973), p. 13. According to Bellamy, there were sheriffs known to have put outlaws on juries (*ibid.*). On specific instances of corrupt sheriffs, see Kaeuper, 'An Historian's Reading,' p. 56.

The company of outlaws is itself an idealized parody of feudal society.[51] Its leader, 'i-crouned · of outlawes kyng' (l. 660) and called 'the kyng with his croune' (l. 671), behaves with a greater degree of courtesy than anyone else in the romance. The outlaw company's reception of Adam and Gamelyn conforms to the conventions of welcome to knights errant in chivalric romance. Only in this section of the narrative does the limited 'courtly' lexis of Middle English romance (*hende, milde, gentil, lewte, pris, aventure, fyn*) appear. Gamelyn, for instance, assures the apprehensive Adam that, if he is 'hende . and come of gentil blood' (l. 663), the leader of the band will not refuse them hospitality; its members address them 'myldely and stille' (l. 655); Gamelyn asks them to identify their leader by their *lewte* (l. 657); and the outlaws themselves, '3onge men of prys' (ll. 772, 804), answer Gamelyn's questions 'withoute lesyng' (l. 659), a common romance formula but also another reminder of the disparity between the noble outlaws and the mendacious Johan. The food and drink which the company offers is 'of the beste' (l. 680), and they dine 'well and fyn' (l. 681). When Gamelyn, who succeeds the 'maister outlaw' as king of the greenwood when the latter is pardoned (l. 689), returns there for a second time to see how his men are faring, they tell him 'of aventures . that they hadde founde' (l. 777). Greenwood society is very much like life at Arthur's court in twelfth-century French chivalric romance: gracious and hospitable, its members entertaining the king with tales of *aventure*.

At the end of the narrative, when Gamelyn has been vindicated and his property restored, his 'kingship' of the greenwood is legitimized in terms of the 'real' world, when the king makes him Chief Justice of the royal 'fre forest' (l. 892) with jurisdiction extending across the kingdom ('bothe in est and west,' l. 891). The use of the term *forest* here (l. 892), its only occurrence in the tale, contrasts with that used of the outlaws' territory (*wode*) and signifies the transition of Gamelyn's sphere of authority from the marginal society of the greenwood to legally defined territory.[52]

The hero's progress from dispossessed outlaw to lord of the manor and Chief Justice of the Forest is marked by an increasing ability to ask for, assess, and give sage counsel. Adam, the only source of *consilium et auxilium* in the first part of the narrative, is a lower-class version of the faithful companions in *Beves of Hamtoun* and *Guy of Warwick*. But

---

[51] As Maurice Keen notes in *The Outlaws of Medieval Legend* (London, 1961; rev. edn., 1977), p. 93.

[52] In the *OED* sense (2) of 'forest': 'A woodland district, usually belonging to the king, set apart for hunting wild beasts and game, etc. . . . having special laws and officers of its own.' On the administration of medieval forests, see Charles R. Young, *The Royal Forests of Medieval England* (Philadelphia, 1979).

whereas Saber in *Beves* and Heraud in *Guy* tender their services out of loyalty and affection, Adam's aid, which is initially limited to the provision of food and drink (ll. 423–25), has to be bought with the promise of advancement (l. 418). Adam remains an essentially comic figure, his values and horizons, despite his initiative to flee to the greenwood, delimited by the pantry. As a fugitive, his chief concern is for his clothes (ll. 620–22) and the source of his next meal (ll. 633–36).

Nevertheless, Gamelyn's appeal to Adam for *red* is the first indication of progress from youth to maturity. Up to this point he has simply reacted to Johan's abuse and attempted to counter it with a show of physical strength. As a result, he has managed no more than to inspire Johan with thoughts of vengeance after his assault on the porter and the wine cellar, and to be tricked into being tied up and declared insane. Although the advice which Gamelyn anticipates from Adam is confirmation of his own rash inclination ('Adam,' seyde Gamelyn · 'what is now thy reed?/ Wher I go to my brother · and girde of his heed?' ll. 429–30), it is only through this appeal that his fortunes begin to take a turn for the better. Adam anticipates the possibility of failure (ll. 443–44) but advises a more prudent course of action ('I can teche thee a reed · that is worth the two,' l. 432): to appeal for assistance from the abbots, priors, and other clerics, who will be Johan's guests at a feast the following Sunday, counsel which Gamelyn considers to be 'a good counseil · ȝeuen for the nones' (l. 456).

Adam loosens Gamelyn's bonds, and when the clergy prove to be as stony-hearted towards his plight and as greedy as Johan, the two of them initiate a brawl with the host and his guests. When the sheriff and his men are summoned to the scene, Gamelyn again seeks counsel from Adam: 'Adam', seyde Gamelyn · 'what be now thy reedes?' (l. 601); to which Adam replies, 'Gamelyn · my reed is now this' (l. 603): 'I rede that we to wode goon · ar that we be founde' (l. 605). The spencer's counsel may be crude, but this time it is effective. Although the banquet episode results in enforced flight, Adam, Gamelyn, and, vicariously, the audience, have the satisfaction of meting out some rough justice to the callous and gluttonous men of religion, teaching them the lesson that, as one friar laments, their attendance at the feast was 'a cold reed' (l. 531).

Gamelyn's transformation from victim to leader begins with a radical role reversal when he and Adam enter the woods. Although Adam asserts his protective authority by taking Gamelyn by the hand as they set off (l. 607), as soon as they enter the greenwood, he becomes disoriented, scared, and hungry. Gamelyn takes charge. For the first time he is confident and optimistic:

'Adam,' seyde Gamelyn · 'now haue we no doute,
After bale cometh boote · thurgh grace of god almight;

> Me thynketh of mete and drynk · that I haue a sight'
>
> (ll. 630–32)

and with good reason, for the fugitives are warmly welcomed by the company of outlaws. When Gamelyn becomes their king, they acknowledge his authority by a declaration of willingness to follow his counsel: 'By seint Iame!' saide his ȝonge men · 'and thou rede therto,/ Ordeyne how it shall be · and it shall be do' (ll. 797–98).

Ote, the third brother, volunteers to act as surety for Gamelyn, although he doubts the wisdom of the hero's decision to return to the woods to await trial at the next assize ('Be god!' seyde sire Ote · 'that is a cold reed!,' l. 759) after his appearance at the shire court to protest the sentence of outlawry imposed upon him through Johan's contrivance. Johan bribes the jurors, but Gamelyn comes up with a more effective course of action. Adam proposes the slaughter of everyone present in the *moot-halle* ('And thou wilt, Gamelyn · do after my reed/ Ther is noon in the halle · schal bere away his heed,' ll. 819–20), in words reminiscent of Gamelyn's earlier suggestion ('Wher I go to my brother · and girde of his heed?' l. 430). Gamelyn's restriction of Adam's *red* to the guilty only (ll. 821–22), a more circumspect if still unorthodox courtroom strategy, underlines the extent of their role reversal and the fact that Gamelyn has indeed reached the age 'whan he good cowde' (l. 48).

Like *Havelok*, *The Tale of Gamelyn* has a double conclusion, one 'judicial' and the other more typical of romance. In the first, Gamelyn assumes the role of judge at his own trial and oversees the execution of Johan and his bribed jurors:

> Thus ended the fals knight · with his treccherie,
> That euer had i-lad his lyf · in falsnes and folye.
> He was hanged by the neck · and nouȝt by the purs,
> That was the meede that he hadde · for his fadres curs
>
> (ll. 883–86)

Then the conventions of romance reassert themselves: the unnamed king makes Ote a justice; Gamelyn not only regains his patrimony but is also rewarded with high honour for his part in expunging judicial corruption; and the young men of the greenwood are pardoned and given 'good office' (l. 894). Finally, and almost, it seems, as an afterthought, Gamelyn marries 'a wyf bothe good and feyr' (l. 898). Surprisingly, there are no rewards for Adam, who disappears from the narrative after Gamelyn rejects his counsel to kill everyone in the courtroom. The spencer's exclusion from the prize-giving may be a mark of authorial censure for his reluctance, in contrast with Bertram the cook and Grim the fisherman, helper-figures of low rank in *Havelok*, to assist the hero other than '[i]n hope of auauncement' (l. 418).

51

Through the unwise *red* of his father's neighbours, Gamelyn loses his patrimony; through Adam's *red* he shapes the appropriate action to regain it. When Johan becomes sheriff, however, the repercussions of the ill-considered judgment by Sir John's neighbours extend well beyond the manor. The conventional 'romance' ending of *The Tale of Gamelyn* supplies a simple, wish-fulfilling, idealized solution to an all too plausible account of corruption and injustice which invites the appellation, 'romance of complaint'.

The fifteenth-century romance of *Sir Degrevant* (*ca.* 1400–10),[53] an apparently 'original' English composition, with some 'courtly' embellishments (Degrevant and Meliador, daughter of his feudal superior, are secret lovers), has an element of 'complaint', comparable in some respects to *Gamelyn*, but with a chivalric gloss. The world of this narrative is also a provincial one; its operational centre is estate rather than court, and its main concerns local disputes of a type recorded in fourteenth-century court records and parliamentary petitions.[54] Degrevant's lord hunts his game, fishes his rivers, kills his foresters, and harasses his tenants, while he, like the lost ideal of knighthood mourned in *The Simonie*, is on a crusade. The hero's response to this provocation is to seek, successfully, redress by the law rather than the sword: 'He thoghte to wyrke by þe lawe/ And by no noþer schore' (Lincoln MS, ll. 151–52). Only at the end of the narrative is the world of local affairs abandoned for the more glamorous shores of 'romance', when Degrevant, now married to Meliador, leaves his manorial wealth to return to the Holy Land, where he dies gloriously in battle.

Athelston

The prerogative of the medieval king to summon and, by the same token, to exclude ' "whom he will" to and from his councils'[55] is the catalyst for personal and constitutional conflict in *Athelston* (1375–1400).[56] Encoded in the narrative, whose relatively late date puts it

---

53 On the dating of the work, see L.F. Casson, ed., *The Romance of Sir Degrevant*, EETS 221 (London, New York, Toronto, 1949; rpr. 1970), lxxii–lxxiii.

54 Casson, *The Romance of Sir Degrevant*, p. lxiii.

55 Baldwin, *The King's Council*, p. 106. 'The peers, for instance, gained a right to be summoned to parliaments, but no such right was acknowledged in regard to councils' (*ibid.*).

56 The work appears to be sourceless. On analogues in the Middle English *Amis and Amiloun*, Old French, and Middle German, and on dating, see Trounce, *Athelston*, pp. 4–25, 60–61.

within the scope of the Ricardian 'discourse of counsel', is a critical investigation of the propriety and validity of some of the many sources of royal advice in the fourteenth century:

> bodies of fixed membership and binding powers, imposed upon the Crown in periods of crisis and often bearing some representative capacity; convenient groupings of administrative officials; and an informal dialogue between the king and his leading subjects, supplemented by great councils and specially-summoned councils for the discussion of particular issues,[57]

which focusses on the potential for political instability and intrigue in possible clashes of interest between public duty and formally constituted councils on the one hand, and private contracts and 'counsel' given informally, or in private, on the other.

King Athelston describes the business of ruling as 'to wysse and rede' (l. 661), but he is, in fact, a ruler who is essentially *redeless*. Eventually, only the *red* of the Archbishop of Canterbury saves the kingdom from tyranny and ecclesiastical interdict. As in the case of the trumped up charge against Lunet by Alundyne's barons in *Ywain and Gawain*, jealousy of a preferred counsellor precipitates the crisis. Royal councils, formal and informal, are the source of the villain's disaffection and the means of his revenge.

Athelston begins with a brief account of four messengers, Athelston, Wymound, Egeland, and Alryke, who cement their friendship by sworn brotherhood in the days before Athelston, who is of royal blood, becomes king. On his succession, Athelston creates Egeland, who is, says the narrator, a man 'off gret renoun' (l. 45), Earl of Stane and does him the additional honour of giving him his sister, Edith, in marriage. Alryke, a learned (ll. 50, 56) and noble (l. 56) *clerk*, is appointed Archbishop of Canterbury. There are unmistakable signs that Wymound is the odd man out in this quartet: he alone merits no mention of positive qualities and appears to be in straightened circumstances. His elevation to the earldom of Dover is described solely in material terms: 'And þus þe pore man gan couere – /Lord off tour and toun' (ll. 41–42).

The favour that Athelston has previously shown Egeland continues during his rule. Egeland, Edith, and their two sons become part of the king's intimate circle, summoned to councils in *halle* and in *boure*:

> And offtensyþe he gan hem calle
> Boþe to boure and to halle,
> To counsayl whenne þey scholde goo   (ll. 76–78).

[57] J.L. Watts, 'The Counsels of King Henry VI, c.1435–1445,' *The English Historical Review* 106 (1991), 282.

Either resentful of the inclusion of Egeland's family, or, more probably, embittered by his own exclusion from these sessions,[58] Wymound is consumed with envy and plots their downfall. He invites Athelston to hear some private *counsayl* in the royal *chaumbyr*:

> 'Sere kyng,' he saide, '3iff it be þi wille,
> To chaumbyr þat þou woldest wenden tylle,
> Counsayl for to here' (ll. 121–24).

The different connotations of *boure, halle,* and *chaumbyr* are interesting here and perhaps thematically significant. *Boure* and *halle* denote different types of space: the *halle* is a place for social gatherings on a large scale or 'for the more gregarious aspects of private life.'[59] ME *boure* is something more akin to a parlour; the term usually refers to women's quarters and often denotes 'bedroom', but in the modern sense of 'sitting room' or 'living room' rather than of individual private space.[60] The formula *to boure and to halle* therefore suggests a distinction between 'private' and 'public' consultation, or, perhaps more appropriately, 'informal' and 'formal' counsel.[61] The distinctions between *boure* and the loan-word *chaumbre* are more subtle, the latter having connotations of 'total privacy' and 'professional transaction' lacking in *boure* and *halle*. The MED defines *chaumbre* as 'room or apartment for personal use; a private room or suite', especially one in the residence of a ruler; and, in many contexts, a *chaumbre* is a room for consultation or official business.[62]

Although the author of *Athelston* does not specifically use the term 'private' for this one-on-one session instituted by Wymound, its secluded setting recalls the bad reputation which *secretum* or *privatum consilium* (*privé conseil*) acquired during the reign of Edward II.[63] Wymound waits until he and the king are sequestered within the *chaum-*

---

[58] The narrative is not explicit on this point here, although Wymond finally concedes that the reason for his bitterness is that the king '. . . lovid hym [Egeland] to mekyl and me to lyte' (l. 799).

[59] Danielle Régnier-Bohler, 'Imagining the Self,' in Georges Duby, ed., Arthur Goldhammer trans., *Revelations of the Medieval World: A History of Private Life*, ed. Philippe Ariès and Georges Duby, II [Cambridge, Mass., and London, 1988]), 323.

[60] *MED*, s.v. *bour*, 2(a; b; c ['any kind of small room']).

[61] Trounce glosses it thus: 'literally "to private and public counsel" . . . but probably here implying "on numerous occasions" ' (*Athelston*, p. 99). He does, however, argue for a distinction between the elements of the formula 'tour and toun' (l. 42): 'Since there are signs . . . that the author of *Athelston* does manipulate these phrases, I think it worth suggesting that he may have had in mind the nature of Dover, which was distinctly a town *and* a castle, both famous' (*Athelston*, p. 98). The analogy perhaps lends some support to the argument for a semantic distinction between *bour* and *halle*.

[62] *MED*, s.v. *chaumbre*, 1; 4a); 5a).

[63] See Baldwin, *The King's Council*, pp. 105–06.

byr (l. 130) before revealing his 'counsel' for the slander ('false lesyngys,' l. 131) it is. Exploiting his fraudulently won status of royal confidant, he plays on the royal sense of honour and makes Athelston pledge his *trowþe* (l. 158) that he will conceal this *counsayl* (l. 159). He offers no advice to the king, who accepts, without question, the false intelligence that Egeland is plotting to poison him. Wymound leaves it to Athelston to adopt whatever course of action he can with his parting shot: 'But do þy beste rede' (l. 177). Although this formula is idiomatic,[64] it could be interpreted as an ironic rejoinder by Wymound to his presumed previous exclusion from the inner circle of counsellors. With further irony, Athelston's next actions show that he is indeed a king who is *redeless*. He acts like a tyrant in rejecting appeals, first by his unnamed queen and then by Alryke, that Wymound's accusation against Egeland be publicly considered 'be comoun (a)sent/ In þe playne parlement' (ll. 265–66, 447–48).

The terms *comoun asent* and *playne parlement* appear frequently in parliamentary records of the fourteenth century.[65] Helen Cam's survey of occurrences of the latter term in the parliamentary rolls of Edward I, Edward II, Edward III, and Richard II, where it is most frequently applied to the judicial business of parliament, indicates that *playne parlement* 'emphasizes a distinction between the formal or plenary session and the less formal and less public proceedings of smaller groups . . . The connotation is of a court where the most solemn proceedings must be done in the sight of all men.'[66] In a more general sense, such publicity gives validity to the proceedings. The appeal for a *playne parlement* by queen and archbishop in *Athelston* thus underlines the qualitative difference between Wymound's false, treasonable, private *counsayl* and the public deliberations of a properly constituted assembly.

These references to *comoun asent* and *playne parlement* point to a composer and audience familiar with fourteenth-century parliamentary procedure. More specifically, the intrigue and injustice which precipitate hostility between Alryke and Athelston recall, and perhaps discreetly allude to, the clash of crown and mitre between Edward III and John

---

[64] Trounce suggests that its meaning 'is obviously: "Do as you think best",' but he finally glosses it as 'But please yourself' (*Athelston*, p. 105).

[65] For example, at the Westminster Epiphany-Candlemas parliament of 1327, the last of Edward II, which became the first of Edward III, a petition from the *communalte du roialme* (the shire knights and urban representatives) asks that the king's advisers be chosen wisely and *par assent de la comune* (*Rotuli Parliamentorum Anglie Hactenus Inediti MCCLXXIX–MCCCLXXIII*, ed. H.G. Richardson and George Sayles [London, 1935], Item 13, p. 121).

[66] 'From Witness of the Shire to Full Parliament,' in Helen Cam, *Law-Finders and Law-Makers in Medieval England. Collected Studies in Legal and Constitutional History* (London, 1962), pp. 111, 126.

Stratford, Archbishop of Canterbury and presiding officer (*consiliarius principalis*)[67] of the royal council, in the political crisis of 1340–41. Edward was in France, desperate for funds to conduct his war; Stratford was the target of a private grudge by another of the king's councillors. The background is summarized by Michael Prestwich:

> The ambitious keeper of the privy seal, William Kilsby, regarded Stratford as responsible for blocking his promotion to the see of York, and he . . . influenced the king against Stratford. An unnamed councillor in England wrote secretly to the king, revealing the reality behind Stratford's bland excuses for failing to supply adequate funds. This man suggested that the king should return to England and arrest Stratford and his colleagues.[68]

Edward was only too ready to believe in the archbishop's duplicity. He dismissed his treasurer and chancellor, and charges were laid against Stratford, who retaliated with vigour from the pulpit against defamatory attacks from the king's side[69] and accused Edward not only of listening to bad advice but also of contravening the provisions of Magna Carta. In the parliament of April, 1341, which the king delayed calling for several months despite the archbishop's requests from December of the previous year, Stratford demanded to be tried by his peers *en pleyn Parlement*.[70]

The sole copy of *Athelston*, MS 175 Gonville and Caius College, Cambridge (early fifteenth century), contains its own brand of intrigue on the subject of *playne parlement*. Immediately after the queen's (ll. 265–66) and Alryke's (ll. 447–48) pleas that Egeland's case be judged by *comoun asent* in *playne parlement*, the manuscript becomes defective for the space of four lines in each case. A failure of sense in the first instance:

> Þat we mowe wete be comoun sent
> In þe playne parlement . . .
> 'Dame,' he seyde, 'goo fro me;
> Þy bone schal nouȝt igrauntyd be' (ll. 265–68)

---

[67] See Baldwin, *The King's Council*, p. 369.

[68] *The Three Edwards. War and State in England 1272–1377* (New York, 1980), p. 218. For a detailed and entertaining account of the intrigue and crisis, see Gaillard Lapsley, 'Archbishop Stratford and the Parliamentary Crisis of 1341,' *English Historical Review* 30 (1915), 6–18; 193–215. Trounce, however, commenting that 'Alryke does impress us by his air of reality, and such a lively portrait, unlike the mere *chanson*-type in Wymound, almost presupposes some immediate model' (p. 119), nominates Bishop William Bateman, who held his episcopate from 1344–53 (pp. 118–19).

[69] Isabel Aspin suggests that the *maveis consiler* referred to in Against the king's taxes (l. 37) may be Stratford himself and that 'this remark . . . may be part of a campaign of slander directed against him' (*Anglo-Norman Political Songs*, note to l. 37, p. 115).

[70] *Rotuli parliamentorum; ut et petitiones, et placita in parliamento, tempore Edwardi r. I* (London, 1767–77), II, 127.

is followed by a deviation from the tail-rhyme pattern in the second:

> Þat we mowe enquere
> And weten alle be comoun asent
> In þe playne parlement . . .
>   'Who is wurþy be schent'   (ll. 446–49):

'A coincidence', Trounce comments, '(if it is mere coincidence), for which I should like to find the explanation.'[71] Speculation that one or both instances of *playne parlement* in *Athelston* were followed by an identifiable and possibly inflammatory reference to the events of 1340–41, or by an allusion to a contentious item of parliamentary business from the reign of Richard II (where the term is found frequently in accounts of treason trials),[72] which either the Gonville and Caius or an earlier scribe felt it prudent to suppress, is irresistible.

Anticlimactically, the confrontation between king and archbishop ended there, 'effectively shelved by being referred to a committee'[73] at the April parliament of 1341. In another curious parallel with this *cause célèbre*, the *playne parlement* is never convened in *Athelston* either. When Egeland and his family are delivered into Alryke's jurisdiction, the narrative makes an abrupt leap from the 'historical' to the 'legendary' mode, when the prisoners instead undergo the ordeal of walking through fire on red-hot ploughshares, from which they emerge miraculously unblemished (ll. 579–38).

The accused are saved from death, as Athelston duly acknowledges, through the *red* of Alryke (l. 672). Nevertheless, even as the king so concedes, conflict between public duty and private contract continues. Implying that his pact with Wymound not to reveal his identity (ll. 150–53) should take precedence over his obligation to oversee justice (ll. 669–74), Athelston is reluctant to name the traitor. Irony is surely intended in the king's simultaneous acknowledgment that it is Alryke's *red* which has saved the day and plea that his confidential *counsayl* with the villain remain so:

> Þey arn sauyd þorwȝ þy red;
> Now lat al þis be ded,
>   And kepe þis counseyl hale.   (ll. 672–74)

It takes Alryke's threat that Athelston will suffer the same ordeal by

71 *Athelston*, note to ll. 265–66 (p. 108). Trounce also remarks that: 'At 266 there are other signs of trouble: it is the end of column and of a page, and the adj. *playne* has been inadvertently repeated' (*ibid.*).
72 See Cam, 'From Witness of the Shire to Full Parliament,' p. 113.
73 Prestwich, *The Three Edwards*, p. 220.

which Egeland and his family have proved their innocence to persuade him to testify. Only when the king has followed the archbishop's counsel, acknowledged Egeland's innocence, renounced his private alliance with the traitor, and is about to order that Wymound tread the ploughshares does the author give epithetic endorsement of Athelston's rehabilitation: 'Thenne said þe goode King Athelston' (l. 774).

Tyrants and incompetent kings in Middle English romance are those who are without *red*, who ignore good *red*, or who take bad. The *redeless* king of Maydenland may be guilty of youthful folly in *Ywain and Gawain*, but the Æthelred of Middle English romance is Athelston, an *unrede* king in every sense: he accepts Wymound's false *counsail* without question and then pursues his own brand of underhandedness by summoning Egeland to London on the pretext that he intends to make his sons knights. The narrator suggests that Athelston has indeed lost his wits ('Þe kyng as wood ferde in þat stede,' l. 250) when he begins to act like a tyrant. Those who demonstrate good judgment and *red* in this narrative are the queen, who receives a physically brutal acknowledgment of her efforts on Egeland's behalf (and, as a result, miscarries Athelston's heir), and Archbishop Alryke. By ignoring Alryke's exhortation to change his tyrannical course of action ('Goode weddyd broþer, now turne þy rede,' l. 441) and put the charge against Egeland before the *playne parlement*, Athelston also puts the kingdom at risk of spiritual alienation by incurring the archbishop's wrath and threat of interdict.

The crisis in *Athelston* has parallels with the concluding episode of *Beves of Hamtoun*,[74] in its depiction of a king who fails to check evil counsel and its setting within the geographically identifiable locations of London and Westminster. Although *Athelston* begins with the topographical vagueness characteristic of folktale and romance ('By a forest gan þey mete/ Wiþ a cros, stood in a strete,/ Be leff vndyr a lynde,' ll. 16–18), its main action takes place in London, with specific reference to Charing Cross, Fleet Street, London Bridge (ll. 335–40; 385; 498), St Paul's (ll. 592, 616), Westminster (l. 407), the distances from London to Stone, Canterbury (ll. 321–24), and Gravesend (l. 751), and to places enroute (ll. 341–46). The final episode of Beves contains similar references: to Tower Street, Cheapside, Ludgate, Gose Lane,[75] Bow Street, the Thames, and Leadenhall (ll. 4294–452; 4483–538).[76] In both cases, topographical

[74] A copy of *Beves of Hamtoun* follows *Athelston* in MS 175 Gonville and Caius (see further, ch. 3, below).

[75] 'a narrow winding alley that used to run behind St Mary le Bow from Cordwainer Street to Cheapside' (Judith Weiss, 'The Major Interpolations in *Sir Beues of Hamtoun*,' *Medium Ævum* 48 [1979], 73).

[76] All *Beves* references are to Eugen Kölbing, *The Romance of Sir Beues of Hamtoun. Edited Six Manuscripts and the Old Printed Copy, with Introduction, Notes, and Glossary*, EETS, e.s. 46, 47, 48 [London, 1885, 1886, 1894].

familiarity gives exemplary force to the disturbing plausibility of the events of the narrative.

Although the narrator introduces his story as an *exemplum* about the evils of falsehood ('Lystnes, lordyngys þat ben hende,/ Off falsnesse, hou it wil ende,' ll. 7–8),[77] *Athelston* is a cautionary tale, less 'moral' than 'political', about tyranny. But whereas the wages of sin for usurper-tyrants like Godrich, Godard, and Johan, are death, *Athelston* at least holds out the possibility of rehabilitation for rightful monarchs, whose misplaced trust in bad counsel has steered them in the direction of despotism. Of the poem's four contexts for royal counsel – *bour, halle, chaumbyr*, and *playne parlement* – the merits of all but the last are implicitly rejected.

From different perspectives in each case, *Havelok, Gamelyn*, and *Athelston* show that the ramifications of a single instance of bad counsel – as 'advice' or 'confidence', well-intentioned or otherwise – are injustice, tyranny, and anarchy. Wymound's 'counsel' to Athelston is itself an act of treason; in *Havelok*, royal deathbed councils have apparently satisfactory outcomes, but they demonstrate how good intentions can be undone by treachery; the deliberations of the council of John's peers in *Gamelyn* deliberately contravene his legally sanctioned wishes. Godrich, Godard, and Johan gain power, and Wymound influence, by manipulating or failing to honour the determinations of councils which lack any mechanism to check that power when it runs riot. In each case, peace, justice, and the hero's rightful station are restored through the sage advice and strategy of 'outsider' figures: Grim, Goldeboru, Adam, Alryke. But although, in conformity with the wish-fulfilling conventions of romance, good counsel eventually triumphs over bad in these three narratives, *Havelok* and *Gamelyn* implicitly address an issue which, it will be argued in chapter 5, is considered in greater depth in *Sir Gawain and the Green Knight*: the fallibility of earthly counsel.

---

[77] The same formula appears at the conclusion of the battle which follows the evil counsel of the steward to King Edgar in the Gonville and Caius manuscript (Kölbing's 'E') of *Beves*: 'As we tellen in oure talkyng:/ Falsnesse cam neuere to good endyng,' ll. 199–200, p. 213).

CHAPTER THREE

'Working by counsel':
the Auchinleck manuscript (i)

Of Arthour and of Merlin,
Guy of Warwick, Beves of Hamtoun

Although the provenance of the Auchinleck manuscript remains something of a mystery, its contents show clear evidence of deliberate division and ordering.[1] Religious and didactic works, including two, *Amis and Amiloun* and *The King of Tars*, which have the formal features of romance, are followed by secular romances, and the volume ends with historical pieces, among them the 'B' or shorter version of *Richard Coer de Lion*. The positioning of individual items within these groupings of 'pious', 'secular', and 'historical' is suggestive of an editorial hand: for example, the three 'Guy' romances – the couplet *Guy of Warwick* (Item 22), its stanzaic continuation (Item 23), and *Reinbrun* (Item 24), the adventures of Guy's son – which are grouped with *Beves of Hamtoun* (Item 25) and *Of Arthour and of Merlin* (Item 26), form a collection of romances of English heroes. Intertextual evidence, by way of shared lines, common motifs, and stylistic and metrical parallels and contrasts, points to design and collaboration.[2] Common authorship has been proposed for the '*Kyng Alisaunder*

---

1 Timothy Shonk concludes that the manuscript's unity of format is suggestive of 'a predetermined design' ('A Study of the Auchinleck Manuscript,' p. 77) and that the major one of its six scribes ('Scribe I') was 'a professional copyist who compiled, copied, and sold books' (p. 87) and assumed editorial responsibility for the overall organization of the manuscript. For further studies, see, for example, A.J. Bliss, 'Notes on the Auchinleck Manuscript,' *Speculum* 26 (1951), 652–58; Judith Weiss, 'The Auchinleck MS and the Edwardes MSS,' *Notes and Queries* 214 (1969), 444–46; Derek Pearsall and I.C. Cunningham, introd., *The Auchinleck Manuscript. National Library of Scotland Advocates' MS. 19.2.1.* (London, 1977), pp. vii–xvi. Fewster's discussion of the manuscript includes a review of earlier scholarship (*Traditionality and Genre*, pp. 38–49).

2 Judith Weiss proposes *Sir Tristrem* as one possible source for the dragon fight in *Sir Beues of Hamtoun* ('The Major Interpolations in *Sir Beues of Haumtone*,' *Medium Ævum* 48 [1979], 75–76, n.8); Nicolas Jacobs has demonstrated possible borrowings from *Beves* in *Degare* ('Sir Degarré, Lay le Freine, Beves of Hamtoun* and the 'Auchinleck Bookshop,' *Notes and Queries* 227 [1982], 294–301); Laura Hibbard Loomis argues that the stanzaic romances of *Guy* and *Reinbrun* are deliberately linked and apparently

group': *Kyng Alisaunder* (Item 33), *Of Arthour and of Merlin, Richard Coer de Lion* (Item 43), and *The Seven Sages of Rome* (Item 18).[3]

As in the case of *Ywain and Gawain, Havelok, Gamelyn,* and *Athelston,* the procedural formula proposed for the Auchinleck romances discussed in this chapter and the next is 'counsel and strategy'. The Auchinleck selection, however, invites categorization as two distinct groups: those romances in which the balance tilts towards 'counsel' as a theme in itself (*Of Arthour and of Merlin, Beves of Hamtoun, Guy of Warwick*) and those (*Floris and Blauncheflur, The Seven Sages, Sir Tristem, Kyng Alisaunder, Richard Coer de Lion*) where the emphasis is on 'strategy'.

Not without justification, Derek Pearsall is dismissive of the literary merit of the Auchinleck romances here labelled as the 'counsel' group: *Guy of Warwick* is 'hack-work, a flat recital of battles which increase only in length,' *Beves of Hamtoun* a 'vulgar thriller', with a hero 'admired for his physical strength, bravado and low cunning,' and *Of Arthour and of Merlin* 'an interminable catalogue of Arthur's first battles against the barbarians, preceded by some account of the marvels surrounding Merlin's birth and early career.'[4] Nevertheless, despite their lack of literary polish, these narratives have an ethical dimension, concerned with the exercise and regulation of political and chivalric power. In *Of Arthour and of Merlin,* the issue is the principles of good government; in *Beves,* the problem of tyranny; and in *Guy,* the legitimate uses of prowess.

'made in conjunction with each other' ('The Auchinleck MS,' p. 612). Textual borrowing is apparent between the stanzaic *Guy* and *Amis and Amiloun* (see Loomis, 'The Auchinleck MS,' pp. 613–21; Fewster, *Traditionality and Genre,* pp. 60–65; Pearsall, *The Auchinleck Manuscript,* pp. x–xi; p. xvii, n.12). As noted in Chapter 1 (p. 13), above, John Finlayson sees the grouping of the *Liber Regum Anglie, Horn Childe, Richard Coer de Lion,* and *The Simonie* as significant ('*Richard, Coer de Lyon,*' pp. 161–64). Basing her study on the *Speculum Gy de Warewyke* (Item 10), *Amis and Amiloun* (Item 11), *Guy of Warwick,* and the *Liber Regum Anglie,* Jean Harpham Burrows posits an overall didactic design in the contents of the manuscript and a patriotic audience, 'the editor/redactor . . . adapting or modifying different kinds of literary selections in order to teach various lessons in proper spiritual and secular behavior' (*The Auchinleck Manuscript: Contexts, Texts and Audience,* unpubl. Washington University PhD. diss. [1984]), pp. 7–8).

3 G.V. Smithers puts forward this argument in his edition of *Kyng Alisaunder, EETS* 227, 237 (London, 1952, 1957), suggesting that 'all are the work of a single author (or so we may say at least of those parts of SS and RCL that are contained in the Auchinleck MS., as of KA and AM),' (II, 41). The conclusion of O.D. Macrae-Gibson's discussion of the dialect and style of the four romances in his edition of *Of Arthour and of Merlin, EETS* 268, 279 (London, 1973, 1979) reaches the different conclusion 'that SS could quite well be by the same author as KA, that this author might at an earlier stage in his career have written AM (though if so his poetic technique changed considerably as his career developed), but that RCL is in all probability of distinct authorship' (II, 75).

4 'The Development of Middle English Romance,' *Mediaeval Studies* 27 (1965), 99,100,101 (rpr. in Derek Brewer, ed., *Studies in Medieval English Romances. Some New Approaches* [Cambridge, 1988]), pp. 11–35).

Of Arthour and of Merlin

Its main source a version of the French prose *Merlin*,[5] *Of Arthour and of Merlin* is one of four accounts of the life of Merlin in Middle English.[6] The action of this romance does, as Pearsall notes, consist for the most part of a string of battles fought by Arthur against rebels and pagans, but, underlying the undisputed monotony of the narrative, is a serious message: the importance of judicious counsel to the survival of Britain in the face of invasion, insurrection, and royal incompetence.

The most important source of wise counsel in *Of Arthour and of Merlin* is Merlin, a figure variously represented in medieval literature as prophet, sage, trickster, fool, counsellor, devil, and magician, sometimes with a touch of the demonic.[7] In the French prose *Merlin* he is primarily an adviser in diplomatic and military matters, who happens to have a gift for magic.[8] In *Of Arthour and of Merlin*, Merlin's wizardry is further reduced,[9] and he becomes, first and foremost, the Wise Counsellor.[10] But although the range of his activities may be somewhat narrower in *Of Arthour and of Merlin* than in its presumed source, as chief counsellor to four kings of England, who include Arthur and his father, Uter, Merlin is the key figure in the narrative. Merlin's position as counsellor extends beyond the functions of political adviser and military strategist to those of priest, father-figure, and, effectively, ruler of the kingdom: it is by his *red*, for example, that high office, such as the appointment of Duke Do as

5　O.D. Macrae-Gibson, *Of Arthour and of Merlin*, II, 2. Although the second section of *Of Arthour and Merlin* is clearly derived from the French ('Vulgate') prose *Merlin*, Macrae-Gibson suggests that the first section may be a conflation of sources (II, 26), although it closely follows the prose *Merlin* in the 'whole elaborate and circumstantial story of the conception, birth, and early childhood of Merlin' (II, p. 20). For further detailed study of the manuscripts of *Of Arthour and of Merlin*, see William E. Holland, 'Formulaic Diction and the Descent of a Middle English Romance,' *Speculum* 48 (1973), 89–109.

6　The others are Henry Louelich's verse translation (ca.1425) of the first half of the French prose *Merlin*, the Middle English prose Merlin (ca.1450), and the first book of Malory's *Morte d'Arthur*.

7　See, for example, Carol E. Harding, *Merlin and Legendary Romance* (New York and London, 1988), p. 155.

8　See Harding, *Merlin and Legendary Romance*, p. 106.

9　The story of his bringing Stonehenge to England from Ireland, for example, is omitted (see Macrae-Gibson, *Of Arthour and of Merlin*, II, 34, n.4).

10　Merlin's origins are as obscure as those of the Arthurian legend. In the twelfth century, the figure of Merlin Celidonius, the second of two Merlin figures in his work, is represented by Giraldus Cambrensis and the earlier of two lives of St Kentigern as a demented prophet and wild man of the woods. See Welsford, *The Fool*, pp. 103–05; Sonya Jensen, 'Merlin: Ambrosius and Silvester,' in *Words and Wordsmiths: a volume for H.L. Rogers*, ed. Geraldine Barnes, John Gunn, Sonya Jensen, Lee Jobling (Sydney, 1989), pp. 45–48.

constable of London (ll. 4115–18),[11] is granted. Most importantly, Merlin is the sole source of the most powerful weapon in the beleaguered Arthur's armory: shrewd and benign counsel.

The display of Merlin's prophetic and magical powers may be reduced in *Of Arthour and of Merlin*, but his talents are not diminished. There are, however, some interesting distinctions between the exercise of his wizardry on the one hand and counsel-giving on the other. The latter is never used for questionable ends, whereas, by transforming Uter into the likeness of her husband (ll. 2513–16) and instructing the king's forces to storm the duke's castle by cunning means ('And tau3t hem gin and eke way,' l. 2501), Merlin engineers the seduction of Ygerne, wife of the Duke of Cornwall. The eventual marriage of Uter and Ygerne is sanctioned by the king's council ('Þurth hei3e mennes conseyling,' l. 2596) and, to reinforce the point, 'Bi hei3e mennes conseyl' (l. 2598), but Merlin's stratagem for adultery is not attributed to his *counseil* or *red*. Similarly, when Arthur conceives a passion for Li3anor, daughter of Earl Siweinis, the affair is consummated 'þurth Merlin' (l. 4189), without further specification. By contrast, Arthur's marriage to Guinevere is explicitly the product of Merlin's direction: 'For bi mi rede he schal spouse/ Gvenour . . . (ll. 3611–12), he states; and duly, some 5,000 lines later, 'Arthour hir nome saun fail/ For Merlin him 3af swiche conseil' (ll. 8625–26).

The first part of the narrative, which covers events immediately preceding Arthur's reign, illustrates the effects on the kingdom of bad or ineffectual counsel. Almost every action of the first five hundred lines in *Of Arthour and of Merlin* is the direct result of some form of malign counsel. Like *Havelok*, the narrative begins with an exemplar of good kingship, in the person of the terminally ill King Costaunce ('A noble mon in al thyng').[12] As with Athelwold, wisdom in giving counsel is one of this king's two chief qualities ('A dou3hty mon he was of dede/ And ry3t wys he was of rede'),[13] and his barons in council decide the immediate future of the kingdom ('Erls and barouns euerichon/ Token hem to red anon, ll. 99–100), which, in this instance, is under threat of Danish invasion. That same fallibility of human counsel which appointed Godrich regent in *Havelok* is demonstrated in the magnates' choice of Costentine,[14] the eldest of Costaunce's three sons, as his successor. Against his father's advice ('Wiþouten his fader þe kinges rade,' l. 62),

---

[11] All references are to Macrae-Gibson's edition and are, unless otherwise indicated, to the Auchinleck manuscript.

[12] Hale MS. 150, Lincoln's Inn Library, London, l. 12 (the Auchinleck manuscript is defective here).

[13] Hale MS, ll. 15–16.

[14] So named in his first appearance in the Auchinleck manuscript, but thereafter referred to as Costaunt, Costaunce, and Moyne. On the various forms of the names of Costaunce and his sons, see Holland, 'Formulaic Diction,' p. 91.

Costentine has become a monk. He proves a pious but incompetent ruler, incapable of *conseil* in the face of the invading forces of the Danish king, Angys – 'He no can conseil to no gode' (l. 209), states one of the barons – and therefore unfit to rule.

An *unrede* king makes his kingdom vulnerable, not only to foreign invasion but also to treason. If the ruler is incapable of providing counsel, it must be sought elsewhere, and, as demonstrated by Godrich, that villainous but apparently 'wis man of red' in *Havelok*, not all counsellors are to be trusted. The able, but excessively ambitious and treacherous ('Fals and ful of couaitise,' l. 82) steward, Vortigern, capitalizes on the kingdom's desperate need for leadership. Treasonably, he withholds his *consilium et auxilium* from Costentine (ll. 122–32) and then manipulates a council of the king's vassals, who appeal directly to him for counsel ('Þerfore þe conseyl of þe lond / Bad he schuld don his hond,' ll. 189–90), into committing regicide, first by declining their request on the grounds of his non-royal rank:

> 'Y nam noiþer 3our douke no king
> Whi aske 3e me conseiling?' (ll. 195–96),

and then by responding to the further plea of a baron, who states that their fool (*conioun*, l. 206) of a king 'no can conseil to no gode' (l. 209), with a refusal to consider their desperate need ('Conseyl worþ 3ou of me non!' l. 225) so long as Costentine is alive. The barons' summary beheading of Costentine and installation of Vortigern on the throne are thus forcefully presented as the direct result of this failure of royal *red*.[15]

Vortigern soon shows the true measure of his counsel, which leads to the progresssive deterioration of the kingdom. It is his *conseyle* (l. 349), for example, that releases the besieged invader, Angys, soon to become his ally against the English barons. Then, by the *conseyl* (l. 473) of Angys, the lands of dispossessed and executed British barons are given to *Sarra3ins* (Danes and Saxons),[16] and the heathen population of the country increases through intermarriage, including Vortigern's to the daughter of Angys (ll. 477–81). In the meantime, however, and running

---

[15] In her discussion of the Vulgate *Merlin*, Harding points out that the destructive counsellor-king relationship between the opportunistic and evil Vortigern and Cost-entine parallels and contrasts with the beneficial counsellor-king alliance between Merlin and Arthur: 'Unlike the ambitious Vortigern, Merlin has no desire to usurp the kingship for himself, and his efforts are directed at making Arthur self-sufficient as ruler, whereas Vortigern aimed at keeping Constans dependent. This pairing of opposites again emphasizes Merlin's positive role' (*Merlin and Legendary Romance*, p. 102).

[16] On the significance of the term 'Saracens' in English romance and French *chansons de geste*, see Diane Speed, 'The Saracens of *King Horn*,' *Speculum* 65 (1990), 564–95 (esp. , with reference to *Of Arthour and of Merlin*, p. 571, n.32).

counter to the evil military and political counsel by which Vortigern controls the kingdom, the seeds of his downfall are quietly planted at his coronation in some entirely private consultation between two barons. Loyal to the memory of Costentine and aware of Vortigern's treason, they devise a strategy to preserve the lives of the king's younger brothers, Uter Pendragon and Aurilis Brosias:

> And tok rede bitvixen hem to
> Þe to childer ouer þe se bring
> And went hem forþ wiþouten lesing,
> No man wist of her conseyle
> Bot þai alon wiþouten faile.   (ll. 286–90).

This history of failed and evil counsel, relieved only by the barons' benign conspiracy to save the lives of Costentine's brothers, prefaces Merlin's entry into the narrative. His wisdom and eloquence first manifest themselves at the age of five, when his speech in his mother's defence saves her from conviction on a capital charge and persuades the judge in the case to do 'Al bi þat childes conseyl' (l. 1164). After this demonstration of his skills, Merlin announces that his role in life is to be *maister* and adviser to four kings ('To kinges foure y worþ maister/ Hem y mot ȝete alle rade,' ll. 1180–81): Vortigern, Aurilis Brosias, Uter, and Arthur.[17]

Merlin's credentials as royal adviser to his three immediate predecessors are well-established by the time Arthur appears. It is, for instance, by Merlin's 'conseyl and rede and witt' (l. 1597) that Vortigern's castle is finally built after the dragons disrupting its construction have been removed. Merlin's *counseil* is acknowledged by five barons, former allies of Vortigern, as the means of Uther's defeat of Angys ('Bi his conseyl ȝe schuld anon/ Angys ouercomen and slon,' ll. 1923–24) and vaunted in the same terms by Merlin himself: 'Bi mi conseyl he haþ þis niȝt/ Angys slayn, y the pliȝt!' (ll. 2005–06). It is Merlin who warns Uter and Aurilis of the approaching army of 'Saracens', who seek vengeance for Angys, and directs the campaign with such success that Uter 'Bi Merlins red euer . . . wrouȝt' (l. 2167) throughout his reign, in the course of which the Round Table, symbolic centre of the Arthurian world, is established 'þurth Merlines hest' (2197).

The events of Arthur's reign and those leading up to it are even more tightly controlled by Merlin's direction. Whereas, for example, Uter is

---

[17] Macrae-Gibson cites one instance where advice by Merlin to Arthur on the subject of generosity in the prose *Merlin* is omitted in *Of Arthour and of Merlin*, but he suggests that, since the same incident is also absent in Malory's version, both must derive from a common version of *Merlin* defective at this point (*Of Arthour of Merlin*, II, 18).

crowned 'Bi comoun dome, bi comoun rade' (l. 2048), Merlin himself takes credit for the happy outcome 'of gode conseyl and wise rede' (l. 2630) in the parliament which decides that whoever can draw Excalibur from the stone, 'Bi godes wille and our rade' (l. 2824), will be Uter's successor. When Arthur is having difficulty in establishing his entitlement to the throne, Merlin tells his supporters that as long as 'alle doþ bi mi rede' (l. 3198), all will be well, and indeed it is. Throughout Merlin's association with Arthur, his counsel prevails in all practical and strategic matters, and always in the best interests of the king.

Through Merlin's *red* and *counseil*, for example, a fact emphasized by its repetition (e.g., ll. 3384, 3387, 3395, 3418, 3432), Arthur is saved from an assassination conspiracy by eleven kings and dukes which escalates into full-scale conflict, in the course of which Merlin acts not only as military tactician but also as distributor of the spoils of war. His advice to Arthur to collect the gold, silver, and other riches left on the battlefield by the defeated barons is considered by Arthur, perhaps with intentional double meaning, as 'riche conseil' (l. 4058). Similarly, when Merlin presides over the sharing out of booty at the end of the five-year campaign against the rebellious barons and 'Saracens', the division is done *curtaisliche* (l. 6459) and 'Bi Merlins conseil sikerliche' (l. 6460). Twice (ll. 4746, 5359) it is stated that Arthur lends assistance to Guinevere's father, King Leodegan, through Merlin's counsel, and that 'Þurth conseil of Merlin ywis' (l. 6035) Arthur, Leodegan, and the brothers Ban and Bohort go to the help of Cleodalis, Leodegan's steward. Merlin's skills as a military strategist are explicitly acknowledged by the narrator at this point of the campaign: the attack by Cleodalis and Arthur against the pagans would, he says, have incurred heavy losses, had it not been for Merlin's beneficial (*bihef*) counsel to kill the ten giants among the enemy force:

> Þer hadde ben miche mischef
> No had Merlin seyd a conseil bihef   (ll. 6145–46).

Similarly, had Merlin not directed Arthur and Ban to help Bohort, Nacien, Herui, and Agravain in their final battle, against the heathen Irish king, Rion, all four, claims the narrator (ll. 9109–13), would have been killed and the battle lost.

Active and ultimately brilliant in battle, the Arthur in *Of Arthour and of Merlin* is not the *roi fainéant* of Chrétien's narratives, but neither does he have the stature of the other two warrior-kings of the '*Kyng Alisaunder* group', Richard Coer de Lion and Alisaunder. Sometimes he has to be galvanized into action, even on the battlefield (ll. 8820–24, 9114–20), where it is Merlin who remains the leader. Although Arthur acts up to a point as a model king in submitting to the excellent counsel of Merlin, the consultative process is very much a one-way affair, and Arthur's authority limited accordingly. Neither an active seeker nor a giver of counsel, Arthur is, essentially, a puppet figure controlled by a benevolent string-puller. Only in the concluding stages of *Of Arthour and of Merlin*, at the end of the battle with Rion, does Arthur take the initiative and act alone (l. 9347), challenging the Irish king 'with gret vigour' (l. 9348). Up to this point the king has normally been seen in battle, as elsewhere, always in company, and usually flanked by Kings Ban and Bohort.[18]

Despite the importance of counsel as a force for both good and evil in this narrative, *Of Arthour and of Merlin* is a more primitive 'counsel' romance than *Guy* and *Beves*. His *red* and *counseil* may dictate all of Arthur's policies – military, political, and even matrimonial – but Merlin never offers moral counsel; nor does *Of Arthour and of Merlin* contain the implicit equation, found in *Guy* and *Beves*, between the ability to give and to heed sage counsel and the attaining of chivalric maturity. Unlike Guy and Beves, Arthur is never seen as *red* giver: without Merlin, he is as devoid of *red* as Costentine.

Guy of Warwick

Although the fate of the kingdom is in the hero's hands at the climax of the narrative, the focus of *Guy of Warwick*, a close adaptation of the mid-thirteenth-century Anglo-Norman *Gui de Warewic*, is personal rather than nationalistic. In a pattern bearing some superficial similarities to the careers of Chrétien's Erec and Yvain, the more humbly born Guy, son of Earl Rohaut's steward, Syward, begins by using his knightly prowess to win love and glory for himself, but then goes on to perform a series of altruistic and increasingly demanding chivalric tasks, progressing from fighting in his own interests to combat on behalf of other knights, of Christendom, and, in his final battle against the giant Colbrond, of England itself.

The ethical concern of *Guy of Warwick* is not the resolution of the 'courtly dilemma' between love and prowess but the maintenance of the balance between prowess and moral responsibility. Christianity plays a large part in this romance, not only in a 'crusading' but also in a 'moral' sense, whose purpose is to lead the hero to an understanding of the proper use of chivalric prowess. Similarly, Guy's quest for the peerlessness in arms which Felice, daughter of Rohaut, makes the condition of granting him her love (ll. 1151–60)[19] is not an end in itself but a painful

---

[18] e.g. ll. 6251, 6513–14, 8587, 9230, 9297.
[19] References, unless otherwise indicated as being to Caius 107, are to the Auchinleck

lesson about the proper place of 'courtly' love in the chivalric ethos. Owing to some similarities with the legend of St Alexis,[20] *Guy* has often been classified as 'exemplary' or 'hagiographic' romance, but, as Susan Crane has demonstrated, the work is essentially worldly in its concerns. The hero's choices are determined not by God but by himself.[21] Guy is an exemplary narrative,[22] but in the sense that it is about the pursuit of an ideal life on earth; its subject is human potential rather than human limitation.

The key word in M. Dominica Legge's characterization of the story of Guy as 'the progress of a man from childhood through an apprenticeship in arms to real fighting, first for a lady and then for God'[23] is 'progress'. Stylistically, the turning point of Guy's development is signified by changes in metre and mode: the switch from couplets to stanzas (at l. 7306), after Guy has despatched a dragon harrying Northumberland, marks a conclusive break with the values of chivalric romance and a broadening of the hero's ethical horizons;[24] and the conventions of chivalric narrative, which govern the first part of the work, are replaced in the stanzaic section by a code of conduct which is essentially antithetical

manuscript in Julius Zupitza, ed., *The Romance of Guy of Warwick. Edited from the Auchinleck MS. in the Advocates' Library, Edinburgh and from MS. 107 in Caius College, Cambridge*, EETS, e.s. 42, 49, 59 (London, 1883, 1887, 1891; rpr. London, New York, Toronto, 1966).

20 See Hanspeter Schelp, *Exemplarische Romanzen im Mittelenglischen* (Göttingen, 1967), pp. 133–48; Dieter Mehl, *The Middle English Romances*, pp. 223–27. Velma Bourgeois Richmond speaks of the work's 'moral purposefulness' (*The Popularity of Middle English Romance* [Bowling Green, Ohio, 1975], p. 154), which is 'to indicate the significance of Christian values and to suggest, by means of a worthy knightly protagonist, how each human being must strive to free himself of egocentric concerns and submit himself and his will to God (p. 188). David Klausner sees the romance as, in part, 'a secular pastiche of elements from the legend of St. Alexis' ('Didacticism and Drama in *Guy of Warwick*,' *Medievalia et Humanistica*, n.s.6 [1975], 103). Andrea Hopkins classifies *Guy of Warwick* as 'penitential romance' in *The Sinful Knights. A Study of Middle English Penitential Romance* (Oxford, 1990).

21 *Insular Romance*, p. 115; *eadem*, '*Guy of Warwick* and the Question of Exemplary Romance,' *Genre* 17 (1984–85), 351–74. The status of *Guy* as exemplary narrative has been discussed most recently by Hopkins (*The Sinful Knights*, pp. 77–78), who suggests that the 'apparent integration' of worldly and spiritual interests in the poem is achieved 'through the motif of penitence' (p. 78).

22 The prologue to *Guy*, which is missing in the Auchinleck, is explicitly in the didactic mode in the Caius manuscript: 'Therfore shulde man with gladde chere/ Lerne goodnesse, vndirstonde, and here:/ Who myke it hereth and vndirstondeth it/ By resoun he shulde bee wyse of witte;/ And y it holde a fayre mastrye,/ To occupye wisedome and leue folye' (ll. 15–20).

23 *Anglo-Norman Literature and Its Background*, p. 169.

24 Fewster, *Traditionality and Genre*, p. 89 (on the significance of the metrical divisions in *Guy* in the Auchinleck manuscript, see also *ibid*., pp. 42–49).

to the 'courtly' ideal in its rejection of love and renown as the *raison d'être* of chivalric life.[25]

Guy's progress towards becoming, in Felice's words, the 'best doand' (ll. 1154, 1157) in arms is publicly marked by his success in meeting increasing demands on his knightly prowess. Privately, his progress towards an understanding of the proper use of arms is charted by his relationships with a series of counsellors, beginning with Love and ending with God. Guy's invocation to Love for guidance and consolation (ll. 425–44) and the ignoring of sage advice from his elders – father, mother, and Rohaut – early in the work are superseded by a growing willingness to seek sage counsel and the capacity to impart it.

The hero's conduct in matters of love and prowess in the early part of the narrative subscribes to 'courtly' values and conventions of conduct. Guy is the archetypal 'courtly' lover, who weeps, sighs, sorrows for his haughty lady of higher station, curses the time he first set eyes on her (ll. 281–84), and pleads for *consilium et auxilium* from Love and Death (ll. 425–54). Although it endows her with a scholarly education, the introductory portrait of Felice (Caius MS, ll. 64–74),[26] is similarly conventional. In taking issue with the counsel of another maiden ('So thou shuld not rede me,' Caius MS, l. 619), who is sympathetic towards Guy, she delivers a stereotyped statement of the obligations of the 'courtly' wooer:

> Oft þou hast y-herd in speche
> Þat we no schal no man biseche,
> Ac men schul biseche wimen
> In the feirest maner þat þai can,
> & fond to speden ȝif þai may
> Boþe bi niȝtes and bi day. (ll. 621–26)

Guy begins his chivalric career by pursuing honour in the form of public feats of prowess, explicitly undertaken for love. 'Arme for þe ichaue vnder-fong' (l. 729), he tells Felice when he has been dubbed knight, and, he reiterates on his return from a successful first trip abroad, 'Armes y fenge for loue of þe' (l. 1122). When, although flushed with victory in his maiden tournament at Rouen, and others in Spain, 'Almaine', Lombardy, France, and Normandy (ll. 1065–68), Felice continues to refuse his suit until he is acknowledged as the best knight in arms in the world, he sets out again for 'oþer cuntres' (l. 1173) to 'winne

---

[25] Fewster characterizes this code of conduct as one which evokes 'a tradition of wisdom literature that exemplifies the ages of humankind through the life of a single figure' (*Traditionality and Genre*, p. 100).

[26] The Auchinleck is defective here.

priis' (ll. 1192, 1223) and become a knight without peer. Guy's declared ambition at this point of the narrative is to be '. . . þe best y-teld,/ Þat be fiȝtand wiþ spere & scheld' (ll. 1169–70).

In this first section of *Guy*, both Guy and Felice measure knightly peerlessness solely in terms of superiority in arms. Even after the tournament successes of his first trip abroad, she rejects his proposal on the grounds that marriage might make him lazy and discourage him from 'armes loue', expressing sentiments reminiscent of Gauvain's advice to Yvain on his marriage to Laudine in *Yvain*:

> & ȝif ich þe hadde mi loue y-ȝeue,
> To welden it while þat y liue,
> Sleuþe þe shuld ouercome:
> Namore wostow of armes loue,
> No comen in turnamant no in fiȝt.
> So amerous þou were anon riȝt.   (ll. 1137–42)

A different perspective on chivalric life is offered by Rohaut (ll. 1199–1212) and Guy's parents (ll. 1233–46), who suggest that a young man, even with a few tournament victories under his belt, should not be too hasty to pursue knightly renown or to sever himself from kith and kin. When Guy puts it to Rohaut that his success 'of armes' (l. 1194) in 'vncouþe lond' (l. 1192) will reflect well on the earl's *worþschip* (l. 1196) and make him widely held in awe (ll. 1195–98), Rohaut counsels him not to be hasty, to stay at home, and to join him in the social pursuits of hunting and hawking. To his father, Syward, Guy announces that he must undertake this quest as a youthful obligation ('So ȝong man schal in ȝouþe do,' l. 1224), so that in old age he may live 'in mirþe & ayse' (l. 1230).[27] Syward's response is that he and Guy will both be happier if the latter remains at home for another two years (ll. 1233–36), and his mother urges him to heed that advice: 'Leue son,' his moder him sede,/ 'Þou do bi þi faders rede' (ll. 1238–39).

Guy disregards the advice of this trio of counsellors,[28] but the proof of the wisdom of age and the ignorance of youth is demonstrated by the first serious challenge to his prowess, which is not the simulacrum of battle in which he has wounded Duke Otoun of Pavia in the tournament

---

[27] Fewster discerns a dialectic in *Guy of Warwick* between youth and age. The narrative, she suggests, is one in which the *sapientia* of age and experience is endorsed over youthful *fortitudo*: 'The poem presents simultaneously two opposite views of age: while young heroes state that age is decline, an ongoing debate develops thematically to suggest the alternative that ageing is growth' (*Traditionality and Genre*, p. 99).

[28] His rejection of his mother's appeal and subsequent abrupt departure (ll. 1247–50) parallel Perceval's conduct at the beginning of *Li Contes del Graal*. As a narrative dealing with the chivalric and spiritual education of the hero, *Guy* is sometimes reminiscent of Chrétien's unfinished poem.

at Rouen, but an ambush by the forces of this vengeful and villainous knight.[29] The engagement ends disastrously in the deaths of, among others, Guy's loyal companions Urry and Torald. The despairing hero is bereft of counsel and devoid of strategy: he 'not what to do' (l. 1471). The episode ends with Guy's first explicit repudiation of the values of courtly narrative, when he lays the blame for the deaths of his men squarely at the feet of Felice: 'For þi loue, Felice, the feir may,/ Þe flour of kniȝtes is sleyn þis day' (ll. 1559–60).

This is the second of three occasions on which Guy curses his passion for Felice. The first is a conventional 'courtly' lament early in the narrative:

> He acursed þe time þat [he] hir say,
> Felice wiþ her eyȝen gray,
> Hir gray eyȝen, hir nebbis schene:
> 'For hir mi liif is miche in wene' (ll. 281–84),

and the last a piece of bitter self-accusation, in which he cites her as the cause of his killing many men:

> Þi loue me haþ so y-bounde,
> Þat neuer seþþen no dede y gode,
> Bot in wer schadde mannes blode
> Wiþ mani a griseli wounde (st.24, ll. 6–9).

Guy has won a degree of renown in tournaments, but, in terms of motivation and effect, his acts of prowess up to the time of the ambush by Otoun amount to failure. The victory at Rouen has made the duke his mortal enemy (ll. 895–96), and his continued pursuit of *priis* has led to his defeat and the death of his fellows. What began as a courtly metaphor ('Felice . . . þou miȝt m[e] sle,' ll. 569–70) has become a gruesome reality, affecting many knights. After this debacle, Guy explicitly offers himself to others as a cautionary example – and, he predicts, by no means the last – of a man undone by a woman:

---

[29] The promoting of hate and the desire for revenge are mentioned by Jacques de Vitry as reasons for his disapproval of tournaments (see Maurice Keen, *Chivalry* [New Haven and London, 1984], citing *Exempla*, ed. T.F, Crane [London, 1890], CXL, p. 88). On the controversial issue of medieval tournaments, which were condemned by the Church and strictly regulated in England, see Noël Denholm-Young, 'The Tournament in the Thirteenth Century,' in *Studies in Medieval History Presented to Frederick Maurice Powicke*, ed. R.W. Hunt, W.A. Pantin, R.W. Southern (Oxford, 1948), pp. 240–68; Keen, *Chivalry*, Ch.5; Kaeuper, *War, Justice, Public Order*, pp. 199–208.

For þe last no worþ y nou3t
Þat wimen han to gronde y-brou3t.
Ac alle oþer may bi me,
3if þai wil, y-warned be' (1563–66).

The bloody encounter with Otoun has, however, served one positive
cause in teaching Guy, who now expresses regret for not having listened
to Rohaut and his father, the value of the advice of his elders:

'Allas! allas! Rohaut, mi lord,
Þat y no hadde leued þi word!
Þan hadde y nou3t y-passed þe se,
Ich hadde bileued at hom wiþ þe;
Þus yuel nere me nou3t bifalle,
Y no hadde nou3t lorn min felawes alle.
Who so nil nou3t do bi his faders red,
Oft-siþes it falleþ him qued' (ll. 1583–90).

Some five years later, restored to health and his knightly reputation
consolidated by further tournament victories, which bring adulation and
respect rather than enmity (ll. 1675–82), Guy determines to return to
England. His first thought is for his friends and relatives:

Into Inglond he wald wende,
For to speke wiþ his frende;
For it was ago fif 3er
Þat he was last þer (ll. 1693–96).

Felice is mentioned by name, with reference to Guy's rejection of the
suits of queens and countesses, as she whom 'he loued so miche' (l.
1702), but only incidentally, and at the conclusion of this report of his
state of mind. Despite Guy's reported determination to return to England, the upshot of his joyful reunion shortly after (ll. 1720–68) with
Heraud, his foster-father and companion-in-arms, who has been
wounded in the battle with Otoun, is the postponement of the homeward voyage in order to lend assistance to Duke Segyn of Louvain,
under siege by the emperor of Almaine for killing his nephew, Sadok, in
a tournament. Felice subsequently disappears from the narrative until,
some 2,500 lines later, Guy finds himself confronted with the prospect of
marriage to the daughter of the emperor of Constantinople.

In a gesture indicative of his increased maturity, Guy asks his foster-
father for advice as to whether he should give aid to the duke: 'He seyd
to Heraud, 'what rede [3e]?/ Sum gode conseyle 3if thou me' (ll. 1902–3).
This time Guy not only seeks counsel, he explicitly resolves to heed it:
'Þat tow me redest, don y wille;/ Þi counsyl forsake y nille' (ll. 1905–06).

In his response, Heraud first reminds Guy of the obligation to help those in need, and only then of the prospective personal benefits of winning honour and renown for himself and his family:

> Hem to help men schul spede
> Þat to help han gret nede.
> For los and priis þou miȝt þer winne,
> & manschip to þe & al þi kinne.   (ll. 1909–12)

The significance of Guy's gesture in asking for advice here is highlighted by the repetition of the words 'gode' and 'conseyl' in Heraud's reply ('Y ȝif conseyl, & gode it is,' l. 1908) and Guy's explicit endorsement of his statement: 'For gode conseyl ȝif[es]tow me' (l. 1916).

This consultative dialogue marks a significant turning-point in the hero's development[30] in that, for the first time, it prompts him to do battle on behalf of a second party. Armed with Heraud's counsel, he overwhelms the forces of the emperor's steward. The grateful Segyn confers power over his dukedom upon Guy and defers to his counsel: 'Bi þi conseyl ichil nov don,/ For to greue mi dedli fon' (ll. 1917–18, p. 114). Guy duly devises some successful battle strategy, and other castles and towns in the hands of the emperor are recovered through his *consilium et auxilium* ('Bi him & bi his conseyl also,' l. 1941 [p. 116]). Guy's superiority as tactician and fighter is underlined by the parallel scene of council between the emperor and his barons (ll. 1949–82 [p. 116]) which follows: Otoun's advice that the siege against Segyn be renewed results in another defeat for the emperor's troops at Guy's hands.

After further battles, Segyn appeals to a council, composed of Guy, Heraud, and four others (ll. 2477–81), for guidance in his dealings with the emperor: 'Lordinges,' he sayd, 'what rede ȝe?' (l. 2485). Guy promises his 'best rede' (l. 2490), and peace is finally made when he (Caius MS, ll. 2687–90)[31] and other allies of both Segyn and the emperor successfully plead for mercy instead of vengeance in the matter of Sadok's death. In the counsel to which he is party here, Guy shows himself to have progressed from the ability merely to devise military strategy to an understanding of the importance of Christian values in judging the rights and wrongs of prowess. Symptomatic of Guy's fundamental immaturity, however, is his assault upon Otoun (ll. 2737–44), whom he unceremoniously punches in the teeth for his objection to the

---

30 In her discussion of Guy's relationship with Heraud (*The Sinful Knights*, pp. 87–90), Hopkins suggests that each of the four occasions on which Guy either takes or seeks Heraud's advice (on the first [ll. 1075–80] the advice is unsolicited) 'shows Guy becoming more independent of Heraud's guidance' (p. 88).

31 The Auchinleck manuscript is defective here.

emperor's preparedness to concede that forgiveness is preferable to vengeance.[32]

Guy's next series of exploits, the defence of Constantinople on behalf of Ernis, the Eastern Emperor, are a triumph of prowess but something of a failure of moral responsibility. The offer of the hand of Ernis's daughter, Clarice, and a string of military victories over the Saracens incite the envy of the emperor's steward, Morgadour, who falsely accuses Guy of seducing the princess (ll. 3221–28). Ernis's refusal to rise to the bait notwithstanding, Morgadour informs Guy that he has been charged with the rape of Clarice, that the emperor is determined to kill him, and that his best option is to flee. In his response to this intelligence, Guy displays an alarming readiness to exercise prowess in a morally reprehensible cause. Bluffed completely, and without any attempt to confront the emperor, he orders his knights to head with him for the Saracen camp to offer their services (ll. 3312–15) to the infidel. Only the emperor's query to Heraud about the puzzling sight of Guy leaving the city with an armed company (ll. 3320–24) provides him with explanation and Guy with an abject apology (ll. 3333–46).

A serious infraction of chivalric conduct is thus averted here, but not so in the 'Florentine' episode, where, in an act of hubris, the hero kills an unarmed and inexperienced opponent and reveals that he still has much to learn about the proper use of prowess. After Guy slays a boar in a forest in Britanny belonging to a certain Earl Florentine, the earl's son, a young knight, is sent to challenge the trespasser. Guy refuses to surrender his horse to the youth, who strikes him with his staff, an insult for which Guy promptly kills him and then proceeds, unwittingly, to Florentine's castle, where he asks for and receives hospitality before he is identified as the killer of his host's son. Guy's attempted justification of his action on the grounds of self-defence (ll. 6888–90) is unconvincing, and his subsequent treatment of the elderly Florentine as callous and arrogant as this act of manslaughter.[33] Guy began his chivalric career by fighting in the name of the 'courtly' values discredited early in the narrative; now, implicitly, he subscribes to the 'epic' code of vengeance, explicitly rejected in the settlement of the dispute between Segyn and the emperor. But whereas Segyn was reluctantly forced, with fatal results, to

---

[32] See the comments by Barron (*English Medieval Romance*, p. 77) and Richmond (*The Popularity of Middle English Romance*, pp. 159–60).

[33] Richmond sees this episode as one of many in the narrative which show 'essential contradictions between the requirements of the knightly code that is Guy's initial standard and the essential Christian values which increasingly determine his attitudes and behaviour. As a striving knight he cannot allow himself to be insulted and must destroy whoever dares to abuse him' (*The Popularity of Middle English Romance*, p. 160).

joust with his lord's nephew (ll. 1861–80), Guy overreacts to a mild affront.

Other less than exemplary conduct on Guy's part in the couplet section of the narrative is indirectly associated with Felice. When he finally accedes to Ernis's thrice-proposed marriage (ll. 2887, 3070–71, 4104) with Clarice, so far, it seems, has Felice been from his thoughts, that it is not until he is at the altar and on the brink of marrying the princess that he suddenly remembers her (ll. 4196–99).[34] He swoons, asks that the ceremony be postponed until he is restored to health, and takes to his bed for a fortnight. At this point, Guy takes Heraud into his confidence ('& alle his conseyl schewed him þo,' l. 4246) and solicits his advice ('Sir Herhaud,' he seyd, 'conseyl me:/ Of mi conseyl ich oxi þe,' ll. 4247–48) as to which of the two he should wed. But when Heraud presents the case for union with the princess – power and riches (ll. 4257–68) – Guy angrily retorts: 'Now ich wot þou louest me nou3t,/ When þou conseyls me mi leman fro' (ll. 4270–71). In self-justificatory reply to this outburst, Heraud, whose advice has been offered in good faith, points out that he had previously had no idea of Guy's feelings towards Felice (l. 4275). Guy's unjustifiably petulant response to Heraud's counsel here is further illustration, this time in a social rather than martial context, of the potential which 'courtly' values have to damage chivalric alliances.[35]

That he could have forgotten her in the first place, and that Heraud, his companion and confidant, could have been unaware of Guy's alleged devotion to her in the second,[36] is symptomatic of Felice's essentially marginal role in the hero's life. The narrative, moreover, ignores Felice for the next 3,000 lines. Rising from his sickbed, Guy happily prepares to resume life at Ernis's court, but his departure from Constantinople is swiftly precipitated when a lion, which he has earlier rescued from a dragon, is killed by Morgadour. Guy takes vengeance on the steward and protests to the emperor about this poor return for services rendered (ll. 4404–22). When Ernis promises, once again, to make amends and undertakes to arrange the wedding with Clarice the next day, Guy, with a degree of slick diplomacy on the one hand and a blatant lack of candour on the other, expresses the fear that the Greeks will regard the

[34] George Ellis comments, with characteristic dryness: 'If the reader has not yet forgotten the all-accomplished Felice . . . it is probably because the laborious campaigns in Germany and in Turkey have not occupied in the recital quite so much time as they consumed in the acting' (*Specimens of Early English Metrical Romances*, rev. J.C. Halliwell [London, 1848], p. 211).

[35] Hopkins, however, makes the interesting suggestion that Guy's behaviour here indicates that he 'has matured sufficiently to know his own mind and be independent of the guidance of Felice and Heraud' (*The Sinful Knights*, p. 89).

[36] Burrows suggests that Guy's silence on this score shows that he has been scrupulous in observing 'courtly' discretion (*The Auchinleck Manuscript*, p. 115).

match as unworthy (ll. 4432–44) and announces his intention to 'Whende . . . in-to mi cuntre,/ Mine frendes to visite & to se' (ll. 4449–50).

Any audience expectations of Felice's reappearance raised by the *reverdie* (ll. 4502–05) which follows Guy's departure from Constantinople, are, however, quickly dispelled, since it is not the revival of the hero's love affair which is heralded here but his involvement in that of another knight. As he rides through the forest, alone, melancholy, and deep in thought ('So michel he herd þo foules sing,/ Þat him þouȝt he was in gret longing,' ll. 4519–20) about 'mani þinges' (l. 4512), although the subject of Felice is not specifically mentioned, Guy's mournful reverie is interrupted by the appearance of an equally sorrowful knight, Tirry of Gormoise. Tirry, Guy's former adversary and ally of the emperor of Almaine, is grief-stricken over events precipitated by his romance with Oisel, daughter of the Duke of Lorraine.

Tirry's predicament provides another example of the deleterious effects of love upon the ties of chivalry and kinship: his elopement with Oisel has already led to the death of many knights; and, in the course of the lengthy episode which follows his meeting with Guy, it claims further victims and endangers the life of Tirry's elderly father. When, with Guy's help, the matter is satisfactorily resolved and Guy takes leave of Tirry, now married to Oisel, and his father, once again he is reluctant to make a declaration of his commitment to Felice: his stated reason for wishing to return to England is to see '[m]ine fader & min frendes' (l. 7045). Sixty lines elapse before Guy tells Tirry that his departure is actually precipitated by the love of his unnamed *leman* (l. 7105). The couplet section of *Guy* ends – without further reference to Felice, friends, or relatives – some three hundred lines later (at l. 7306), after Guy returns to Warwick, where he takes up residence with King Athelstan and kills an Irish dragon harrying Northumberland.

The first part of the stanzaic *Guy of Warwick* returns to the clichés of romance which dominate the early scenes of the couplet section. Guy's reunion with Felice is a stylized affair which takes exactly two lines: 'On a day sir Gij gan fond,/ & feir Felice he tok bi hond' (st.5, ll. 1–2). Felice herself is reduced to the formulaic abstractions of 'bird so bliþe' (st.5, l. 3), 'swete wiȝt' (st.7, l. 6), and 'bird so briȝt' (st.7, l. 9); Guy's response to her declaration of love (st.6, ll. 7–12) is equally formulaic: 'He kist þat swete wiȝt./ Þan was he boþe glad & bliþe' (st.7, ll. 6–7).[37] The scene contrasts markedly with the reunion of Guy and Heraud after their long

---

[37] Hopkins comments of Guy's behaviour here that: 'It is noticeable how Guy's former impetuous wooing of Felice has become something more cold and formal' (*The Sinful Knights*, p. 101).

separation following the ambush by Otoun, when, bursting with emotion and weeping for joy, Guy kisses and embraces his foster-father:

> When Gij herd Herhaud speke,
> Him thou3t his hert wald to-breke,
> & in his armes he haþ him take,
> & gret ioie wiþ him gan make;
> Him he kist wel mani siþe:
> For ioie he wepe, so was he bliþe. (ll. 1749–54)

The subsequent betrothal and marriage of Guy and Felice (sts.5–18), events characteristic of narrative closure,[38] give the opening of the stanzaic section of *Guy* something of the appearance of romance in reverse. After the wedding, however, the conventions of romance are altogether abandoned in a scene which mirrors Felice's instruction to Guy to seek fame abroad, and Syward's attempt to dissuade him, at the beginning of the couplet section. This time, and in vain, it is Felice, his wife of a fortnight, who, after listening to Guy's announcement that he intends to forsake both her and bloodshed in her name for a life of pilgrimage, exhorts him not to leave, but to atone for his sins by founding churches and abbeys (st.28, ll. 7–12). Nevertheless, just as Guy renounced deeds of arms in the name of love after the battle with Otoun, now he expresses a desire to repudiate worldly chivalry altogether. His 'conversion', as Fewster terms this sudden 'increased awareness of Christianity',[39] is as much a final repudiation of 'courtly' values (sts.24–25) as an awakening of Christian conscience, with echoes of that earlier lament for the fallen: 'Ac for þi loue ich haue al wrou3t' (st.25, l. 7).

Guy of Warwick is, paradoxically, an anti-love romance. In a complete reversal of the chivalric topos, love is presented as hindrance to, not as inspiration for, the quest for knightly perfection. Initially set up as chivalric goal, love quickly becomes chivalric obstacle: deeds of prowess in its name lead to the death of worthy knights. The important relationships in this work are not the bonds of love and marriage but of knighthood.[40] Guy's love for Felice serves merely as catalyst for the deeds through which he learns, by way of hard won experience, the proper use of prowess.

---

[38] As Ellis remarks: 'Here, therefore, the reader will naturally expect a termination of this long-winded story' (*Specimens of Early English Metrical Romances*, p. 219).

[39] *Traditionality and Genre*, p. 85.

[40] As William Calin comments of *Gui de Warewic*, 'The most moving sentimental scenes . . . in the narrative as a whole, the episodes which are truly love scenes, recount and dramatize, in moving detail, recognition and separation between Gui and his male friends, Tierri and Heralt' ('*Gui de Warewic* and the Nature of Late Anglo-Norman Romance,' *Fifteenth-Century Studies* 17 [1990], 25).

Felice herself undergoes a kind of 'rehabilitation', from disdainful lady of courtly convention in the early part of the narrative to exemplary doer of good works in its latter stages: 'In þis warld was non better wiman,/ In gest as-so we rede' (st.279, ll. 2–3). Ultimately, however, Guy rejects both her charity and her love. After defeating the giant, Colbrond, Guy, emaciated, unrecognized, and in pilgrim dress, joins a group of indigents in Warwick for whom Felice provides daily sustenance. When she sends him dishes from her table and offers to do so for the rest of his life (st.281), Guy thanks her, but his thoughts are elsewhere: 'all anoþer was his þou3t' (st.282, l. 2). He leaves Warwick and takes up residence in the hermitage where he dies nine months later, summoning his wife only on his deathbed. After he sets eyes on her, his soul departs (st.293). Felice dies fifteen days later, and they are finally reunited in eternal bliss.

Guy does not abandon knightly prowess in the stanzaic section of the narrative, but the enterprises to which he devotes it are as much a form of atonement for the bloodshed he has committed in the name of love[41] as the final steps to chivalric perfection. He takes up arms only at the request of others and in patently just causes, his new found humility symbolized by the abandonment of knightly for pilgrim status. Guy's principal adversaries in his last three great fights, for which he is actively sought as champion but which he undertakes, incognito, as pilgrim first and knight second (thereby becoming something of a medieval Clark Kent-Superman) are formidable: two giants, Amoraunt and Colbrond, and Duke Berard, wicked steward to the emperor of Almaine.

The vanquishing of Amoraunt not only achieves its immediate object, the release of Earl Jonas of Durras and his fifteen sons from imprisonment by the Saracen king, Triamour of Alexandria, but also obtains a guarantee of freedom for all of Triamour's Christian prisoners (st.88). In his penultimate exploit, Guy once again comes to Tirry's rescue. On the homeward trip to England after slaying Amoraunt, he encounters Tirry, now his sworn brother (l. 4916), sorrowing and destitute, and similarly dressed as a pilgrim. Neither recognizes the other, but Guy offers help in the form of the counsel which, he says, a disinterested party can often provide:

> Conseyl y can 3iue þe gode,
> & tow telle me þi þou3t;
> For oft it falleth vncouþe man
> That gode conseyle 3iue can   (st.144, ll. 8–11)

---

[41] 'A certain amount of bloodletting is the lot of the warrior; but his own past, romping around Europe killing, wounding, and destroying for the sake of gaining fame in order to win Felice's love, he now sees, rightly, as a disgusting occupation, not worthy of a serious, dedicated knight' (Hopkins, *The Sinful Knights*, p. 104).

Tirry explains that he has been unjustly accused by Berard of having caused, through his *red* (st.151, l. 5), the death of the emperor's cousin, Otoun.[42] The indictment has led to the seizure of his lands, imprisonment, and the exile of his wife. Tirry's friends, however, have taken counsel amongst themselves (st.153, l. 4), pleaded with the emperor on his behalf, and gained his freedom on the condition that Guy of Warwick champion him in judicial combat against the steward. After a year-long search, Tirry has concluded that Guy is dead and that he is without remedy: 'Þerfore y wot þat Gij is ded: /For sorwe can y me no red' (st.154, ll. 10–11).

Without revealing his identity either to Tirry or the emperor, Guy appears before the emperor's court, pleads his friend's case, offers himself as champion, asks for horse and armour, and has his request granted (sts.170–79) After a day of combat, in which the spectators take him for an angel (st.188), and Tirry himself decides that he is 'non erþelich man' (st.191, l. 7), Guy and the bed in which he is sleeping are tossed into the sea by allies of Berard. Waking to the sight of stars and waves, he raises the issue of prowess in an anguished prayer to the Creator. For the first time, he articulates his understanding of its proper use:

> & y no fiʒt for to win no þing,
>   Noiþer gold no fe,
> For no cite no no castel,
> But for mi felawe y loued so wel.   (st.197, ll. 5–8)

and his life is saved by a miracle in the following stanza. Berard is killed, Tirry has his lands and wife restored, and succeeds to the stewardship. Guy exchanges his borrowed armour for pilgrim's mantle, but his final words to Tirry (sts.230–31), delivered in his own identity, become a homiletic speech in which he exhorts his friend to serve the emperor faithfully and not to commit the sins of his predecessor.

Just as Guy supplied the *red*, as remedy, which Tirry needed against Berard, so, in his last and greatest fight, he does for King Athelstan against Colbrond, Anlaf of Denmark's African giant. On his return to England, Guy learns that Anlaf is terrorizing England with Colbrond and a force of 15,000 knights and has called upon Athelstan to surrender, unless a champion can be found to do battle with the giant. The king asks for counsel from a parliament of barons, earls, bishops, knights, priors, and abbots summoned to Winchester:

---

[42] Otoun has, in fact, been killed by Guy himself, during the Oisel episode (l. 6427).

> For godes loue y pray 3ou,
> Gode conseyl 3iue me now,
>   Or elles we ben al schent.   (st.238, ll. 10–12)

> Þerfore ich axi 3ou ichon,
>   What rede is best for to don?   (st.239, ll. 5–6)

Instead of making the wrong recommendation, like Athelwold's and Birkabein's councils in *Havelok*, this parliament makes none. Devoid of *red*, Athelstan's earls and barons respond to his plea with the silence of those whose heads have been struck off (st.240, ll. 10–12). The king retires for the night in despair and prays to Christ for a champion. Heavenly *red* is immediately forthcoming in a dream in which an angel tells him to ask a pilgrim, whom he will see the next day at the north gate of the city, to undertake the duel with Colbrond. Guy, the pilgrim in question, reluctantly accepts the challenge.

The hero's ultimate act of prowess thus receives both divine and earthly endorsement. The measure of Guy's progress towards an understanding of the proper use of prowess is demonstrated in his prayer before the battle. Whereas he unceremoniously called upon God's help when he first set out in courtly fervour on his quest for Felice,

> 'God,' quod Gij, 'y do foliliche:
> Y sle me seluen sikerliche;
> Mine owhen [deþ] y go now secheinde.
> God,' he seyd, 'be mine helpinde!'   (ll. 553–56),

now, on his knees (st.251, l. 10), he prays to God, not simply for 'help', but for guidance and counsel:

> 'Lord,' seyd Gij, 'þat rered Lazeroun,
> & for man þoled passioun,
>   & on þe rode gan blede,
> Tat saued Sussan fram þe feloun,
> & halp Daniel fram þe lyoun,
>   To-day wisse me & rede'   (st.252, ll. 1–6).

As sheer 'epic' entertainment *Guy of Warwick* is a rousing, if protracted, tale of knightly triumph over the villains from Central Casting: Danes, Saracens, giants, and evil dukes and stewards. As chivalric romance, it tells the history of a knight who wins in love and war. But *Guy* also encodes a serious exploration of the ethos of chivalry, which focusses on the relationship between prowess and moral responsibility. The quest for love is not endorsed as a valid motive for taking up arms. Feats of arms, the narrative establishes early on, are not sufficient in themselves to establish chivalric excellence; prowess exercised solely for personal glory can be irresponsible (it provokes the mortal enmity of Otoun and all its consequences) and morally wrong (as in the Florentine episode). As *Guy* moves towards a definition of ideal chivalry, which places altruism above earthly renown, it abandons not only the conventions of 'courtly' love but also re-writes the definition of chivalry as deeds of derring-do, which inspired the hero at the outset of his chivalric career. In the stanzaic section of the narrative, the quest for renown is displaced by the quest for atonement. Arms, relinquished in favour of pilgrim's mantle, are taken up only in altruistic causes.

Wise counsel is the medium through which Guy discovers the proper balance between prowess and moral responsibility and arrives at a true understanding of the knightly vocation. Although *Guy of Warwick* follows a ' "penitential pattern" '[43] in the hero's reparative quest in the stanzaic section of the narrative, it never abandons the 'political' model of procedure. By heeding the counsel of his elders, acquiring the capacity to advise others and to evaluate his own conduct in the light of experience, and, finally, by turning to heaven for guidance, Guy becomes a knight without peer in his command of chivalric prowess and true understanding of the chivalric ethos.

Beves of Hamtoun

An adaptation, with some emendations and interpolations,[44] of the Anglo-Norman *Boeve d'Hamtoune*,[45] *Beves of Hamtoun* shares certain superficial similarities of theme and structure with *Guy of Warwick*. In this instance, however, the role of counsel in the hero's life is not directed towards an understanding of the ethos of chivalry but to the overcoming of tyranny and injustice.

Although they are not marked by a change in verse form, *Beves*, like *Guy*, falls into two distinct and self-contained parts on the diptych pattern, which chart the loss and restoration of the hero's patrimony.[46] The

---

[43] Hopkins, *The Sinful Knights*, p. 115.

[44] See Judith Weiss, 'The Major Interpolations in *Sir Beues of Hamtoun*,' *Medium Ævum* 48 (1979), 71–76.

[45] Which probably dates from: 'in its existing shape . . . the last decade of the twelfth century' (Judith Weiss, 'The Date of the Anglo-Norman *Boeve de Haumtone*,' *Medium Ævum* 55 [1986], 240).

[46] There is, however, a switch in verse form from stanzas to couplets early in the narrative, at line 475. Fewster sees this metrical shift as having thematic significance in that it constitutes 'a new opening that points to the establishment of Beues as the hero of this romance. Like the *Guy* metrical change, the break signals a new set of adventures for the hero' (*Traditionality and Genre*, p. 48).

first, and longer, section (to l. 3510)[47] deals with Beves's fight against a private wrong motivated by lust; the second, his efforts to overcome a public act of royal tyranny, precipitated by material greed, which has far-reaching consequences for the kingdom. Whereas *Guy* is the account of the life of a national hero, whose defence of England against the threat of Danish invasion is only one, albeit the greatest, of his chivalric exploits, the political concerns of *Beves* are actually closer to those of *Havelok*. Like Guy, Beves progresses from a disregard for good counsel to the recognition of its importance for knightly success, but his ultimate mission is to save England, not from the external threat of dragons, giants, or invasion, but from the internal threat of royal tyranny.

As a child, Beves is the helpless victim of evil counsel. When he is seven years old, his mother conspires with her lover, Devoun, emperor of Almaine, to murder her elderly husband Guy, Earl of Southampton. The first explicit act of 'counsel' in the narrative is one of conspiracy, in which Beves's mother reveals her plot against his father to a 'messenger': 'Anon ri3t þat leuedi fer/ To consaile cleped hir masager' (ll. 70–71). As acknowledged by Beves's uncle, tutor, and designated killer, Saber, who saves Beves and fakes evidence of his death by soaking his clothes in pig's blood (ll. 347–52), it is her *red* to have her son murdered as well: 'Dame,' a seide, 'ich dede him of dawe/ Be þe red and be þe sawe' (ll. 481–82).

Attired in poor clothes and unrecognized, Beves receives, and rejects, his first piece of *red*, which takes the form of an abusive warning ('Scherewe houre son, y þe rede,' l. 398) by a porter against entering the family castle, now occupied by Devoun. Nevertheless, Beves enters the hall and 'counsels' the usurper in a similar vein: 'Aris! Fle hennes, I þe rede' (l. 436). He rants, raves ('Beues was ni3 wod for grame,' l. 439), and strikes the emperor with a club in a display of impotent anger which serves merely to illustrate his youthful vulnerability. Only another, more reasoned form of action restrains the tyrannical exercise of authority and saves him from death, when the knights in the hall, distressed on the child's account, ignore his mother's demand that they seize him (ll. 452–56).

Alarmed at the possible consequences of Beves's actions, Saber warns that unless he heeds his counsel ('Boute þow be me consaile do,' l. 472), both of them will be imperilled. Beves, like Guy, ignores the sage advice

---

[47] References, unless otherwise indicated, are to the Auchinleck version of *Beves*, in Kölbing, *The Romance of Sir Beues of Hamtoun*. On the relationships between the manuscripts and printed versions, see Mehl, *The Middle English Romances*, pp. 211–13; Jennifer Fellows, 'Editing Middle English Romances,' in *Romance in Medieval England*, ed. Mills, Fellows, Meale, pp. 7–10.

of his elder – in this case, to remain in hiding[48] – and soon, on his mother's orders, finds himself captured and sold into heathendom, where he soon becomes the prized property of King Ermin of Armenia and object of the love of the king's daughter, Josian. Beves repeats his mistake later in the narrative when Terry, Saber's son, offers him life-saving advice in different circumstances: rightly guessing that a letter in Beves's possession actually contains his death warrant on a false charge of seducing Josian, Terry asks to read it.[49] Just as Beves has previously ignored Saber's advice, he rejects Terry's request, walks straight into the trap (ll. 1387–88), and spends the next seven years in a snake-infested dungeon.

The fortunes of Beves begin to improve only when he learns to act on good advice, beginning with that of Josian's servant, Boniface. Although she loves Beves, Josian is wooed by another, unwanted suitor. Boniface counters Beves's rash proposal to flee with the princess, now the reluctant but virgin bride of King Yvor of Mombraunt, with a plan of his own: 'Sire, þe is beter do be me rede!' (l. 2210). 'It schel be so!,' says Beves (l. 2236). The first part of the strategy, to remove Yvor from the scene, is successful, and Boniface prefaces the details of the next step – to drug old King Garcy, who has been left to guard Josian, and then to flee – with the words: '3if 3e wil by my consaile do' (l. 2296). When Beves declares that he is, in fact, ready to do battle with Garcy and all his host (ll. 2332–38), Boniface once more sagely counsels discretion: 'Sir, 30w is better do by my reed' (l. 2340). Beves heeds this counsel, the plan is successful, and he and Josian take ship for Cologne. Three times Boniface has tendered his counsel, and three times Beves has curbed his rashness and successfully followed good advice.[50]

Having conclusively proved his prowess in battle with a dragon who has taken up residence in Cologne, Beves is now fully qualified, physically and mentally, to reclaim his inheritance. In a significant step towards maturity, he actively solicits wise counsel before taking action and, instead of following his own rash inclinations, seeks advice, this time from another uncle, Saber Florentin, bishop of Cologne: 'Leue em, what is to rede/ Of me stifader Deuoun,/ Þat holdeþ me londes at Hamtoun?' (ll. 2912–14). The bishop duly provides *red* (l. 2922), in the form of one hundred men to support Beves and Saber in mounting an attack on the emperor. Following hard upon this indication of maturity is

48 Although Ellis is of the opinion that, by concealing Beves in a closet, 'Saber was unable to devise any counsel worth following' (*Specimens of Early English Metrical Romances*, p. 243), this seems to be a logical strategy in the circumstances.
49 Unlike Josian, the heroine of the romance, Beves never receives a scholarly education.
50 The pagan Boniface now appears to have served his purpose and is slain by lions (ll. 2378–86).

the first endorsement of Beves's own credentials as counsellor; converted and baptised by Saber Florentin but stranded in Cologne, Josian appeals to him as he prepares to leave for England: 'Who schel me þanne wisse & rede?' (ll. 2942).

It is not, however, until Beves and his company are one mile out of Southampton that he is represented as a military leader, capable of providing battle strategy. He addresses his men thus: 'Lordinges,' to his men a sede,/ '3e scholle do be mine rede!' (ll. 2957–58), the plan being to trick Devoun into thinking that the force, led by a certain 'Gerard', has come to lend assistance against attacks by Saber. Beves's good counsel here is, however, directly challenged by evil, when his mother re-enters the narrative with her own strategy for the emperor ('Sire,' 3he seide, 'doute 3ow nou3t!/ Of gode consaile icham be-þou3t,' ll. 3313–14): to muster forces from Almaine and Scotland. Beves is nevertheless victorious, has Devoun put to death – his mother, beside herself with grief at the sight of her husband 'in þe pich' (l. 3460) conveniently falls and breaks her neck – and, within the space of thirty lines, marries Josian and follows Saber's advice to go to King Edgar in London to claim his patrimony (ll. 3487–88), a request which is immediately granted. Like his father before him, Beves becomes the king's marshall.

Marriage and restoration of birthright are usually signals to narrative closure, and the rapidly moving events of these thirty-five lines (ll. 3475–510), which also make reference to the children of Beves and Josian, constitute a stereotyped conclusion to a Middle English romance.[51] But *Beves* has some some thousand lines to go, and the concerns of this last quarter of the narrative enter the arena of public affairs. At issue are the duties of kingship and the problem of tyranny. Tyranny is shown to be an insidious thing: some despots may be instantly recognizable, like Devoun, but they may also be less immediately obvious, like the apparently worthy King Edgar. In the first part of *Beves*, a criminal act robs the hero of his father and his birthright; in this last part, the abuse of legitimate authority drives him from his lands and leads to the loss of his wife and children.

Beves's second exile is precipitated by the attempted theft, by Edgar's foolish son, of Josian's gift, the magnificent warhorse Arundel, who retaliates by kicking out the prince's brains (ll. 3561–63). Arundel has been left unattended only because Beves has left the stable to fulfil the obligations of the office of king's marshall, a point emphasized by the narrative:

[51] 'The reader will now be disposed to flatter himself that this prodigious and eventful history is terminated; that Sir Bevis will in future sleep quietly in his bed, Arundel in his stable, and Morglay in its scabbard' (Ellis, *Specimens of Early English Romances*, p. 272).

> Hit is lawe of kinges alle,
> At mete were croune in halle,
> & þanne eueriche marchal
> His ȝerde an honde bere schal.
> While Beues was in that office,
> Þe kinges sone, þat was so nice,
> What helpeþ for to make fable?
> A ȝede to Beues stable   (ll. 3551–58).

Disregarding Beves's adherence to his duty on the one hand and his son's felonious action on the other, Edgar orders the hero's execution. But, taking into account his previous record of loyal service, the barons exercise their right of counsel and suggest that Arundel be hanged instead (ll. 3571–74), a proposal to which Beves responds by making his estate over to Saber and emigrating to Armenia. This incident, where royal tyranny is restrained only by baronial counsel, offers something of a parallel with events in the early part of the narrative, when refusal by the knights of Southampton to comply with an unjust order saves Beves from the homicidal wrath of his mother.

Creating an impression of competing narrative modes, *chanson de geste* and 'political romance', this last part of *Beves* presents a striking contrast between the lurid and fantastic nature of those episodes which take place abroad, mainly in 'Armenia', and the more 'realistic' tenor of those set in England.[52] Take, for example, the two attempts to steal Arundel, the unsuccessful one by Edgar's son and a second, successful one in Armenia: whereas we are given the plausible details and consequences of the English prince's actions, Arundel is simply whisked away in Armenia by unspecified 'charmes' (l. 4033). Beves achieves his goals in Armenia by the sword, but in England he regains his patrimony 'Ase hit was lawe and riȝt vsage' (l. 3470).[53] Deviating from the topographical vagueness of *Boeve d'Hamtoune*,[54] the final episodes of *Beves* convey an impression of geographical versimilitude. We are a long way from exotic and unhistorical 'Armenia' when the narrative moves into the concrete and recognizable world of London and its environs: Putney, the Thames, Westminster, Cheapside, Ludgate.

The events of Beves's second exile parallel those of the first. Having

---

[52] On the geographical boundaries of *Beves*, see Metlitzki, *The Matter of Araby*, pp. 126–33.

[53] As Crane comments: 'Bevis wins back his heritage from King Edgar not by invasion but by pressing his legal claim and winning the support of the king's counselors' (*Insular Romance*, p. 87).

[54] See Albert C. Baugh, 'Convention and Individuality in the Middle English Romance,' in *Medieval Literature and Folklore Studies. Essays in Honor of Francis Lee Utley*, ed. Jerome Mandel and Bruce A. Rosenberg (New Brunswick, N.J., 1970), pp. 138–39.

originally lost his birthright and his father to the evil machinations of his mother, he is now deprived of the family assets through royal tyranny and of his wife through the treachery of the giant, Ascopard, who abducts Josian after she delivers twins in a forest enroute to Armenia. In Armenia, Beves inspires the love of another lady, who persuades him to marry her in a bigamous but chaste union (ll. 3829–40). The work of conversion continues, too: with the aid of his son, Guy, Beves forcibly brings Christianity to the entire kingdom of Armenia (ll. 4019–20), to which the dying Ermin makes Guy heir (ll. 4008–13). After defeating Yvor in single combat, Beves himself is crowned king of Mombraunt (ll. 4253–54). He has achieved all that the exotic world of *chanson de geste* can offer but is a dispossessed person in the 'real' world of England.

Beves makes a final journey to his homeland, this time with a force of 60,000 (l. 4276), to lend support to Saber's son, Robant, in the face of the ursurpation of the ancestral lands by King Edgar. Beves argues his case before the king's court in Westminster, but there is a lone dissenter to the decision of king and barons to restore his property in the person of Edgar's steward. The steward's denunciation of Beves as outlaw and traitor to the king (ll. 4309–14) and to the people of London (ll. 4324–38) leads to a conflict of epic proportions – 32,000 die and the Thames turns red with blood (ll. 4530–32) – in claustrophobically familiar surroundings.[55]

This episode is one of two major interpolations by the English adapter of *Boeve de Haumtone*,[56] and, despite its likely association with the incident involving Simon de Montfort and a crowd of Londoners in December, 1263,[57] its immediate narratorial significance is not overtly clear. Dieter Mehl suggests that it is intended for local appeal to English, specifically London audiences, 'of less refined tastes',[58] and Susan Crane, that: 'In terms of the poem's professed national feeling, the best we can do is to read this episode non-mimetically as a "good baron" triumphing over slander.'[59] The episode can, however, be interpreted as another illustration of the power of malign counsel to corrupt justice and promote anarchy, a notion supported by the more forthcoming version of *Beves* in Gonville and Caius manuscript 175, where the baleful effects of the steward's *red* are presented in a similar light to the potentially dire consequences of Wymound's slanderous *counseil* in *Athelston*, which, as it happens, follows *Beves* in that manuscript. The Gonville and Caius narrator ascribes the bloodshed to 'þe fals stywardys red' (l. 198, p. 213),

---

55 As Judith Weiss remarks: 'His Pass of Roncesvalles is Gose Lane' ('The Major Interpolations in *Sir Beues of Hamtoun*,' p. 73).
56 The other being the dragon fight in Cologne (see Weiss, 'The Major Interpolations,' pp. 71–72).
57 See Weiss, 'The Major Interpolations,' p. 74, and above, ch. 1, p. 37.
58 *The Middle English Romances*, p. 216.
59 *Insular Romance*, p. 61.

commenting, like his counterpart in *Athelston*, that: 'Falsnesse cam neuere to good endyng' (l. 200, p. 213);[60] likewise, the Gonville and Caius Edgar summons his earls, barons, and knights in order to make the same attribution: 'And tolde hem, hou hys men were ded/ Þorw3 þe false stywardys red' (l. 214, p. 214).

Edgar's crime is not, like Athelston's, to act upon the advice of one evil counsellor, but not to act at all. This *redeless* king offers no response to the steward's slanderous attack upon Beves and simply disappears from the narrative until the battle is all but over. The steward's actions in the king's name (he incites the Londoners by claiming that Beves has been outlawed by royal *comaundement* [l. 4332]) remain unchecked, and the next we hear of Edgar is that he is eager to make peace by marrying his daughter to Beves's son, Miles (ll. 4539–60).

As in *Guy*, love is a problematic issue in *Beves*, but instead of being a seductive obstacle on the hero's path to a true understanding of chivalry, it is actively eschewed by him from the outset. Whereas *Guy* initially subscribes to the 'courtly' values of love service, *Beves* displays a consistent streak of misogyny: Guy eventually denounces the negative effects of 'courtly' love upon chivalry and acknowledges God, rather than Felice, as the inspiration for his noble deeds, but Beves, although spurred throughout by Christian zeal, is also driven by the desire for vengeance upon his mother. In the *curriculum vitae* with which he identifies himself to Ermin, he accuses his mother of treacherously engineering his father's death, condemns the wickedness of many other women, and swears vengeance for Earl Guy, without making any reference to Devoun, the willing instrument of the deed itself:

> 'For gode,' a seide, 'ich hatte Bef,
> Iboren ich was in Ingelonde,
> At Hamtoun, be þe se stronde;
> Me fader was erl þar a while,
> Me moder him let sle wiþ gile,
> Wikked beþ fele wimmen to fonde!
> Ac sire, 3if it euer so be-tide,
> Þat ich mowe an horse ride
> And armes bere & scheft to-breke,
> Me fader deþ ich schel wel wreke!' (ll. 542–52).

It is tempting, although it credits the narrative with an unwarranted depth of psychological insight, to see the influence of his childhood trauma in all of Beves's dealings with women, which end in disaster, or near disaster, until his mother is dead. The single kiss which he gives

---

[60] 'Lystnes, lordyngys þat ben hende,/ Off falsnesse, hou it wil ende' (*Athelston*, ll. 7–8).

Josian at the announcement of her pending conversion (ll. 1194–99), for example, leads directly to the false accusation of seduction (ll. 1200–10) and his seven-year incarceration in Brademond's dungeon. Then, having escaped and been advised by the bishop of Jerusalem to marry only a virgin (ll. 1967–69), he returns to Armenia to learn that King Yvor has Josian 'to bord and to bedde' (l. 2012).

Other incidents, too, recall the horrific events of Beves's early years. Like Guy, he kills a wild boar; but while Guy's boar fight and subsequent killing of Florentine's son illustrate the wrongful use of chivalric prowess, Beves's despatch of the beast, whose head he presents to Ermin, has a different, symbolic significance. His mother's plot to murder his father begins with a feigned illness, which, she tells her husband, can be cured only by the meat of a wild boar (ll. 184–86). When Guy duly sets out on the hunt, Devoun waylays him with a company of 10,000 knights, kills, and beheads him. Beves's boar slaying is a reverse metaphorical representation of that murder:[61] Devoun sends Guy's head to his mistress as a trophy (ll. 277–85), whereas Beves intends giving the boar's to Josian (l. 832). In the course of the hunt, Beves is also assailed, by Ermin's wicked steward; but after defeating his attackers, he presents the head to Ermin (ll. 903–04) without further reference to Josian.[62]

Although Josian eventually becomes his wife, and on one occasion is called Beves's *lemman* (l. 1984) by the narrator and, on another, by Beves himself (l. 713), he remains the passive and reluctant partner in their relationship. The first, and decidedly ill-timed, offer of her hand comes from King Ermin, who makes his proposal immediately after the statement of disgust for his mother and all womankind with which Beves introduces himself. The hero's declaration, in response to Ermin's offer, that 'I nolde for-sake in none manere/ Iesu, þat bouȝte me so dere' (ll. 565–66) is explicitly a rejection of heathendom, but also, implicitly, of sexuality. Beves ceases his comically brutal rejection of Josian's advances (ll. 1093–132; 1179–99)[63] when she announces her readiness to embrace Christianity, but not until Devoun and his mother are dead, and Beves is

---

61 And, to engage in speculation about unconscious symbolism, possibly of his desired revenge upon Devoun: the boar is castrated (l. 815), although Devoun meets his end in a cauldron of boiling pitch and brimstone (ll. 3451–57).

62 To venture into Beves's subconscious once again, possibly he associates his plan to give the boar's head to Josian with the attack which follows almost immediately (ll. 837–88).

63 On Josiane's wooing of Boeve in *Boeve de Haumtone* and its comic potential, see Judith Weiss, 'The wooing woman in Anglo-Norman romance,' in *Romance in Medieval England*, ed. Mills, Fellows, Meale, pp. 152–53. On the figure of the 'bele Sarrasine', see also William Calin, 'Rapports entre chanson de geste et romans courtois au XIIe siècle,' in *Essor et Fortune de la Chanson de geste dans l'Europe et l'Orient latin. Actes du XIe Congrès International de la Société Rencesvals pour l'Etude des Epopées Romanes (Padoue-Venise, 29 août – 4 septembre 1982)*, 2 vols. (Modena, 1984), II, 415–16.

said, for only the second time in his life,[64] to be 'glad & bliþe' (l. 3471), do they marry.

The talented, loving, and faithful Josian is the antithesis of Beves's lascivious mother and the (initially) aloof Felice, but she is also the object of his transferred resentment and, as Lee Ramsey argues, 'clearly punished'[65] for her first two marriages, unwanted and unconsummated though they are. Condemned to death for the murder of her second husband, Earl Miles, she is stripped to her shift and tied to the stake before Beves rides to the rescue (ll. 3289–93). Even after marriage to Beves, and moments after giving birth to twin sons on the flight from England to Armenia, she is beaten, bound, and kidnapped.

During and despite these hardships, Josian, well-versed in the Eastern arts of magic and trickery and possessed of healing and musical skills, is no passive Griselda and emerges as one of the most enterprising women in Middle English romance. Her ingenuity gives her more in common with *Ywain and Gawain*'s Lunet than with *Guy of Warwick*'s Felice. Like Felice, she dispenses charity to Christian pilgrims for her beloved's sake during his seven years of imprisonment (ll. 2080–88), but her outstanding quality is her talent for *gyn*. While Beves shows himself to be progressively more receptive to wholesome counsel, Josian, successfully contriving to remain a virgin throughout her first two marriages, becomes an exponent of stratagem to virtuous ends. The means by which she manages this in the first instance are not revealed, but she avoids consummation of the second forced union by strangling the bridegroom (ll. 3175–224). No practical use is made of Felice's education in *Guy*, whereas Josian uses the knowledge of medicine she has acquired from the 'meisters grete' (l. 3672) of Bologna and Toledo to give herself the temporary appearance of a leper in order to discourage the renewed advances of Yvor (ll. 3671–700). She exercises her healing skills upon Beves when he is wounded in a skirmish with Ermin's knights on Christmas Day (ll. 715–34) and is also well-tutored in music, a talent which she employs to practical advantage to support herself and the temporarily ailing Saber (ll. 3906–16), after he rescues her from her postpartum abductor (ll. 3852–88), and they commence a seven-year search for Beves.

Nevertheless, even on her deathbed, Josian fails to capture her husband's full attention. Mortally ill, she summons her son, Guy, and Beves's cousin, Terry, to her side. The first mention of Beves in this final scene concerns his thoughts not for Josian, but for Arundel. Upon the arrival of Guy and Terry, Beves goes abruptly to the stables, where he

---

[64] The first (l. 2497) follows his victory over two lions in the forest where he and Josian take refuge after their flight from Garcy and Yvor.

[65] *Chivalric Romances*, p. 59.

finds his horse dead (ll. 4595–97). Stricken with grief, he returns to see, apparently for the first time, that Josian is on the brink of death. He embraces her, and they die together.

Like the first, the second conclusion of *Beves of Hamtoun* returns to the conventional framework of romance, with the marriage of Edgar's daughter and Beves's son, and the reconcilation of king and hero. Instead of returning to Southampton, however, Beves bestows his earldom upon Saber and returns to Armenia to take up residence in Mombraunt, where he and Josian spend the last twenty years of their lives. Beves thus fulfils a threefold mission in life: personal, patriotic, and religious. Through his efforts to regain his patrimony and the family honour, he delivers England from tyranny and Armenia from heathendom. The continued success of these achievements is assured by the succession of his sons, Guy and Miles, to these respective kingdoms, and achieved in no small part through the faithful lifetime service of his uncle, Saber.

Beves follows a pattern, common to *Havelok*, *Gamelyn*, and *Guy*, in which the hero's maturity is signalled by his capacity to receive, to act upon, and to impart wise counsel. With the exception of Havelok, who never rejects good advice, the heroes of these romances progress from initially ignoring sage *red* and *counseil* to heeding their mentors and showing themselves to be capable givers of counsel. Knights who spurn wholesome counsel invite failure and dishonour; *unrede* kings, like Athelston (*Athelston*), the king of Maydenland (*Ywain and Gawain*), Costentine (*Of Arthour and of Merlin*), and Edgar (*Beves*), who are deficient in judgment and receptive, actively or passively, to evil counsel, or averse to good, are either cyphers or tyrants.

CHAPTER FOUR

'Winning by *gyn*':
the Auchinleck manuscript (ii)

Sir Tristrem, Kyng Alisaunder,
Richard Coer de Lion, Floris and Blauncheflur,
The Seven Sages of Rome, Sir Orfeo

As evidence that parliamentary attendance for shire knights may not have been the chore which it has seemed to some modern historians,[1] J.R. Maddicott cites a delightful instance of life in imitation of art from the *Chronicon Angliæ*'s account of the 'Good Parliament' of 1376. The case of the knights and the friar is the very stuff of successful stratagem in Middle English romance:

'. . . two shire knights, Sir John de la Mare of Wiltshire and Sir John Kentwode of Berkshire, tricked a suspected accomplice of Alice Perrers, the king's mistress, into giving himself up. The suspect was a Dominican friar, known both as a physician and a magician, whom the knights approached at Alice's manor of Pallenswick under the pretext of seeking advice about their health. The phials of urine which they carried deceived the friar into receiving them, thus effecting his own capture, and it was only the subsequent intervention of the Archbishop of Canterbury that saved him from burning.'[2]

The pursuit of objectives by such devious and ingenious means (*gyn*; less frequently, *queyntise*), which are often devised through *red* and *counseil*, is the preferred *modus operandi* of the Auchinleck 'strategy' romances: *Kyng Alisaunder, Richard Coer de Lion, Floris and Blauncheflur, Sir Tristrem,* and *The Seven Sages of Rome*. Such *gyn* may be concrete or abstract, martial (engines of war; battlefield strategy) or 'social' (usually some form of deception). In *Floris* and *Blauncheflur, Sir Tristrem, The Seven*

---

1 'It is as hard for us as it may have been for contemporaries to weigh up the burdens and benefits of parliamentary service, but the probability is that it brought pleasure more often than distress' ('Parliament and the Constituencies,' p. 72).
2 'Parliament and the Constituencies,' pp. 79–80 (citing the *Chronicon Angliæ*, pp. 98–99).

Sages, and *Sir Orfeo*, *gyn* is predominantly 'social', with verbal *gyn* also playing a significant role in the latter two narratives. *Kyng Alisaunder* and *Richard Coer de Lion*, on the other hand, maintain a more even balance between the exercise of chivalric prowess and various forms of martial and social *gyn*.

ME *gyn* (and *engin*) derive from OFr *engin* ('habileté, adresse, ruse, fraude, tromperie, artifice, expedient'),[3] and the medieval sense of Latin *ingenium* ('ars, machinatio, fraus').[4] The *MED* has separate entries for *engin* and *gyn*. *Gyn* has four main senses: (1) 'Inventive talent, ingenuity, cleverness, skill'; (2) 'A means of effecting a purpose, an expedient scheme'; (3) 'An ingenious device or contrivance'; (4) 'A machine or structure used in assaulting or defending fortifications, a siege machine or tower'. *Engin* has three similar definitions: sense (2) of *gyn* is not among them, but 1(b) of *engin* ('deceitfulness, trickery; evil intention or design; a trick, a snare') introduces the notion of 'scheme' with negative connotations which are absent from *gyn* (2).[5] The negative senses of *engin* tend to be formed with the addition of a modifier (*vuel enginne, fendes engyn, fals engyn*, etc.)[6] or doublet ('bi losengerie an bi engin', 'false engyn and conspiracioun'). *Gyn* also occurs in a negative sense with *craft* ('deceit') to refer to the failure of Wymound's characteristic mode of conduct ('neuere with crafft ne gynne', l. 771), when he is finally called to account in *Athelston*. ME *engin* and *gyn* are therefore virtually synonymous, except that in the sense of 'evil scheme' *engin*, with an appropriate qualifier, is the more common term.

As R.W. Hanning sums it up in his definition of OFr *engin* in twelfth-century romance: 'the word *engin* has a variety of meanings, applicable to human abilities of an intellectual rather than a heroic nature, but also

3   Frédéric Godefroy, *Dictionnaire de l'ancienne langue française*, s.v. *engin*, III.
4   Charles du Fresne (Seigneur du Cange), *Glossarium ad scriptores mediæ et infimæ Latinitatis*, IV, 360 (cited by Robert W. Hanning, *The Individual in Twelfth-Century Romance* [London and New Haven, 1977], p. 106). Hanning also notes Greek *méchané* as a 'classical parallel to the range of meanings of *ingenium* '(*The Individual*, p. 107). The Greeks had another word for it: *metis* or 'cunning intelligence', which can be defined as a combination of 'flair, wisdom, forethought, subtlety of mind, deception, resourcefulness, vigilance, opportunism, various skills, and experience acquired over the years' (Marcel Detienne and Jean-Pierre Vernant, trans. Janet Lloyd, *Cunning Intelligence in Greek Culture and Society*, [Hassocks, Sussex, and Atlantic Highlands, N.J.], p. 3).
5   ME *queyntise* (OFr *cointise*) has the same range of meanings, including its negative senses, as *engin*: 'wisdom, intelligence, skill' (1a), 'guile, cunning; deceit, trickery' (1b); 'ingenuity or strategy' (2a), 'a plan, ruse, or stratagem' (2b), 'a plot, scheme, trick, or trap; a dishonest act or deceptive statement' (2c). Unlike *gyn* and *engin*, however, *queyntise* can also denote 'supernatural means, magic' (4b).
6   The *MED* provides a separate entry for the term *mal engin* (Med. Lat. *malum ingenium* [Du Cange, *Glossarium*, IV, 360]): 'deceit, trickery; also a treacherous scheme'.

to specific achievements that issue from these abilities: marvellous arti-
facts, war machines, and the like.'[7] In insular romance the context of *gyn*
ranges from battlefield to bedroom. Military strategy and the engines of
war (siege ladders, towers, mangonels), along with a large element of
gyn as trickery, are prominent in *Kyng Alisaunder* and *Richard Coer de
Lion*. In *Beves of Hamtoun*, *gyn*'s field of reference is particularly wide,
ranging from engines of war (ll. 3356, 4115) and the hero's ingenuity (l.
2003) to the architectural design of the chapel (l. 4610) in which Beves
and Josian are buried. By the mid-fifteenth century, however, in *The
Squyr of Low Degre*, *gyn* is confined to the elaborate gadgetry of the
window latches in the princess of Hungary's boudoir ('Every wyndowe
by and by,/ On eche syde had there a ginne,/ Sperde with many a divers
pynne,' ll. 96–98), and the embellishments on the sarcophagus at the
head of her bed ('She put him in a marble stone,/ With quaynt gynnes
many one, 'll. 691–92),[8] where she keeps the presumed remains of her
lover.

The objective of 'winning by *gyn*' is expressed with formulaic fre-
quency in Middle English romance,[9] although the goal itself varies considerably. In *Beves*, for instance, it refers both to the regaining of the
hero's birthright:

> 3if ich mi3te with eni ginne
> Me kende eritage to winne   (ll. 2939–40)

and to the unspecified means of the capture of Arundel by Ermin and
Yvor:

> And er hii mi3te þat hors winne,
> Þai lau3te him wiþ queinte ginne   (ll. 1525–26).

Elsewhere, the *gyn/wynne* couplet is used of military strategy and

---

7 *The Individual*, p. 105. On non-military forms of concrete *engin* in medieval narrative,
   see Merriam Sherwood, 'Magic and Mechanics in Medieval Fiction,' *Studies in Philology* 44 (1947), 567–92.
8 *The Squyr of Lowe Degre. A Middle English Metrical Romance*, ed. William Edward Mead
   (Boston, 1904).
9 *Gyn* is found as a rhyme with *wynne* in Middle English verse as early as *ca.*1200 in the
   Owl and the Nightingale: 'He mot gon to al mid ginne,/ Wan þe horte boþ on winne'
   (ll. 669–70); 'Mid lutle strengþe þur3 ginne/ Castel & bur3 me mai iwinne' (ll. 765–
   66). Eric Gerald Stanley, ed., *The Owl and the Nightingale* (London, 1960). In his edition
   of *King Horn* (Oxford, 1901), J.B. Hall cites further examples of the couplet in
   La3amon's *Brut*, *Generides*, *Kyng Alisaunder*, and *Le Morte Arthur*, in a note to l. 1456
   (p. 174).

engines of war,[10] and, most frequently in *Floris and Blauncheflur*, of strategy in the cause of love.[11]

Middle English romance may be spare in the lexicon of *courteisie*, but it is rich in the terminology of subterfuge. There are two, lexically distinctive, kinds of trickery in Middle English romance: the hero tends to use *gyn* or *queyntise*, and his adversaries *gile*, *wyle*, *trecherie*; and, less commonly, *male engynne*. *Gyn* can have a certain moral ambivalence in its association with trickery and guile,[12] but, occurring as it does most often in the service of the hero, its connotations are predominantly positive.[13] Similarly, *gile* is regularly, but by no means exclusively, employed by villains. Beves escapes from Brademond's gaol with the help of *gile* (l. 1621), although later he refers to the means of his release as 'godes grace & min engyn' (l. 2003) and to Ermin's *gile* (l. 1995) in sending him on a mission to deliver his own death warrant. *Gile* appears more frequently in the latter stages of *Beves*: Devoun claims that Beves, who is posing as a French knight called 'Gerard', is seeking to reclaim his supposedly forfeited heritage with 'gret gile' (l. 3003); 'Gerard' replies that if the emperor will give him arms, ships, and men against Saber, he will soon hear of a 'queinte gile' (l. 3022) to his benefit; and when Beves is reunited with Saber, he tells him of the successful *gile* (l. 3060) which he has engineered against their common adversary.

Hanning sums up the significance of *engin* for twelfth-century courtly audiences thus:

> This ability to create an advantage by calculation, manipulation, and the use of illusion is particularly admired and cultivated in a courtly society, where it is the only power available to most.[14]

---

[10] See, for example, *Of Arthour and of Merlin*, ll. 2222–23 (Percy Folio); *Roland and Vernagu*, ed. Sidney J. Herrtage, *EETS*, e.s. 39 (London, 1882), st.25, ll. 282–86 (as tail-rhyme); *Richard Coer de Lion*, ed. Karl Brunner, *Der mittelenglische Versroman über Richard Löwenherz. Kritische Ausgabe nach allen Handschriften mit Einleitung, Anmerkungen und Deutscher Übersetzung* (Vienna and Leipzig, 1913), ll. 2653–54, 5259–60, 6389–90); *Kyng Alisaunder*, ed. G.V. Smithers, *EETS* 227, 237 (London, 1952, 1957), ll. 1219–20. (Subsequent references are to these editions.)

[11] See, in addition to the instances in *Ywain and Gawain*, *Floris and Blauncheflur* and *The Seven Sages of Rome*, which are cited below, *Sir Degrevant*, ll. 917–18, 722–23.

[12] Hanning, *The Individual*, p. 105. J. B. Hall suggests that in Middle English romance *gyn* 'is often contrasted with open force' (*King Horn*, note to l. 1456, p. 174). *Gyn* is used, on one occasion, to malign purposes by the wicked empress in the Cotton Galba E.ix manuscript of *The Seven Sages of Rome*, edited from the manuscripts, with introduction, notes and glossary by Killis Campbell (Boston, New York, Chicago, London, 1907), l. 3055.

[13] For a list of the various types of deception found in Middle English romance, see Gerald Bordman, *Motif-Index of The English Metrical Romances* (Helsinki, 1963), pp. 53–61.

[14] *The Individual*, p. 111.

This line of argument is developed further by C. Stephen Jaeger, who makes both locative and ethical distinction between 'courtier' narrative, like Gottfried's *Tristan*, and the 'chivalric' narratives of Chrétien.[15] In Jaeger's 'courtier' narrative, the hero's struggle takes place in the closed world of the court, a place where 'courtliness' may be merely a veneer of fellowship and good manners, and conflict becomes intrigue rather than armed challenge.[16] In 'chivalric' narrative, however, the arena of action is away from the court, and courtliness becomes 'a sublime ethical code'.[17]

The spatially restricted world of much Middle English romance frequently gives rise to such 'courtier' *gyn*. Most of *Sir Gawain and the Green Knight*, for example, takes place at Arthur's and Bertilak's courts, where the hero is challenged by various forms of dissimulation. *Sir Cleges*, *Sir Tristrem*, and *Athelston* could likewise be regarded as 'courtier' narrative, while substantial 'courtier' episodes are embedded in *Ywain and Gawain*, *Beves*, *Guy*, *Richard Coer de Lion*, and *Kyng Alisaunder*. The principal mode of *gyn*, 'courtier' and otherwise, is simple disguise – most often the hero's assumption of pilgrim (e.g. *Richard Coer de Lion*),[18] merchant (*Havelok*, *Floris and Blauncheflur*), minstrel (*Sir Orfeo*), or beggar (*Sir Orfeo*, *Sir Tristrem*) persona, a ploy which may or not may not be successful[19] – but 'courtier' masquerade can become a form of theatre, as in the elaborately staged deceptions of *The Erle of Toulouse*, in which murder is masked as courtly charade,[20] and *Sir Gawain and the Green Knight*, where the shape-shifting Green Knight/Bertilak loses his head in circumstances reminiscent of the beheading and revival of grotesque fool figures in medieval mummers' plays.[21]

---

[15] *The Origins of Courtliness. Civilizing trends and the formation of courtly ideals 939–1210* (Philadelphia, 1985), pp. 236–54.

[16] *The Origins of Courtliness*, p. 238.

[17] *The Origins of Courtliness*, p. 242.

[18] *Guy of Warwick*, *Richard Coer de Lion*, and *Sir Orfeo* offer interesting distinctions between the hero's adoption of pilgrim status as vocation on the one hand, and as mask on the other. Guy dons the mantle of pilgrim in the spirit of penitence in the stanzaic section of *Guy*, and Orfeo sheds royal finery for *sclavin* (l. 228 [ed. Speed, *Medieval English Romances*]) in despair rather than as disguise when he abandons his kingdom after the abduction of Heurodis. Richard, on the other hand, masquerades, unsuccessfully, as a pilgrim to avoid recognition in hostile territory.

[19] The hero's disguises are treated with scepticism, or discovered, in *Floris and Blauncheflur*, *Kyng Alisaunder*, and *Richard Coer de Lion*. Havelok's self-representation as merchant on his return to Denmark is also not entirely convincing, since his bearing appears better suited to a chivalric rather than a commercial career (*Havelok*, ll. 1465–74).

[20] See Geraldine Barnes, 'Deception and Game in *The Earl of Toulouse*,' *Poetica* (Tokyo) 17 (1984), 34, 39.

[21] On the theatrical qualities of this scene, see E.K. Chambers, *The Mediaeval Stage* (London, 1903), I, 185–86; Laura Hibbard Loomis, '*Gawain and the Green Knight*,' in

Although the terms are similar in meaning, the uses of OFr *engin* and ME *gyn* differ in the *romans courtois* of Chrétien de Troyes on the one hand, and earlier French and insular romance on the other. Hanning's analysis of *engin* in the *Roman d'Enéas*, which pre-dates Chrétien's *Erec*, *Cligès*, and *Yvain*, and in the Anglo-Norman *Ipomedon* by Hue de Rotelande reveals a distinct shift from the frequent, explicit application of the term *engin* in the *Roman d'Enéas* with reference to behavioural stratagem and architectural artifice to a more comprehensive, and implicit, integration of the concept into Chrétien's narratives, where the signifier itself is rarely found.[22] Insular romance, by contrast, delights in the construction, mechanics, and application of *engin/gyn* in both its concrete and abstract senses. *Ipomedon*, for instance, is imbued, both implicitly and explicity,[23] with various forms of *engin*.

By way of direct comparison between the application of *engin* in French and insular romance, a higher proportion of references to *gyn* appears in *Floris and Blauncheflur* than in its presumed direct source, 'Version A' of the Old French *Floire et Blancheflor* (ca.1150).[24] But perhaps the best illustration of the foregrounding of *gyn* in Middle English romance is to be found in *Ywain and Gawain*: whereas Lunete's manipulation of Laudine into marriage with Yvain, the grateful but passive recipient of her ingenuity in *Yvain*, is never defined as such, even when he is gripped by despair over his apparently hopeless love for Alundyne, the hero of *Ywain and Gawain* thinks actively and explicitly, although negatively, in terms of winning the lady by *gyn*:

> I can noght se by nakyn gyn
> How þat I hir luf sold wyn   (ll. 897–98)

Arthurian Literature in the Middle Ages: A Collaborative History, ed. Roger Sherman Loomis (Oxford, 1959), p. 538 (rpr. in Howard and Zacher, *Critical Studies of 'Sir Gawain and the Green Knight,'* pp. 3–23); Judith Perryman, 'Decapitating Drama in *Sir Gawain and the Green Knight*,' *The Dutch Quarterly Review of Anglo-American Letters* 8 (1978), 283–300; Wendy M. Reid, 'The Drama of *Sir Gawain and the Green Knight*,' *Parergon* 20 (1978), 11–23; Victoria L. Weiss, 'The "laykyng of enterludez" at King Arthur's Court: The Beheading Scene in *Sir Gawain and the Green Knight*,' in *The Medieval Court in Europe*, ed. Edward R. Haymes (München, 1986), pp. 189–99; Frederick B. Jonassen, 'Elements from the Traditional Drama of England in *Sir Gawain and the Green Knight*,' *Viator* 17 (1986), 221–54.

[22] See *The Individual*, pp. 107–36.

[23] See ll. 205, 1912, 2147–48, 2486, 2576, 3297, 5021, 7746, 7781–83, 9283 (*Ipomedon. Ein Französischer Abenteuerroman des 12 Jahrhunderts*, ed. Eugen Kölbing [Breslau, 1889; rpr. Geneva, 1975]).

[24] See Geraldine Barnes, 'Cunning and Ingenuity in the Middle English *Floris and Blauncheflur*,' *Medium Ævum* 53 (1984), 15. For a summary of views on the dating of the French poem, see Jean-Luc Leclanche, ed., *Le Conte de Floire et Blancheflor* (Paris, 1980).

Sir Tristrem

Sir Tristrem, the Middle English version[25] of Thomas of England's 'courtier' romance of plot and counterplot, is a condensed and sometimes
elliptical narrative. Lacking any sustained moral dimension, the narrative manifests little interest in love and none in the ethical problems
raised by Thomas in his story of the fateful passion of Tristan, nephew of
King Mark of Cornwall, and Iseut, Mark's wife. The emphasis in *Sir
Tristrem* is on the process of deception, trick, and countertrick, through
which the lovers communicate with each other and escape detection.
Tristrem is strategist, counsellor, and lover, in that order. Unlike Guy and
Beves, his gift for counsel and strategy is instinctive. Tristrem has little
need of his tutor and foster-father, Rohand, once his life has been saved
by Rohand's ploy of claiming him as his own child, after Tristrem's
father is slain by Duke Morgan through *gile* (l. 208).[26]

The frequent references to Tristrem as *trewe* (e.g. ll. 2167, 2400, 2567,
3336) indicate that, despite his mastery of *gyn*, the narrator does not
regard the cunning hero ('of loue si slei3e,' l. 3160) as unchivalrous or
immoral. Tristrem's talents as strategist are demonstrated by his skill at
chess, switch of knightly identity (as 'Tramtris', l. 1216) on a perilous
mission, and disguise (as merchant, beggar, leper), although his reper-
toire in *Sir Tristrem* does not extend to the roles of pilgrim, fool, and
minstrel, found in other versions of the legend. Although *gyn* is used
explicitly only once of Tristrem's various strategies – to describe a
dwarf's observation of the means ('Þe duerwe ysei3e her ginne,' l. 2062)
by which, to thwart a plot to trap them, Tristrem sends Isonde a message
of warning in runes inscribed on woodchips – it is the means of preserv-
ing not only his love but, in his early years, life itself.

On the other hand, treachery on the part of Tristrem's adversaries
masquerades as *red* and *counseil*. The feudal privilege of giving counsel is
abused by Mark's barons, who are jealous of Tristrem's favoured
position at court and hatch their scheme to send him on a hazardous trip
to Ireland under the guise of advising the king to marry: 'Þe king þai rad
to ride' (l. 1347).[27] Similarly, the plot to trap Tristrem and Isonde,

---

25 Probably with a northern English intermediary. See Crane, *Insular Romance*, p. 189.
26 References are to Eugen Kölbing, *Die englische Version von Tristan-Sage Sir Tristrem*
(Heilbronn, 1882; rpr. Hildesheim, Zürich, New York, 1985). The Auchinleck manuscript contains the unique copy of the poem.
27 Charles Edward Long points out that Holthausen's emendation of *ride* to *bride* in this
line ('Zur erklärung und textkritik der me. romanze "Sir Tristrem",' [*Anglia* 39, 1916],
378), which he cites in his edition of *Sir Tristrem* (University of Arkansas Ph.D. [1963],
note to l. 1347, p. 170), gives a better reading than *ride* as 'free' or 'ride'.

frustrated by the woodchip *gyn*, is presented to Mark by Meriadok as feudal counsel (l. 2036).

Tristrem plays an active role in three key scenes of royal counsel. The first is a council convened by Mark to consider the ransom demanded by Moraunt, king of Ireland. Tristrem has already proved his prowess and wisdom by avenging his father, killing the tyrant Morgan – who, like others of his ilk, 'to conseil he calleþ neiȝe' (l. 269) – and establishing law and order in 'Ermonie'. Now, like Guy and Beves at a similar stage of development, he demonstrates his maturity by offering the king the benefit of his *red* (ll. 984–990). Later in the narrative, when the barons propose the bridal quest to Ireland, Tristrem's opposition to the plan is expressed as advice to the king: 'Y rede, ȝe nouȝt no striue' (l. 1365). He is absent when 'Mark to conseyl ȝede/ And asked rede of þo to' (ll. 1838–39) about his rash boon to a harper, who demands Isonde as payment for his playing. What counsel, if any, Mark may have received is not recorded; all the poet tells us is that the king decides that he must preserve his *manhed* (l. 1840) and fulfil his promise. Tristrem returns just as the harper has left with the queen, chides Mark for his action, and goes successfully in pursuit. The implication is that, had Tristram been present, the king would have been given, and followed, a better *red*.

In Crane's view, *Sir Tristrem* 'has lost the significance developed for it by Thomas, and it has not gained a new one.'[28] Nevertheless, the Middle English narrative is, for the most part, the archetypal story of survival and success through *gyn*. In reducing the matter of Thomas's Tristan to its bare bones, *Sir Tristrem* offers a paradigm of the 'counsel and strategy' formula proposed for the Middle English romances in this study.

Elaborate types of *gyn* control the action of three Auchinleck romances belonging to, or inspired by, the 'Matter of Araby' (the fragmentary *Kyng Alisaunder*, *The Seven Sages of Rome*, and *Floris and Blauncheflur*) and a fourth, *Richard Coer de Lion*, which takes place largely in the East. Apart from *Richard Coer de Lion*, whose hero expresses the conviction that the Holy Land is Christendom's rightful heritage, to be won back from its pagan usurpers, the primary goal in these narratives is not restoration of the hero's birthright or the attainment of chivalric excellence, but the amassing of wealth and power in *Kyng Alisaunder*; survival and vindication in *The Seven Sages*; and the reunion of sweethearts in *Floris and Blauncheflur*.

28 *Insular Romance*, p. 195.

Kyng Alisaunder

Alexander the Great is the Arthur of the ancient world (or perhaps more accurately, Arthur is the Alexander of the medieval world): both are conceived by *gyn*; their respective tutor-counsellors, Aristotle and Merlin, are famous in their own right; both found empires, and die, without issue, by treachery. But, while the legend of Arthur endows him with a measure of immortality as the *rex quondam rexque futurus*,[29] for medieval moralists, Alexander was the prime symbol of the transience of earthly things.[30] As told by Chaucer's Monk in the *Canterbury Tales*, for example, his story is a *de casibus* tragedy. The references to Alexander in the *Policraticus* are a mixture of positive and negative: he is compassionate (IV:11, V:7), but also 'a greater man than his father in both his virtues and his vices' (V:12)[31] and numbered among those who have destroyed their dynasties through pride (IV:12). The hero of *Kyng Alisaunder* is, likewise, neither an entirely positive or negative model: his is the tale of the fall of a powerful ruler, not directly through the turns of Fortune's wheel, but indirectly, through over reliance on his own *gyn*.

Like many versions of the Alexander legend, *Kyng Alisaunder*, an adaptation of Thomas of Kent's *Roman de toute chevalerie* (ca.1250),[32] closely associates its hero with the marvels, or gyn, of the natural world.[33] Alexander's victories and the 'wondres of worme and beest' (l. 37) are, says the narrator, to be the subject of his poem. Although *Kyng Alisaunder* can be read as a *de casibus* tragedy, inasmuch as the hero is not in control of his own destiny and his downfall is explicitly attributed to

---

29 *Malory: Works*, ed. Eugène Vinaver, 2nd ed. (London, New York, Toronto, 1971), p. 717.

30 See George Cary, *The Medieval Alexander* (Cambridge, 1956), pp. 80–117; 143–62.

31 John Dickinson, trans., *The Statesman's Book of John of Salisbury* (New York, 1967), p. 131; 'Huic Alexander filius successit, et uirtute et uitiis patre maior' (Clemens C.I. Webb, ed., *Joannis Saresberiensis Episcopi Carnotensis Policratici* [London, 1909; rpr Frankfurt am Main, 1965], I, 571a).

32 See Cary, *The Medieval Alexander*, pp. 35–37. *Kyng Alisaunder* is complete only in the late fourteenth-century Laud Misc.622. On the Auchinleck fragments, see G.V. Smithers, *Kyng Alisaunder*, II, EETS 237 (London, 1957), 4–6; idem, 'Two newly-discovered fragments from the Auchinleck Manuscript,' *Medium Ævum* 18 (1949), 1–11; 'Another Fragment of the Auchinleck MS,' in Pearsall and Waldron, ed., *Medieval Literature and Civilization*, pp. 192–210. See also G.H.V. Bunt, 'Alexander's Last Days in the Middle English *Kyng Alisaunder*,' in *Alexander the Great in the Middle Ages*, pp. 202–04, 209–10, 217–220. All references are to MS Laud Misc.622 in the edition by Smithers.

33 On the treatment of the marvellous element of the story in the Middle Ages, see Cary, *The Medieval Alexander*, pp. 234–46; Dieter Mehl calls *Kyng Alisaunder* 'in a way, chiefly a collection of *mirabilia*, of geographical, zoological, and anthropological curiosities' (*The Middle English Romances*, p. 231).

auenture (l. 7831), Alisaunder is not a symbol of the transience of earthly things or of the fickleness of fortune, but rather, like Tristrem, a master strategist. *Gyn*, both on and off the battlefield, in the form of engines of war, military strategy, disguise, trickery, astrology, and necromancy, is the principal *modus operandi* of the narrative. Whereas *gyn* is the instrument of Alisaunder's success, however, it is also the instrument of Fortune, which precipitates his own downfall and that of his chief adversary, the Persian king, Darius.

The prologue makes the claim that all of Alexander's achievements are the direct result of Aristotle's tutelage (he 'dude by his mais[t]res techyng,' l. 32), and the product of that *counseil* is later specified by the emperor of Athens to be the art of *gyn*: 'He dooþ by Aristotles conseile,/ By hym he is so ful of gynne/ Þat alle men he may wynne' (ll. 3008–10). Conceived, like Arthur, by *gyn*, when an astrologer, disguised as a god, seduces his mother, Olympias, Alisaunder displays a masterly virtuosity of *gyn*. More than once he successfully invokes the formula by 'strengthe/bataille or by gynne' (for example, determining to do battle with King Porus of India with 'boþe strengþe and gynne', l. 7256, and with the people of Gog and Magog, either 'by bataille oiþer by gynne', l. 5995). He also devises military *queyntise* (l. 2813), and, like Tristrem, practises the art of disguise.

Alisaunder poses as either messenger or chamberlain on three occasions. On the first, in an essentially comic episode, he purports to be a certain 'Antigon', a messenger from his own court to that of Darius. Suspecting the messenger's real identity, Darius challenges 'Antigon', who counters by claiming that Alisaunder is fairer, not so curly-haired, and fatter (ll. 4156–58). The target of Alisaunder's next disguise ('a queynt gyle,' l. 5456), this time as a royal chamberlain, is Porus. Once again, he delights in giving a naturalistic, but false, representation of himself: when Porus asks him what Alisaunder is like, he describes him as a noble but little old man who feels the cold (ll. 5490–93).

His third and last disguise is, however, foiled by a woman. After successfully carrying out another mission as 'Antigon' to rescue the abducted wife of Prince Candeluk, to whom he initially represents himself as Alisaunder's 'first conseiler' (l. 7475), and, after changing clothes with his steward, Alisaunder pays a visit to Candeluk's mother, Candace, who has conceived a passion for him. As in *Guy* and *Beves*, love gets short shrift in *Kyng Alisaunder*, which is one of a number of 'anticourtly' versions of the Alexander story in which Candace is either presented negatively or not at all.[34] The only significance for Alisaunder

---

[34] See Cary, *The Medieval Alexander*, pp. 218–20. For the view that the author of *Kyng Alisaunder* has tried to improve on Candace's character in the *Roman de toute chevalerie*, see Martin Camargo, 'The Metamorphosis of Candace and the Earliest

in the unwelcome attentions of Queen Candace is the failure of *gyn* on his part and its success on hers, which results in his becoming her prisoner of love (ll. 7610–765). Candace is not deceived by the 'Antigon' disguise because she has own form of *gyn*: a metal statue of Alisaunder which accurately represents him in face, eyes, nose, mouth, height, and limb (ll. 6729–31). Once again he protests that the 'real' Alisaunder has different physical characteristics, that he is ruddier of complexion and older (ll. 7645–47), but to no avail. Like Gawain, Alisaunder joins the list, enunciated by Candace herself, of men who have been undone by women (ll. 7703–09).[35] Her superior *gyn*, she crows, has proved mightier than Alisaunder's prowess: 'Al þi strengþe ne gayneþ þe nauȝth,/ For a womman þee haþ ycauȝth' (ll. 7690–9).

The central conflict of the story, that between Darius and Alisaunder, is as much a test of *gyn* as of military might. At one point Darius offers half his kingdom, along with his daughter, to anyone who can overcome Alisaunder, 'Oiþer with gyle oiþer with gynne' (l. 3987). A Persian knight, disguised as a Greek, briefly seizes Alisaunder 'bi gynne' (l. 3891) and later admits that he *engyned* (l. 3916) to kill him. The hero's response is to praise the knight's action as a 'hardy dede in grete queyntise' (l. 4047).[36] This episode marks both the halfway point of the 8121 lines of the Laud manuscript and an increase in various forms of *gyn*. From this time on, Alisaunder wages war against Darius primarily on that basis: for example, by tying the branches of trees to the tales of his men's horses and creating a dust storm which persuades the Persian king and his army that the whole world is marching on them (ll. 4069–76), Alisaunder contrives their departure from a desirable campsite and then occupies it himself. When Darius dies by treachery, Alisaunder discovers his slayers by means of a simple trick: publicly promising them great honour as the killer of his foe if they make themselves known, he hangs them when they do.

English Love Epistle,' in *Court and Poet. Selected Proceedings of the Third Congress of the International Courtly Literature Society* (Liverpool 1980), ed. Glyn S. Burgess (Liverpool, 1981): 'Perhaps the *Kyng Alisaunder* poet was troubled by the unfavourable light cast upon his hero through his involvement in so sordid an affair. By making the lady less reprehensible, he makes Alexander's curiosity and lack of vigilance appear less serious' (p. 107).

35 A comparison also noted by R.W. King, 'A Note on 'Sir Gawayn and the Green Knight,' 2414ff.,' *Modern Language Review* 29 (1934), 435; Mary Dove, 'Gawain and the *blasme des femmes tradition*,' *Medium Ævum* 41 (1972), 21–22; John Eadie, 'Sir Gawain and the Ladies of Ill-Repute,' *Annuale Medievale* 20 (1981), 55–56.

36 Ojars Kratins suggests that Alisaunder's decision to drop charges of treason against the Persian knight, when one of his knights defends him at his trial on the grounds that the Persian's bond of loyalty is to Darius, not to Alisaunder 'provides the poet with an opportunity to show Alexander as a just king who respects the supremacy of the feudal vow' ('Treason in Middle English Metrical Romances,' *Philological Quarterly* 45 [1966], 670).

A formal division of the narrative shortly after this episode ('Nov agynneþ þe oþere partye/ Of Alisaunders dedes hardye,' ll. 4747–48) serves as the introduction to Alisaunder's adventures in India and Egypt: 'Of selkouþ trowes, of selkouþ beeste-/ Al ȝou shal telle the oþere gest' (ll. 4761–62). The 'wondres of worme and beest' are nature's own form of *gyn*, and India, Ethiopia, and Egypt prove a veritable encyclopedia of natural and human *gyn*. The inhabitants of 'Gangarides', for example, are said to be *engyneful* (l. 4860) and the *queyntest* (l. 4864). The people of the 'water island' of Meopante, between India and Egypt, are similarly enterprising: they secure their windows from the tides 'by on gynne' (l. 6170) and travel in submarines, 'By her gynnes and by her crokes' (l. 6183). Some beasts in the land between Ethiopa and the Atlas tribes are not only examples of nature's *gyn*, but are also *engyneful* themselves: the dolphin, for example, is *queyntere* than the crocodile (l. 6608), concealing himself in the water below and piercing the reptile's belly with his 'bristles' (l. 6611).

This world of wonders, which Alisaunder determines to conquer 'oiþer bi strengþe or elles by sum gynne' (l. 4891), tests his own capability for ingenuity to the full. Neither military nor any other kind of *gyn*, for example, will persuade the terrified inhabitants of a fortified town in India to tell him where to find water: 'With mangenels ne wiþ gynne/ Ne miȝth he on word ywynne' (ll. 5135–36). He sends a party of two hundred knights to the town, 'Forto wyte, wiþ sum gynne,/ What folk þere weren jnne' (ll. 5146–47), but the expedition fails when they are devoured by hippopotamuses (ll. 5157–62). Alisaunder himself has something in common with some of these extraordinary beasts in that, like the *monoceros* (l. 6529), he too, says the narrator, can be captured only 'by gyle and by snacche' (l. 6549).

The greatest test of Alisaunder's prowess and *gyn* comes from the cunning people of Taracun, Gog, and Magog. As he is about to turn his attention from the East to Europe, a neckless, one-eyed uniped tells him that in Taracun he will find the tribe of Nebrot, builder of that monument to architectural *gyn*, the tower of *Babiloyne* (l. 5955), and issues a direct challenge: if Alisaunder can overcome the monstrous reptile-eating cannibals of these regions 'by bataile and gynne' (l. 5978), he will win worldwide renown. In accepting the challenge, Alisaunder specifically repeats these terms to his barons and knights, appealing to them for their support in an enterprise which will be won 'Oiþer by bataille oiþer by gyn' (l. 5995). The contests with Taracun, Gog, and Magog fittingly meet the terms of the challenge. The inhabitants of Taracun, capital of Magog, set *calktrappes*[37] (l. 6060) for Alisaunder and his army, intending to kill

[37] 'A device with sharp iron spikes set on the ground to cripple the feet of an advancing enemy' (*MED*, s.v. *calketrappe*).

them *gilefullich* (l. 6063). But Alisaunder fights *gyn* with *gyn*: he has gangways made so that he can cross fen country (ll. 6094–95) and wins the first skirmish. After this victory he determines to save civilization 'by queyntise . . . oþer disceyte' (l. 6147) and devises a brilliant piece of *gyn*, the walling up of the residents of Gog and Magog, and of other undesirables, through the *queyntise* (l. 6245) of bitumen provided by the people of Meopante.[38]

Although his education by Aristotle is related in many versions of the Alexander legend,[39] the hero of *Kyng Alisaunder* is confident to the point of arrogance of his own wisdom and judgment, giving the lie somewhat to those lines in the prologue which credit the hero's success to the following of 'his maistres techyng' (l. 32). Aristotle is mentioned by name on only three occasions: as one of Alisaunder's two dozen tutors (l. 667), as the source of his talent for *gyn* (l. 3008), and as his companion and chronicler of the marvels of the East (ll. 4763–70).

In the second part of *Kyng Alisaunder*, however, Alisaunder asks for guidance from a variety of sources, including, oracles, idols, magicians, heaven, and his own barons. He asks for heaven's *rede* to destroy the monstrous citizens of Magog (ll. 6151–57); and, after his successful progress through India, it is said to be 'By al his baronage consent' (l. 5933) that he decides to make war on Europe (cf. ll. 5984–85, 6004). It is 'by conseil of his beste' (l. 6774) that he consults the trees of the Sun and Moon in Egypt and thereby learns that the manner of his death will, like that of Darius, be 'Þorouȝ envie and by tresouns' (l. 6892). When wild beasts attack him at the Caspian gates, his vulnerability is expressed in terms of his loss of 'many a conseiler' (l. 7109), an ominous portent. Finally, as the end approaches, Alisaunder takes counsel from his surviving barons (ll. 7269–71) to pursue Porus to Facen, where he kills him.

Alisaunder makes little use of counsel, and his enemies find that theirs is ineffectual against him. The counsel of Darius's knights and barons, solicited (ll. 1681–87; 3295–401; 4494) and unsolicited (1816–26; 2005–30), is to no avail. A scene of public consultation by the nobles of Athens, from whom Alisaunder has demanded tribute, illustrates the only outcome of counsel which Alisaunder will permit his opponents: the decision to surrender. Whereas the young Athenians are determined to fight on, their elders win 'þe maistrie of þe consaile' (l. 3116), submit, and win the conqueror's mercy. To be seen to counsel resistance against Alisaunder, as in the case of an unfortunate duke of Macedonia, is to invite swift and brutal retribution:

---

38 On this episode of the Alexander legend, see Andrew Runni Anderson, *Alexander's Gate, Gog and Magog, and the Inclosed Nations* (Cambridge, Mass., 1932).
39 Cary, *The Medieval Alexander*, pp. 105–110.

> He smoot a duk hote Coronde,
> Þat ȝaf hem conseil hym wiþstonde,
> Þorouȝ shelde and breny, and þorouȝ þe chyne –
> He most nedes his lijf fyne (ll. 3239–42).

In his failure to take counsel and prompt condemnation of the policies of others, who, like the Athenians, initially resist his attack ('Her wicked conseil hij shullen abyne,' l. 2988), Alisaunder manifests some despotic tendencies. The narrative does not charge him with tyranny; but neither does it represent him as an ideal monarch. A moralistic evaluation of Alisaunder's use of *gyn* appears in the two different reported reactions to the escapade in which he visits Darius in the guise of 'Antigon': the young soldiers of Alisaunder's army find it amusing; unamused, the older men regard it as folly (ll. 4271–72).

The ethically ambiguous representation of the hero in *Kyng Alisaunder* hinges on the uneven balance between counsel and strategy in his ethos of leadership. The narrative maintains an apparently objective stance throughout, but there is, perhaps, an implicit moral, to the effect that the ruler who operates solely by *gyn*, without the checks and balances of counsel, and who is over confident in his capacity to prevail by *gyn*, will also die by it. Twice Alisaunder is trapped by *gyn* (capture by the Persian soldier; the backfiring of his own *gyn* when Candace penetrates his disguise), but successfully extricates himself. On a third occasion, however, he is the victim of fatal guile, in the form of poisoned wine sent to him by the deposed justice, Antipater. Fortune has turned and is poised to strike Alisaunder, says the narrator: 'Auenture haþ terned his paas,/ Aȝeins þe kyng and rered maas' (ll. 7831–32). Olympias warns him against the traitor (ll. 7833–36), but, heedlessly, he downs the potion.

Although *Kyng Alisaunder* is lacking in overt moral,[40] its message seems to be that, no matter how brilliant he may be, a ruler cannot succeed by *gyn* alone. While Beves has 'God's grace' as well as his own *gyn* to thank for his success, as a pagan, Alisaunder is at an unstated disadvantage. Without the appropriate earthly, and a measure of heavenly counsel, no king, despite the cleverness of his own strategy, can overcome *gyn* in the employ of Fortune.

Richard Coer de Lion

The royal legatees of Alexander's talents in Middle English romance are Arthur and Richard Coeur de Lion, the latter inheriting the mantle of

---

[40] Richmond sees the work's message as the folly of the pursuit of renown (*The Popularity of Middle English Romance*, p. 36).

Alexander's heroism and his skills as a tactician. Structurally, *Richard Coer de Lion*, a work without identifiable source,[41] is a 'loss and restoration' romance of the *Havelok* and *Beves* pattern: the Holy Land has been usurped by Saracens; Richard's goal, as he clearly states at the battle of Jaffa, is 'to cleyme oure herytage' (l. 6797). Procedurally, however, *Richard Coer de Lion* is a 'strategy' romance, in which the Saracens are defeated through various forms of *gyn*.

Richard Coer de Lion exists in two versions, A and B, the former younger, and longer than B by some 1200 lines.[42] B, preserved in the Auchinleck and four other manuscripts,[43] has less fabulous material than A, which appears to be an expansion of the earlier narrative. John Finlayson distinguishes between them on the grounds that B is 'exemplary history presented in the epic mode,'[44] whereas A embroiders the story of Richard with material which is patently fictitious. In addition to its tendency to 'romanticize' the Richard legend, A also introduces the 'counsel' topos, which makes Richard's mission a twofold one: to win back the Holy Land from the Saracens and to inspire and reform his chief ally, the French king, Philippe Auguste.

Richard Coeur de Lion has his affinities with all the heroes (Roland, Oliver, Alexander, Charlemagne, Arthur, Gawain, Turpin, Ogier the Dane, Hector, and Achilles) listed in the opening lines of the work (ll. 11–19) as the subjects of other romances. The parallels with Alexander, Arthur, and Charlemagne, with whom Richard is compared on other occasions (Alexander and Charlemagne, ll. 6727, 7082; Arthur and Gawain, l. 6728), are the most pointed. Like Alexander, he dies of poison.[45]

But, unlike Alexander, Richard's success is not even nominally attributed to a tutor or counsellor. Neither A nor B tells us anything of

41 Brunner postulates a lost Anglo-Norman original (*Richard Löwenherz*, pp. 51–70).
42 See Brunner, *Richard Löwenherz*, pp. 11–17.
43 The Auchinleck text of the poem (L) exists only in fragments from l. 2958. It contains the first 24 lines and material beginning from l. 1287. The other B versions are found in British Library Egerton 2862 (E), Harley 4690 (H), College of Arms Arundel 58 (A), and Bodleian Library MS Douce 228 (D). Brunner groups the Auchinleck with (E) and (D) (*Richard Löwenherz*, p. 13); his composite edition is based on the A version in Gonville and Caius College Cambridge MS 175 (C) and printed versions by Wynkyn de Worde (W). For a comparative line-by-line table of the material in the A and B versions, see *Richard Löwenherz*, pp. 15–17.
44 'Richard, Coer de Lyon: Romance, History or Something in Between,' *Studies in Philology* 87 (1990), 180.
45 Some biographical details of Richard's life which appear in A, such as the element of the supernatural associated with his parentage (ll. 35–240), are reminiscent of the conceptions of both Alexander and Arthur. For the historical background to this legendary account of Richard's birth, see Bradford B. Broughton, *The Legends of King Richard I Coeur de Lion. A Study of Sources and Variations to the year 1600* (The Hague and Paris, 1966), pp. 12–13, 78–86.

Richard's childhood; we learn only that he inherits the throne at the age of fifteen, by which time he appears to be a fully-fledged military leader and tactician. When he addresses the ' . . . bysschop, eerl, baroun honeste,/ Abbotes, kny3tes, swaynes strong' (ll. 1344–45) at a Westminster feast, it is to seek their support for a Crusade (ll. 1348–75). Like Alexander, Richard rarely accepts counsel from any identified source, and, in contrast to his Saracen adversaries, he is not seen in council with military advisers. But the narrator also makes it clear that Richard never acts as a tyrant: when, for example, he makes the Earl of Leicester steward of Cyprus, it is 'Thorugh conseyl of his barony' (l. 2454). Naturally, he angrily rejects ('The deuyll hange 3ow with a corde!/ For your counseyll and your tydynge,' ll. 6932–33) the proffered *red* (l. 6919) of the infidel.

If Richard is the heroic and strategic heir of Alexander, he is the crusading heir of Charlemagne. Dieter Mehl calls *Richard Coer de Lion* a 'militantly Christian novel,'[46] and the bellicose religious fervour of the work is certainly closer to the Auchinleck's Charlemagne romances, *Roland and Vernagu* and *Otuel*, than to *Guy* or *Beves*. As Finlayson comments, the work's 'literary relationships are to the O.F. *chanson de geste* rather than to the romance of adventure'.[47]

The means by which the Saracen strongholds of the Holy Land are conquered, and Richard's unreliable French allies and the hostile 'Griffons' ('Greeks') of Sicily and Cyprus subdued, are *gyn*, *queyntyse*, and prowess. The 'Griffons', vows the English king, will be dealt with by 'queyntyse & wiþ strengþe of honde'.[48] Richard's two principal forms of military *gyn* are the mangonel and a portable siege castle. The former, a 'strong gyn, ffor þe nones' (l. 2923), is named 'Robynet' (ll. 1398–99; 2922); the latter, whose construction is admired by the narrator:

> Off tymbyr grete and schydys long
> He leet make a tour fful strong,
> Þat queynteyly engynours made   (ll. 1393–95)

and described in more detail as a masterpiece of English workmanship by Richard:

> I haue a castell, i vnderstonde,
> Was made of tembre of Englonde,
> With syxe stages full of tourelles
> Well flourysshed with cornelles   (ll. 1849–52)

---

46 *The Middle English Romances*, p. 208.
47 'Richard, Coer de Lyon,' p. 179.
48 Quoted from the 'E fragments' of the Auchinleck, edited by Eugen Kölbing in 'Kleine Publicationen aus der Auchinleck-HS. III: 'Zwei fragmente von King Richard,' *Englische Studien* 8 (1885), l. 94. (*Richard Löwenherz*, l. 1846).

is christened 'Mate-Gryffon' (ll. 1856, 2898)[49] after the skirmishes in Sicily and Cyprus. Enjoying the titular status normally reserved for swords and horses, these engines of war elevate technology to a position equal with courage and Christian zeal in Richard's armoury.

The *gynne/wynne* couplet appears three times, *gyn* twice referring to engines of war (mangonels, scaling ladders, portable castles), and once to a stratagem. The object of *wynne* in the first instance is the entire Holy Land:

> King richard wiþ al his miȝt
> To ward acres gan him diȝt
> & þouȝt wiþ queyntise & ginne
> Þe holy lond for to winne,[50]

and, in the second, the city of Nineveh:

> Wiþ arweblast and wiþ oþer gynne,
> 3if þey myȝte þe cyte wynne' (ll. 5259–60).[51]

On the third occasion, a Saracen offers his *gynne* and *queyntyse*, which are duly rejected by the English king, as the means of gaining booty: 'Þorwȝ my queyntyse and my gynne/ I schal doo þe gret tresore wynne' (ll. 6389–90). Richard scorns such abstract forms of Saracen *gyn*, and its concrete manifestations are no match for his strength: effortlessly, he slashes the iron chain stretched across the harbour at Acre (ll. 2633–36) with his battle-axe. As a Christian he has, of course, the advantage of divine *gyn* with which to combat Saracen guile. When, for example, the treacherous Saracens offer Richard the gift of a demon disguised as a horse (ll. 5530–41), the deception is revealed to Richard by an angel, who provides a counter *gyn* to neutralize its demonic powers and reprogramme it as an effective battle steed.

The narrative also contains some unusual and grisly forms of *gyn*. In a bizarre episode involving the emperor of Cyprus, his chief steward, and Richard, the deliberate perversion of the feudal ritual of counsel into a grotesque form of *gyn* ends with the emperor hoisted on his own petard. Chided by his steward for nearly killing a messenger from Richard, the emperor, eyes twinkling treacherously ('The eyen twynkled of the emperoure,/ And smyled as a vile traytoure,' ll. 2147–48), bids the steward to kneel before him in order to receive a *counsayle* (l. 2152) and promptly

---

[49] Which, as Finlayson notes, means ' "kill the Griffons" – "griffons" being the Frankish term for the local populace of Greek descent.' ('*Richard, Coer de Lyon*,' p. 170).

[50] Kölbing, 'Zwei fragmente,' ll. 15–18. (*Richard Löwenherz*, ll. 2651–54).

[51] These lines are in *A* only.

cuts off his nose. For this injury and abuse of seigneurial power, the victim takes due and poetic revenge: he severs his mutilator from his daughter, from the keys of his castle, and from one hundred of his knights, all of which, along with his own reliable military *counsayle* (l. 2262) he delivers to Richard, who thereby scores a great victory over the emperor.

Even more bizarre than the amputation of the steward's nose are two episodes in which *gyn* involves cannibalism. In the first,[52] Richard is the object of the stratagem: he has succumbed to a fever, and to cater to his convalescent craving for pork, unobtainable in the Holy Land, an enterprising knight, in the hope that God's help as well as his own cleverness ('Þorw3 Goddes my3t, and my counsayl,' l. 3101) will cure the king, successfully substitutes the tasty flesh of a young Saracen. The second such *gyn*[53] is devised by Richard himself and has as its object the intimidation of Saladin's ambassadors, who have come to negotiate the release of hostages. Telling the ambassadors that he will decide the fate of the hostages 'Þorw3 counsayl' (l. 3407) and 'in counsayl' (l. 3411) with his marshall, Richard orders the execution of the prisoners and has their heads served up to the envoys as the first course at dinner.

Neither historical tradition nor the Auchinleck manuscript relates the *gyn* through which the hero is said to acquire his epithet in *Richard Coer de Lion*:[54] when, masquerading as a pilgrim, he is recognised and betrayed by a disgruntled English minstrel and imprisoned by King Modred of Almaine (the fictional counterpart of Leopold of Austria), Richard uses his liaison with Modred's daughter, Margery, to foil the king's plan to have him killed by a lion; Margery supplies Richard with forty silk handkerchiefs in which he wraps his hands, and, by means of this *gyle* (l. 1070), he attacks the lion, rips out its heart, liver, and lungs, sprinkles its heart with salt and eats it (ll. 1090–1109). Like *Beves* and *Kyng Alisaunder*, *Richard Coer de Lion* has no place for love in the hero's career. Alisaunder may be tricked into his affair with Candace, but Richard exploits his entirely voluntary association with Margery to outwit her father.

Richard is faced with with two types of antagonist on his quest: treacherous Saracens, and devious Christians who obstruct his journey to the Holy Land and the smooth course of the Crusade. After being refused supplies in Almaine, Richard is, with Margery's intervention, reconciled with Modred (ll. 1573–605). Later, the Emperor of Cyprus, who refuses to make reparation for the pillage and slaughter by the local populace of

---

[52] This episode appears to belong to A only: it does not appear in manuscripts (D), (A), or (H); (E) and (L) are defective here.

[53] This episode is found in (E).

[54] Other manuscripts of A and B do, although (E) is defective here.

three of Richard's ships when they are wrecked off the coast at Limasour, eventually acknowledges that 'he had done amys' (l. 2348) and does homage to the English king (ll. 2381–88). The King of France, Richard's sworn brother (l. 1674), suffers from chronic treachery.[55] In Sicily, for example, he devises a *tresoun* (l. 1677) in the form of false report to King Tanker (Tancred) that the English king is bent on the conquest of his kingdom. Tanker's son, Roger, persuades his father of Richard's true intentions, but, meanwhile, Philippe joins the 'Griffons' in an attack upon the English in Messina.

In *A* particularly, the English king is obliged to assume the dual commanding roles of military tactician and moral adviser to Philippe, who receives the harshest criticism of all his allies. In an episode exclusive to *A*,[56] Richard counsels the French king to be generous towards the men of his army, both high-born and low, and to follow his orders (' . . . Phelyp, doo as j þe teche,' l. 3816) in the division of their forces and treatment of prisoners ('And looke þou doo as j þe seye' l. 3820) by not sparing the treacherous Saracens for ransom, unless they embrace Christianity (ll. 3786–828). Philippe, says the narrator, 'layde . . . a deff eere' (l. 3795) to the first part of this advice, and he ignores the second by lifting the sieges of Taburette and Archane for payment ('Ffor mede he sparede hys ffoon,' l. 3901) and pledges of loyalty.

Corroboration of the wisdom of Richard's counsel is supplied by Thomas of Moulton's exemplary capture of the fortification of Orgylous (ll. 4069–285), where Christian zeal and *gyn* overcome Saracen *gyle*. A Saracen spy, 'Þat hadde ben Crystene in hys ȝouþe' (l. 4077), who poses as a fugitive Christian familiar with every *gyle* (l. 4086) in Orgylous, promises that, if the English baron will 'doo as je þe teche' (l. 4084), the stronghold will soon be his. Thomas rightly suspects treachery and orders the manner of the apostate's death in terrifying detail, thereby eliciting an immediate confession and the disclosure of the *gyle* which protects Orgylous: a bridge, joined *queyntelyke* (l. 4110) in the middle by a concealed and easily dislodged pin, over a pit sixty fathoms deep. Saracen advice is acceptable in the circumstances, and Thomas demands: ' "Now, Sareyzyn, anon me rede/ Hou we schole doo at þis nede?" ' (ll. 4125–26). The renegade advises the Christians to use their 'goode engynes' (l. 4129), specifically the mangonel, in order to launch an assault without attempting to cross the bridge. The ploy is successful; those within surrender on the advice of the double agent and beg for mercy, offering Thomas all their goods. Thomas ignores the latter proposal but spares their lives on condition that the bridge is immediately destroyed.

---

55 Their conflict on the Third Crusade is historically documented. See Broughton, *The Legends of King Richard I*, pp. 23–28.
56 ll. 3759–4816 are found in *A* only.

Sincerely penitent, the apostate is shriven of his sins. That night, he overhears Saracens devise a 'tresoun queynte' (l. 4232) to kill the baron and his men in their sleep after plying them, 'al ffor a gyle' (l. 4254), with strong wine. He alerts Thomas, who kills every man, woman, and child in Orgylous and shares the spoils with his troops.

By Richard's standards, Thomas is a model crusader and Philippe an abject failure. When, in the course of a celebratory post-mortem of the storming of a number of Saracen towns, Richard discovers that, in defiance of his counsel, the French king has spared the lives of the infidel for *mede* (l. 4693) and protestations of loyalty, he accompanies him back to Taburette and Archane to prove his point that such pledges are worthless and that the only means of dealing with Saracens are death or baptism. Having greeted Philippe with scorn and abuse, the inhabitants of both towns are duly slaughtered to a man. 'I sayde þe soþ' (l. 4725), Richard tells him at Taburette; 'þou art nou3t wys' (l. 4784), he chides at Archane, repeating the exhortation at the end of his speech: 'Be trewe, doo as j 3e teche' (l. 4803). Philippe's sighs and glares are the response of a scolded child rather than a king:

> He gan to moorne, and heeld hym stylle;
> He glouryd, and gan to syke,
> Wiþ Kyng R. gan hym euyl lyke,
> Ffor wordes he gan to hym deyl   (ll. 4798–801).

Although Philippe is reluctant to accept Richard's counsel, Saladin's advisers appreciate his exemplary prowess. In both *A* and *B*, they urge their lord to sue for peace with the English king: 'And he schall teche þe and wysse/ In werre to be bold and wys' (ll. 3694–95).

Both versions contain overt criticism of the corrupt French. In *A*, the Saracens are guileful, and the French cowardly, boastful, and covetous:

> Frenssche men arn arwe and ffeynte,
> And Sarezynys be war, and queynte,
> And off here dedes engynous;
> Þe Ffrenssche men be couaytous.
> Whenne þey sytte at þe tauerne,
> Þere þey be stoute and sterne
> Bostfful wurdes ffor to crake,
> And off here dedes 3elpyng to make   (ll. 3849–56).

Both *A* and *B* make the latter actively treacherous:

> And weren traytours in þat ffy3te.
> He louyd no crownes ffor to crake,
> But doo tresoun, and tresore take   (ll. 5464–66).

Whereas Philippe permits himself to be bribed into sparing the mendacious enemy, Richard scornfully declines Saladin's offer of treasure and
half the Moslem empire for the release of Saracen prisoners, if he renounces his faith. The French king is eventually eliminated from the
narrative and returns home, much, in both *A* and *B* (ll. 5921–26), to the
hero's disgust.

Richard is, in some respects, a Christian version of Alisaunder: a military commander who succeeds through prowess and *gyn*. Unlike
Alisaunder, however, he is not a conqueror ambitious for worldly gain
but the restorer of Christendom's heritage. Although Richard also meets
his death through treachery, *Richard Coer de Lion* in no way demonstrates
the transience of earthly glory but rather celebrates the glory of earthly
achievement in the service of God. The hero of this jingoistic narrative is
an exemplary English king, who successfully pursues a military crusade
against the Saracens through prowess and *gyn* and, concurrently in *A*, a
moral crusade by means of wholesome *counseil* directed at his morally
bankrupt confederates.

Floris and Blauncheflur

Suffused with floral imagery and expressions of tenderness, 'Version A'
of the Old French *roman idyllique*,[57] *Floire et Blancheflor*, source of the
Middle English *Floris and Blauncheflur*, is a 'sentimentalized' version of
the story, told in the 'epic' mode in *Beves of Hamtoun*, of the dispossessed,
fatherless, Christian child sold into heathendom, who eventually marries
an aristocratic pagan. Nevertheless, as the numerous medieval translations and adaptations of *Floire et Blancheflor* attest, its theme of love
between pagan and Christian, lost and found through a combination of
devotion and *engin*, lends itself to a diversity of retelling. The story has
comic as well as hagiographic potential, but its various reworkings tend
to emphasize either the 'religious' (the Old Norse *Flóres saga ok Blankiflúr*;
the Spanish *Flores y Blancaflor*) or 'idyllic' (Konrad Fleck's *Floire und
Blanschesflûr*) elements of the tale, and some (the French 'B' or 'popular'
version; *Flóres saga ok Blankiflúr*) introduce a chivalric component.[58] *Floris
and Blauncheflur* is unique in its focus on the comic potential of the tale.

---

57 As Myrrha Lot-Borodine classifies it (*Le Roman idyllique au moyen âge* [Paris, 1913; rpr.
Geneva, 1972], p. 3).
58 For comparative studies of the story see, for example, Joachim Reinhold, *Floire et
Blancheflor: étude de littérature comparée* (Paris, 1906; rpr. Geneva, 1970); F.C. de Vries,
*Floris and Blauncheflur: a Middle English Romance, edited with introduction, notes and
glossary* (Groningen, 1966), pp. 53–60 (with extensive bibliography); J.B. Smith,
'Konrad Fleck's *Floire und Blanschesflûr* and the Old Norse *Flóres saga ok Blankiflúr*: a

In *Floire et Blancheflor*, Floire, heir to the throne of 'Naples', is deprived through *engin* of his beloved Blancheflor and reunited with her through the force of his love and some subsidiary *engin*.[59] The end result of the consultative dialogue between the king and queen on the means of putting an end to the attachment between their young son and the Christian girl (ll. 284–338),[60] is the elaborate *engin* of her faked death, complete with magnificent tomb,[61] and subsequent sale to 'Babylonian' merchants. When Floire becomes suicidal with grief, his parents relent, confess to their *engin* (ll. 860–62), and finance his quest for her. The hero sets sail for Babylon, posing as a merchant. In the meantime, dazzled by her beauty, the emir of Babylon has designated Blanchefleur as the next in his series of annual consorts and had her sequestered in his splendid and impenetrable 'tour des puceles' (l. 1700), prior to being 'chosen' in a ceremony under 'l'arbre d'amours' (l. 1807) in his paradisical orchard. Floire, having exchanged the guise of merchant for that of engineer, is smuggled into the tower in a basket of flowers, but the lovers are discovered and condemned to death. Spared largely through the pathos of their youth, beauty, and mutual devotion, they marry and return to Naples, where Floire embraces Christianity and converts his kingdom.

Floris and Blauncheflur is a fast-moving, pared down narrative, faithful to the storyline of *Floire et Blancheflor*, but approximately two-thirds shorter.[62] Floral imagery,[63] repetition of the term *amours*, and extended expressions of emotion and descriptions of the beauty of hero and heroine

---

stylistic comparison,' unpubl. M.A. thesis, University of Manchester (1955); Geraldine Barnes, 'Some observations on *Flóres saga ok Blankiflúr*,' *Scandinavian Studies* 46 (1977), 48–66; *eadem*, 'Cunning and Ingenuity in the Middle English *Floris and Blauncheflur*' and 'On the ending of *Flóres saga ok Blankiflúr*,' *Saga-Book of the Viking Society* 22 (1986), 69–73; Roland Lane, 'A critical review of the major studies of the relationship between the Old French *Floire et Blancheflor* and its Germanic adaptations,' *Nottingham Medieval Studies* 30 (1986), 1–19; Karen Pratt, 'The Rhetoric of Adaptation: The Middle Dutch and Middle High German Versions of *Floire et Blancheflor*,' in *Courtly Literature. Culture and Context*, ed. Keith Busby and Erik Kooper (Amsterdam and Philadelpha, 1990), pp. 483–97.

59 On *engin* in *Floire et Blauncheflor*, see Jocelyn Price, '*Floire et Blancheflor*: the Magic and Mechanics of Love,' *Reading Medieval Studies* 8 (1982), pp. 18–20, 27–29; Barnes, 'Cunning and Ingenuity,' pp. 12–13.

60 References are to Margaret M. Pelan, *Floire et Blancheflor: édition du MS. 1447 du fonds français*, 2nd ed. (Paris, 1956).

61 As Price notes: 'Interestingly, and for plot purposes, gratuitously, Floire's parents embody what could have presumably worked as a merely verbal ruse in an intricately elaborate artefact' ('*Floire et Blancheflor*,' p. 18).

62 Approximately 350 lines have been lost from the beginning of the 861-line text in the Auchinleck manuscript (see de Vries, *Floris and Blauncheflur*, p. 3). There are 3040 lines in Margaret Pelan's edition of BN f.fr. 1447, which de Vries (*Floris and Blauncheflur*, pp. 60–62) considers closest to the English version.

63 See William C. Calin, 'Flower imagery in *Floire et Blancheflor*,' *French Studies* 18 (1964), 103–11.

are absent. The conversion of Floris, mentioned only in the Auchinleck manuscript, is a one-line affair (l. 852),[64] which does not extend to the rest of his kingdom. The English narrative becomes, instead, a celebration of *gyn*. Floris loses and is reunited with Blauncheflur through strategy and counter strategy. When he is warned that impregnable Babylon can be penetrated 'Neiþer wiȝ strengȝe ne wiȝ ginne' (l. 234), Floris rises to the challenge and, like Alisaunder, fights *gyn* with *gyn*.

By the time he reaches Babylon, the hero has already demonstrated his aptitude for *gyn* in devising the stratagem whereby he and his company will represent themselves as merchants (E. 'As marchaundes we shull vs lede,' l. 354) on the quest. He also engages briefly in verbal *gyn* with one of his hosts enroute: when asked the reason for his pensiveness, Floris, who, according to the narrator, has Blauncheflur on 'al his þouȝt' (l. 110), replies that: 'Mi þouȝt is on alle wise/Mochel on mi marchaundise' (ll. 117–18). Although the author of the English romance omits the debate between *Savoir* and *Amours* for Floire's allegiance (Fr. ll. 1421–62) on his arrival in Babylon, he seems to have been inspired by *Amours*' final argument, about a lover's capacity for *engin*: 'Car qui ainme, ce sai ge bien,/ Engingneus est sor tote rien' (ll. 1457–58). Whenever Floris announces the object of his mission to Babylon, Blauncheflur shares the spotlight with *gyn*. The burden of his quest, expressed, directly or indirectly, four times in the Auchinleck version, is this: 'Hou he miȝte wiȝ sum ginne,/ þe faire maiden to him awinne' (ll. 157–58).[65] Additional variations of this couplet make it a stylistic feature of the poem:

To comen al þer wiȝinne,
Neiþer wiȝ strenȝe ne wiȝ ginne. (ll. 233–34)

7 a well þer springeȝ inne
þat is wrowt wiȝ mochel ginne. (ll. 290–91)

ȝif þou miȝt þous his loue winne,
He mai þe help wiȝ some ginne. (ll. 392–93)

Wende þou hom into þin in,
Whiles I þink of some ginne. (ll. 418–19)

Who him tawȝte þilke gin,
For to come þi tour wiȝin. (ll. 790–91)

---

64 All references, unless otherwise indicated as being to Egerton 2862 (E), are to the version of the romance in the Auchinleck manuscript, in de Vries's diplomatic edition, cited in n. 58, above.

65 'For to fonde wiȝ som ginne/ þat faire maide to biwinne' (ll. 209–10); 'To fonde wiȝ som ginne/ þe maiden aȝen to him winne' (406–07); 'To fonden wiȝ som gin/ þat faire maiden for to win' (806–07).

A scaled down version of its luxurious French counterpart, Babylon's hallmark in *Floris and Blauncheflur* is its horticultural and architectural *gyn*: the orchard spring with the power to test the chastity of the emir's bridal candidates (ll. 298–309) is wrought with much *ginne* (l. 291); the blossoms of the 'tre of loue' (l. 312) can be manoeuvred into falling, 'þourh art and þourgh enchantement' (l. 321), upon the preferred choice at the yearly nuptials. Applications of the term *gyn* extend to anatomy in the Egerton manuscript: whereas *Floire et Blanchefleur* describes the eunuchs who guard the harem as those who 'Les genitaires pas nen ont' (ll. 1708), the eligibility of guard duty in the tower is defined thus:

> But no serieaunt may serue þerynne
> Þat bereth in his breche þat gynne
> To serue hem day and ny3t,
> But he be as a capon dy3t (E.ll. 591–94).

Floris is advised by Dares, a Babylonian burgess sympathetic to his cause, to represent himself to the tower porter as a *ginour* (ll. 335, 346), or 'engineer',[66] desirous of replicating this feat of construction in his own country. As a doer of *gyn*, Floris does indeed prove a highly successful *ginour*: an unheroic Alisaunder, he breaches the walls of 'Babylon' itself, not with military strategy or mangonel, but with a basket of flowers.

The distinctive character of the English poem is crystallized in the trial scene. In 'Version A' of *Floire et Blancheflor*, the lovers' display of mutual devotion persuades the emir's barons to aquit them of their 'treasonable' behaviour towards him; in *Flóres saga ok Blankiflúr*, Flóres wins Blankiflúr in judicial combat; in *Floris and Blauncheflur*, however, it is the curiosity of their judges to find out the *gyn* by which Floris has managed to penetrate Babylon's defences which reprieves the lovers. They win a stay of execution, which leads to a full reprieve, when one of the judges offers the life-saving counsel ('Þe children þerwi3 fram depe he redde' (l. 785)[67] that the emir spare Floris in order to discover both his *counseile* (l. 789), that is, his means of ingress, and the deviser of that *gyn* (l. 790). Such information is necessary, says the nobleman, so that the emir may guard against other such incursions.

The action of *Floris and Blauncheflur* takes place within a framework of counsel and strategy, beginning with the machinations of the king and

---

[66] According to the *MED*, the application of Middle English *ginour* and *enginour* is limited to the technical senses of (a) 'stone-mason, builder' and (b) 'one who operates siege engines'. In Old French, however, *engigneor* can refer to the devil, 'le trompeur suprême' (Godefroy III, 169).

[67] Following A.B. Taylor's gloss for *redde* as 'saved by advice' (from OE *rædan*), in his edition, *Floris and Blancheflour: a Middle-English Romance* (Oxford, 1927), rather than de Vries's 'saved' (from OE *hreddan*).

queen of Naples and continuing with a succession of helper-figures who provide Floris with *red* or *gyn*: the burgess with whom he lodges at his first port of call endorses the ability of his sworn brother, Dares, to 'wissen 7 reden ariȝt' (l. 164); Dares duly devises the plan whereby Floris deliberately loses at chess in order to win the cooperation of the tower porter, who becomes the inventor of the basket strategy (ll. 424–45); and Blaunchflur's friend, Claris, temporarily manages (ll. 542–45) to conceal Floris's presence in the tower.[68]

The transition of Floris and Blaunchflur from children to adults at the end of the narrative[69] is signalled by Blaunchflur's acquisition of the status of counsellor – it is through her *counsail* (l. 826) that Claris is married to the emir, in a presumably permanent union[70] – and by a summons to Floris from the barons of Naples ('And al þe barnage ȝaf him red,' l. 835) that he return home to claim his inheritance on the death of his father. When the emir counters this piece of feudal *red* by asking him to do 'bi mi conseil' (l. 841) instead and accept a tempting offer to stay in Babylon, Floris replies in self-righteous terms which imply a recognition of his feudal obligations: 'I nel bileue for no winne;/ To bidde me hit were sinne' (ll. 846–47).[71] Whereas *Floire et Blancheflor* ends with full-scale conversion for Floire and his kingdom, and rewards for the helper-figures and Blancheflor's mother, *Floris and Blaunchflur* concludes a few lines later, after Floris's unheralded conversion, with the re-establishment of the feudal *status quo*.

Selective reduction of source material in *Floris and Blaunchflur* produces a shift in register. Although the hero's success in outwitting the obstacles put in the way of his desire by his elders gives *Floire et Blancheflor* an affinity with 'new comedy'[72] and *fabliau*, sentiment overshadows the French narrative's potential for humour. On the other hand, by concentrating on passages of dialogue in his source devoted to the provision of *consoil* and the devising of *engin*,[73] the English adapter makes the machinations of lovers rather than the emotion of love the focal point of the story, and thereby turns 'idyll' into comedy.

68 The role of another 'guide' figure, the chamberlain, whom Floris requests to 'vs both wyssh and reede' (E.l. 353) as he sets out on the journey to 'Babylon', is never developed, in English or in French (Fr. ll. 948–51), beyond this single reference.

69 On the representation of childhood in the original, see Jocelyn Price, '*Floire et Blancheflor, passim*.

70 The emir's custom of beheading the previous year's bride (*Floire et Blancheflor*, ll. 1730–34) is not mentioned in the English version.

71 His response is briefer and expressed indirectly in the French: 'Floires respont, n'i remaindra' (l. 2982).

72 See Barnes, 'Cunning and Ingenuity,' pp. 11–12.

73 See Barnes, 'Cunning and Ingenuity,' pp. 13–14, 16–19.

The Seven Sages of Rome

The act of an editorial hand may account for the juxtaposition of *The Seven Sages of Rome*[74] (Item 18) and *Floris and Blauncheflur* (Item 19). Both are written in the hand of the Auchinleck Scribe III[75] and share certain characteristics of theme and motif: their heroes are young, well-educated princes with similar names (Florentine; Floris), who, having been accused of breaking a sexual taboo and committing an act of *lèse-majesté*, are condemned and reprieved through various forms of counsel and strategy.[76] Particularly reminiscent of *Floris and Blanchefleur* is the story of 'Inclusa', which appears towards the end of the fifteen short narratives enclosed within the frame tale of *The Seven Sages* and tells of the successful entry by a resourceful knight, through the *queyntyse* (l. 3061)[77] of an obliging mason, into a tower in which a lady 'as whyte as flowre' (l. 2938) is imprisoned by her jealous husband. The *gyn/wynne* couplet, with amorous objective, which develops into something of a refrain in *Floris and Blanchefleur*, also appears in the tales of 'Inclusa' ('Thenne thought he vppon sum quente gynne/ Howe he myght to that lady wynne,' ll. 3021–22) and 'Tentamina' (ll. 1811–12; 1829–30).

In the frame tale of *The Seven Sages*, Florentine's seven wise tutors combat the evil counsel and verbal *gyn* of the emperor Diocletian's second wife with their own brand of narrative strategy. Motivated by ambition for her own sons, the empress makes seductive overtures to Florentine and, when repelled, accuses him of attempted rape. Diocletian demands that his son be put to death forthwith. His barons, however, exert their right to feudal counsel in order to prevent this act of injustice,

---

[74] Whose source is a prose redaction of the Old French verse *Roman des sept sages de Rome*. On the Old French versions of the Seven Sages story and their influence, see Mary B. Speer, *Le Roman des Sept Sages de Rome. A Critical Edition of the Two Verse Redactions of a Twelfth-Century Romance* (Lexington, Kentucky, 1989), pp. 17–20.

[75] Since Gathering 15 of the Auchinleck manuscript is missing, approximately the last 1050 lines of *The Seven Sages* and the first 350 lines of *Floris and Blauncheflur* are lost. A leaf containing approximately the first 120 lines of *The Seven Sages* has also been lost between fols. 85 and 86.

[76] On sources and analogues of *The Seven Sages*, see Killis Campbell, *A Study of the Romance of the Seven Sages with special reference to the Middle English Versions* (Baltimore, 1908), pp. 3–34; idem, ed., *The Seven Sages of Rome*, pp. xi–xxxvi. For a summary of scholarship on the question of the origin of the legend, see Catherine van Buren, ed., *The Buke of the Seven Sages* (Leiden, 1982), pp. 182–96.

[77] References are to Karl Brunner's edition of the Auchinleck manuscript (A) in *The Seven Sages of Rome (Southern Version). Edited from the MSS*, EETS 191 (London, 1933), with the exception of ll. 1–119 and l. 2770 ff., where the Auchinleck manuscript is defective and citations are from Brunner's text of the early fifteenth-century MS Egerton 1995 (E). Quotations from MS Cotton Galba E.ix (C) are from Killis Campbell's edition, *The Seven Sages of Rome*.

and, in a week-long duel of wits, the empress attempts to precipitate, and the sages to win stays of, Florentine's execution by telling the emperor tales of filial and household disloyalty and wifely wisdom in the first case, and stories of the personal, political and dynastic consequences of baleful female counsel in the second. After the barons' intervention on the first day, the prince is saved on the next by Master Bancillas's tale of 'Canis', about a man who, 'þourgз þe counseil of his wif' (l. 841), killed his favourite greyhound in the mistaken belief that the dog had slain his son. In 'Roma', on the other hand, the empress tells the story of an emperor of Rome, who is besieged by seven Saracen kings and advised by a wise old man to put the city in the care of seven sages, one of whom dresses up as fool and terrifies the enemy into fleeing, but then himself supplants the emperor.

Not all scholars consider *The Seven Sages* to be a romance,[78] and some classify it as purely didactic narrative,[79] but its *modus operandi* of counsel and strategy gives it a place amongst the romances in this study. Sharing a focus with *Floris and Blauncheflur* on cunning and ingenuity to the exclusion of chivalric action, the narrative could be said to be in the comic mode,[80] although it tends towards the darker side of comedy and delivers a didactic message conspicuously lacking in *Floris and Blauncheflur*.

Like the story of Floris and Blauncheflur, the legend of the Seven Sages is preserved in a number of European adaptations and translations of varying character. The Spanish *Libro de los engaños*, for example, a version of the 'Eastern' branch of the Seven Sages story, has affinities with the *speculum principis* mode, whereas other Iberian versions, all deriving from the 'Western' branch, are more concerned with the issue of female counsel. The *Libro de los engaños*, suggests Alan Deyermond, exhibits an 'obsessive concern with such matters as the limits of royal authority, the

---

78 Among those who do is George Kane (*Middle English Literature. A Critical Study of the Romances, the Religious Lyrics, Piers Plowman* [London, 1951], pp. 60–61). Laura Hibbard calls it 'in actuality a collection of tales rather than a romance' (*Mediæval Romance in England*, p. 174). Derek Pearsall considers its classification as romance 'dubious' (*The Auchinleck Manuscript*, p. viii).

79 See, for example, Wendy Clein, *Concepts of Chivalry in Sir Gawain and the Green Knight* (Norman, Okla., 1987), pp. 33–34. The Middle English *Seven Sages* is found in the company of romances in the Auchinleck manuscript, with *Beues of Hamtoun* in Cambridge University Library MS Ff.II.38 (F), and with *Ywain and Gawain* in (C), and elsewhere among overtly didactic works, such as those in MS Rawlinson poet.175, Bodleian Library (R), and (E).

80 Piero Boitani regards *The Seven Sages* as being 'closer to the comic' than to the romance mode for this reason: 'the *Seven Sages of Rome*, which in its time was classified as a 'romance', is in fact closer to the comic mode, where . . . the primary value is what Detienne and Vernant, speaking of the Greek *metis*, call 'les ruses de l'intelligence' (*English Medieval Narrative in the Thirteenth and Fourteenth Centuries*, trans. Joan Krakover Hall [Cambridge, 1982] p. 116).

reliability of advisers, and the dangerously exposed position of members of the royal family'.[81] In Deyermond's view, the *Libro de los engaños* is a political work, where the motif of the unreliability of female counsel may not be as thematically significant as its statements concerning kingship.[82]

The Middle English *Seven Sages* also inclines towards the 'political'. The dangers of heeding the counsel of women in general, and of one's wife in particular, are a commonplace theme in medieval narrative,[83] but antifeminism is not the central theme of this narrative, although it serves to illustrate it. The principal issue in *The Seven Sages* is the loss of royal integrity and miscarriage of justice, caused by malign counsel and trea-chery and rectified by wholesome counsel and strategy. Three types of counsel – learned, baronial, and wifely – precipitate the crisis. First, there is the learned, collective *kounsail* (l. 146) taken by the seven tutors of the widowed emperor's son to educate their charge at a distance from the distractions of the capital. Then follows the well-intentioned but ill-fated counsel by the barons that the emperor remarry (ll. 211–18).[84] When the new empress cajoles Diocletian into recalling Florentine to Rome,[85] the prince himself interprets the astrological ill omens on the eve of his departure as forecasting his death if he speaks at court before the end of seven days. Master Bancillas urges that the sages take *counseil* (l. 359) to formulate a strategy to protect the prince, whose parting *counseil* (l. 362) is that they should devise the means of making it possible for him to maintain the necessary term of silence.

Throughout the frame narrative, the malign counsel and cunning of

---

81 'The *Libro de los engaños: its Social and Literary Context*,' in *The Spirit of the Court*, ed. Burgess and Taylor, p. 161. The work was written early (1253) in the reign of Alfonso X ('the Wise'), and Deyermond sees it as having topical application to his reign.

82 Different emphases in two other Spanish versions have been demonstrated by Anthony Farrell: in the 1530 printed edition of the *Libro de los siete sabios* the issue of statesmanship is pronounced, whereas the nineteenth-century *Historia de los siete sabios de Roma* has a 'more plebeian' vision of the world' in which the frame story is more of 'an overblown domestic quarrel'. See 'A Late Spanish Survival of the Seven Sages: *Historia de los siete sabios de Roma*, Madrid, 1859,' in *Studies on the Seven Sages of Rome*, ed. H. Niedzielski, H.R. Runte, W.L. Hendrickson (Honolulu, 1978), pp. 96, 101.

83 See Katharine Rogers, *The Troublesome Helpmate* (Seattle and London, 1966), p. 96. For a discussion of antifeminism as the theme of *The Seven Sages*, see R.M. Lumiansky, 'Thematic Antifeminism in the Middle English *Seven Sages of Rome, Tulane Studies in English*,' 7 (1957), 5–16.

84 More specifically, (C) has the barons state: 'We wald 30u rede to wed a wife' (l. 262); and (F): 'Thorow councell of hys bolde barons/ He weddyd a wyfe of grete renowns' (ll. 185–86).

85 In (C), the empress seeks out a *counsailoure* (l. 229) in the person of a witch to contrive the prince's death; in (F) she tries to draw the prince into a conspiracy to kill his father ('But queyntly we schall him slee,' l. 369) and then thinks of some *queyntyse* (l. 388) to destroy her stepson.

the empress are restrained and countered, first by the counsel of the emperor's knights, and then by the counsel and *gyn* of the prince's tutors. The emperor's trust waivers from one source of counsel to the other, as empress and sages engage in a story-*quytyng* contest in which narrative itself becomes a form of *gyn*. The empress's last tale is explicitly represented as such in (C): 'Sho vmbithoght hir of a gyn' (l. 3055). Whereas counsel, for good and ill, is the thematic focus of the frame story and individual tales,[86] the contesting parties tell tales which are governed by *gyn* of various kinds, with the use of the terms *gyn* (ll. 1344, 1811; 1829; 2110; 3021), *engin* (l. 1949), and *queyntise* (ll. 2759; 2764; 2806; 3061)[87] increasing as the storytelling progresses. Within the frame tale itself, the empress tells the emperor that the sages are attempting to deceive him 'thorowe hyr queyntyse' (l. 2818).

Introduced as 'A nobylle man and wyse of dome' (l. 10), and previously accustomed to be merciful (l. 970), the emperor becomes 'a blustering and vacillating tyrant'[88] in the face of his wife's conniving. When, after she delivers her accusation against Florentine, the emperor orders his son beaten and hanged and has him led into the hall for execution, his earls and barons chide him for acting 'Wi3outen counseil and rede' (l. 500) and plead for a reprieve until the following day, when they can give their considered judgment ('Bi conseil of þi gentil men,' l. 504). Twice the emperor is reminded by the sages of the evil consequences of putting his son to death 'Wi3 outen assent of barouns hende' (l. 1386; l. 1700). On a third occasion, Master Catoun reminds him that he will be the object of universal opprobium, if he wilfully ignores their wise counsel in favour of that of his wife: 'Al þe werld þe spise,/ 3if þou do bi here and lete þe wise' (ll. 2301–02).[89]

In the complete Middle English versions of *The Seven Sages*, Florentine is finally vindicated and the empress meets a fiery end. The conclusion varies slightly from manuscript to manuscript, but the motif of 'counsel and strategy' is explicitly highlighted in (F), where Florentine himself condemns his father for his initial intention to have him put to death: 'Without councell slee me þou wylt,/ Agenste ryght, withowten gylte' (ll. 3723–24), and the narrator states that the empress is executed 'For hur queyntyse and hur false redd' (l. 3802). (E) concludes with a moral

---

86 George Kane sees the dominant motif of the individual tales as 'the triumph of evil' (*Middle English Literature*, p. 61).

87 Also 'dede queint' (l. 2032); 'dede of queint list' (l. 2036).

88 John Jaunzems, 'Structure and Meaning in the *Seven Sages of Rome*,' in *Studies on the Seven Sages of Rome*, ed. Niedzielski, Runte, Hendrickson, p. 49.

89 In (F), the emperor is constantly reminded by the sages of the potentially devastating consequences if he has his son hanged 'Thorow councell of þy wyvys redd' (ll. 510, 626, 694, 1065, 1203, 1475, 1581, 1945).

similar to the introduction of *Athelston*,[90] another tale of evil counsel and false accusation: 'And clerkys tellyd in hyr wretynge/ Of falssenys comythe euylle endynge' (ll. 3803–04).

Womanly wiles initiate the action in *The Seven Sages*, but the narrative is more generally concerned with the question of justice than of gender. While Florentine is on trial for his life, morally and constitutionally the emperor is in the dock. Although excluded from the bulk of the narrative of *The Seven Sages*, which is devoted to the fifteen individual tales, in the context of the frame tale itself the feudal *counseil* of the emperor's barons plays a role equal in importance to the learned counsel and *gyn* of the sages in peforming the dual service of vindicating and saving the life of the emperor's heir and restoring his own integrity.

Sir Orfeo

The most sophisticated use of *gyn* in the Auchinleck manuscript is found in the short romance, *Sir Orfeo*, where a range of *gyn*, concrete and abstract, is fully integrated into the narrative. *Gyn* falls into two distinct categories in the poem: Orfeo's artistic and verbal skills on the one hand, and the artifice of the fairy king's world on the other. These two forms of *gyn* oppose each other in a confrontation between civilization and barbarism more subtle than the straightforward tussle between good and evil counsel in *The Seven Sages*.

The technology of the engines of war in *Kyng Alisaunder* and *Richard Coer de Lion* and of magical feats of building in *Floris and Blauncheflur* is replaced in *Sir Orfeo* by that of landscaping and the architectural and decorative arts. But whereas human *gyn*, artistic and horticultural, is a positive force in shaping Orfeo's kingdom, the *gyn* of Fairyland is a negative expression of artifice. Fairyland is a world of deceptive order, which proves to be no more than a dazzling front of architectural, engineering, and artistic *gyn* (355–76),[91] lacking social and political substance and serving only to mask the disorder and horror within.[92]

Neither counsel nor a collective display of prowess by Orfeo's knights can deflect the supernatural *gyn* of Fairyland, which intrudes upon Orfeo's England to steal his queen. Faced with her threatened imminent

---

90 'Lystnes, lordyngys þat ben hende,/ Of falsnesse, how it wil ende/ A man þat ledes hym þerin' (ll. 7–9).

91 All references are to the edition of *Sir Orfeo*, based on the Auchinleck manuscript, in Speed, *Medieval English Romances*.

92 On the various forms of craft and ingenuity in the poem, see Seth Lerer, 'Artifice and Artistry in *Sir Orfeo*,' *Speculum* 60 (1985), 92–109.

abduction by the fairy king, Orfeo vainly seeks the counsel of his court ('He asked conseyl at ich man,/ Ac no man him help no can,' ll. 179–80), but Heurodis simply disappears from the armed guard of sixty knights. Unlike other heroes of Middle English romance, Orfeo, the undeservedly *unrede*, is left to devise his own strategy to win her back. His initial reaction to the loss of his wife, however, is an apparently aimless and perpetual exile. Appointing his steward as regent, Orfeo sheds the trappings of royalty for the persona of pilgrim, retaining only his harp as a token of his former identity:

> Al his kingdom he forsoke;
> Bot a sclavin on him he toke.
> He no hadde kirtel no hode,
> Schert, no no noþer gode,
> Bot his harp he tok algate
> & dede him barfot out atte ʒate.   (ll. 227–32)

Contrary to the usual pattern of Middle English romance, it is not consultative dialogue which galvanizes Orfeo into action but a mute form of communication. After some ten years in the wilderness (l. 266), he glimpses Heurodis among the fairy hunt; neither utters a word to the other ('Ac noiþer to oþer a word no speke,' l. 324), but Orfeo delivers a brief monologue (ll. 331–42) in which he determines to follow the company.

Gaining entry to Fairyland as a minstrel, the hero assumes the role of trickster-counsellor in his dealings with the fairy king, whom the beauty of Orfeo's musical *gyn* inspires with a rash boon: 'Now aske of me what it be,/ Largelich ichil þe pay' (ll. 450–51). Mental *gyn* prompts Orfeo to demand Heurodis as payment and to hold the king to his bargain by appealing, not to his better nature, but to the royal sense of honour. When the king balks at the response to his promise, Orfeo briskly compares his reference to the unseemly pairing of this scruffy minstrel and fair lady with the far more unseemly prospect of a king reneging on his word (ll. 463–68). As trickster, Orfeo acts entirely in his own interest; as counsellor, still to his own advantage, he prevents a king from behaving in an unkingly manner. Finally, *gyn* as disguise serves Orfeo as the means of testing the loyalty of the steward.

Orfeo's minstrel persona is not so much a question of disguise as of dual identity. He is, after all, a talented musician, bereft of all his worldly goods except his harp, by means of which he soothes the savage beasts in the wilderness, gains access to Fairyland, delights the senses of the fairy king, and rescues Heurodis. When he announces himself to the fairy king as 'bot a pover menstrel' (l. 430), he is giving an accurate account of his circumstances; but when he returns to the 'real' world of Winchester,

Orfeo's pose as a 'minstrel of pover liif' (l. 486) becomes a calculated disguise. He borrows clothes from a beggar couple who give him lodging on the outskirts of Winchester, parades around the town claiming to be an indigent foreign minstrel ('Icham an harpour of heþenisse;/ Help me now in þis destresse,' ll. 513–14), and gives the steward, who recognizes his harp as Orfeo's, an entirely fabricated account (ll. 535–41) of its provenance: that he found it in the wilderness ten years earlier beside the body of a man killed by lions.

This final piece of *gyn*, the most detailed in the poem, entails a shift in narrative register. *Beves of Hamtoun* may seem an unlikely work for comparison here, but, as in that romance, when the hero returns to England,[93] *Sir Orfeo* assumes an air of social 'reality' not present – Orfeo's parting instructions to his magnates the tale to call a *parlement* (l. 216) and choose his successor when they have confirmation of his death notwithstanding – in the earlier part of the narrative. In the concluding section of the work, Winchester is described in terms of fourteenth-century town planning: it has suburbs, humble dwellings, and a city street in which Orfeo encounters his steward ('And as he 3ede in þe strete/ Wiþ his steward he gan mete,' ll. 509–10).[94] This is a very different Winchester from the non-urban paradise, formerly, says the narrator (ll. 49–50), known as Thrace, which is Orfeo's kingdom at the beginning of the poem.

The steward having proved his loyalty, Orfeo discloses his true identity and immediately subjects him to a lecture (ll. 556–74), pompous by comparison with his graceful admonition of the fairy king (ll. 463–68), about the reason for his disguise and the consequences, had he proved disloyal in his regency. When, in an emotional reponse to this speech, the steward knocks over the table in his eagerness to embrace his long lost lord, and Orfeo has a bath and a shave, the transfer from the idealized, stylized Winchester at the beginning of the poem to a more naturalistic world in which 'romance' has been virtually eradicated is complete.

The ultimate concern of *Sir Orfeo* is not the love between Orfeo and Heurodis but the feudal bond, tested through Orfeo's *gyn*, between king and steward. We see the heartfelt reaction, in word and gesture, of the

---

[93] The English setting of *Sir Orfeo* is unique to the Auchinleck manuscript. Critical opinion is divided on the question of the manuscript's authority here (see Speed's textual note to l. 40, *Medieval English Romances*, II, 338), but the anglicizing of the location befits the narrative's concern with the responsibilities of government.

[94] Orfeo goes 'No forþer þan þe tounes ende' (l. 481) on the first day of his return. The beggar's cottage appears to be outside the city gates, since Orfeo goes from there 'in-to þat cité' (l. 501), and Heurodis is later conducted 'in-to þe toun' (l. 588). As Colin Platt writes of Winchester: 'In 1340 . . . over the suburbs a whole, the incidence of the poor, or the relatively poor, was higher than within the walled area' (*The English Medieval Town* [London, 1976], p. 38).

steward to Orfeo's return, but not the response of Orfeo and Heurodis to their own reunion. The subject of the last line in the poem is neither Orfeo nor Heurodis but the steward and his reward for keeping *trawþe* with his lord: 'And seþþen was king the steward' (l. 596). Despite its theme of love lost and found through the triumph of human *gyn*, in the end, as in other Middle English romances, affairs of state take priority over those of the heart.[95]

---

[95] On the treatment of kingship in the poem, see R.H. Nicholson, '*Sir Orfeo*: A 'Kynges Noote,' *Review of English Studies* 36 (1985), 161–79; A.S.G. Edwards, 'Marriage, Harping and Kingship: The Unity of *Sir Orfeo*,' *American Benedictine Review* 32 (1981), 282–91; E.D. Kennedy, '*Sir Orfeo as Rex Inutilis*,' *Annuale Medievale* 17 (1976), 88–110.

CHAPTER FIVE

The Failure of
Counsel and Strategy

Sir Gawain and the Green Knight

The hero's quest in *Sir Gawain and the Green Knight* begins with martyr-
dom in the name of the honour of the Round Table as its apparent object,
but it ends in a flesh wound and humiliation. This most 'courtly' of
Middle English romances is, from beginning to end, a narrative of frequently ambiguous, unfulfilled, or upended generic signals and expectations,[1] including the reversal of 'counsel and strategy' from formula for
success into recipe for failure.

Orfeo prevails through his own ingenuity over a lack of feudal counsel, Havelok and Gamelyn remedy the consequences of bad, although
well-intentioned counsel, and Alisaunder and Richard Coer de Lion ex-
tricate themselves from the consequences of unsuccessful disguises, but
in *Gawain* the Arthurian world is dogged from start to finish by failed
counsel and strategy. For the hero himself, the narrative constitutes the
humiliating double delinquency of a failed attempt at *gyn* and abandonment of heavenly *red*. Ultimately, Gawain as an individual and Arthur's
court as a whole are implicitly condemned for deficiencies of judgment
and faith, which render them vulnerable to an elaborate *gyn* crafted by
the magical powers of Morgan le Fay.

Dating from the second half, and probably from the last years, of the
fourteenth century,[2] *Gawain* is a poem which engages, although without

---

[1] See, for example, W.R.J. Barron, 'The Ambivalence of Adventure: Verbal Ambiguity
in *Sir Gawain and the Green Knight*, Fitt I,' in *The Legend of Arthur in the Middle Ages*, ed.
P.B. Grout *et al.* (Cambridge, 1983), pp. 28–40; *idem*, 'Chrétien and the *Gawain*-poet:
Master and Pupil or Twin Temperaments?,' in *The Legacy of Chrétien de Troyes*, II, ed.
Norris J. Lacy, Douglas Kelly, and Keith Busby, (Amsterdam, 1988), pp. 255–84; John
Finlayson, 'The Expectations of Romance in *Sir Gawain and the Green Knight*,' *Genre* 12
(1979), 1–24; *idem*, 'Definitions of Middle English Romance,' *Chaucer Review* 15 (1980),
44–62, 168–81; Sacvan Bercovitch, 'Romance and Anti-Romance in *Sir Gawain and the
Green Knight*,' *Philological Quarterly* 44 (1965), 30–37 (rpr. in *Critical Studies of Sir
Gawain and the Green Knight*, ed. Donald R. Howard and Christian Zacher [Notre
Dame and London, 1968], pp. 257–66).
[2] Tolkien and Gordon suggest a date of the mid- to late fourteenth century for the
poem, which is extant only in Cotton Nero A.x, Art.3, itself dated to *ca.*1400. See

overt political message, in the Ricardian 'discourse of counsel'.[3] Feudal, 'courtly', female, false, worldly, and divine counsel all have a bearing – with varying degrees of effectiveness – on the outcome of the hero's quest. In the first of the poem's four fitts Arthur is failed by all but one of his 'natural counsellors'; in Fitt II, Gawain is cast in the role of 'courtly' counsellor, but has that role usurped in Fitt III by Lady de Hautdesert, who induces him to break not only his *trawþe* with her husband, Bertilak, but also to reject the counsel of his spiritual preceptor, Mary; in Fitt IV, and not without a degree of hypocrisy, Gawain spurns the morally negative advice of Bertilak's guide.

The failure of the Round Table in the opening scene of the poem to supply counsel in the light of the invitation by the half-man/half-giant (ll. 140–41)[4] figure of the Green Knight to an exchange of axe blows on successive Christmases is more closely reminiscent of the timidity of Athelston's barons in the face of Anlaf of Denmark's challenge to the English king to provide a champion to defend his realm in single combat with the giant, Colbrond, in *Guy of Warwick*, than of the utter helplessness of Orfeo's court in their confrontation with less tangible supernatural threat in *Sir Orfeo*. In response to Athelston's direct appeal to his *parlement* (*Guy*, st.238, l. 3) to nominate a combatant, the magnates sit silent and motionless, 'as if their heads had been struck off': 'Stil seten erls & barouns,/ As men hadde schauen her crounes:/ Nouȝt on answere nold' (st.240, ll. 10–12). Similarly, Arthur's court 'seten stonstil' (l. 242), as if they had all 'slypped vpon slepe' (l. 244), at the first sight of the Green Knight; and, once the challenge has been issued, they become even 'stiller' (l. 301). Only after the king moves to strike the blow himself (ll. 326–27) does Gawain step forward to offer his counsel ('I wolde come to your counseyl bifore your cort ryche,' l. 347) and nominate himself as respondent on the Round Table's behalf. The court's immediate reaction is not to engage in public debate on the issue, but to whisper together, in apparently hasty and perfunctory counsel, in order to rubber-stamp Gawain's initiative:

J.R.R. Tolkien and E.V. Gordon, ed., *Sir Gawain and the Green Knight*, 2nd. edn., revised by Norman Davis (Oxford, 1967), pp. xxv–xxvii.

3   Michael Bennett has argued for direct links between Richard II and the composition of the poem, whose dialect ascribes it to the area of Southeast Cheshire. He proposes the king himself as patron and the author as one of the gentlemen of Cheshire who flocked to his court towards the end of his reign. See '*Sir Gawain and the Green Knight* and the Literary Achievement of the North-West Midlands: the Historical Background,' *Journal of Medieval History* 5 (1979), 63–88; *idem*, 'Courtly Literature and Northwest England in the Later Middle Ages,' in Burgess, ed., *Court and Poet*, pp. 74–76; *idem*, *Community, Class and Careerism. Cheshire and Lancashire Society in the Age of Sir Gawain and the Green Knight* (Cambridge, 1983), pp. 233–35.

4   All line references are to the 2nd. edition by Tolkien and Gordon, revised by Norman Davis (Oxford, 1967).

> Ryche togeder con roun,
> And syþen þay redden alle same
> To ryd þe kyng wyth croun,
> And gif Gawain þe game.   (ll. 362–65)[5]

Arthur's own advice to Gawain is, on the other hand, couched in super-ficially authoritative terms but devoid of explicit direction:

> 'Kepe þe cosyn,' quoþ þe kyng, 'þat þou on kyrf sette,
> And if þou redez hym ry3t, redly I trowe
> Þat þou schal byden þe bur þat he schal bede after.'
>
> (ll. 372–74)[6]

The overall impression is of a youthful but well-meaning king, handi-capped by a *cour fainéante*,[7] who are, with one exception, deficient both in courage and dignity: their childish and indecorous reaction to Gawain's subsequent decapitation of the Green Knight is to treat the severed head like a football (l. 428).[8]

The court is given a degree of compositional substance in Fitt II by being described as a catalogue of some of its members – Ywain, Erec, Doddinaval, the Duke of Clarence, Lancelot, Lionel, Lucan, Bors, Bedivere, Mador de la Porte (ll. 551–55) – when they gather 'to counseyl' (l. 557) Gawain as he leaves for the Green Chapel to receive the return blow. Elizabeth Gee's analysis of this impressive knightly roll call, how-ever, suggests that it strikes an ominous note for the Round Table in its foregrounding of several knights who, elsewhere in medieval narrative, take leading roles either directly in its downfall or in the events sur-rounding the last days of Arthurian society.[9] Moreover, the nature of the lachrymose and unspecified 'counsel' which they give to the departing Gawain (l. 557) seems neither practical nor conducive to comfort or cheer:

---

5 As J.W. Nicholls comments: 'Gawain's clear and eloquent courtesy contrasts sharply with this mode of discussion, and further marks him off as an individual' (*The Matter of Courtesy. A Study of Medieval Courtesy Books and the Gawain-Poet* [Woodbridge and Dover, N.H., 1985], p. 123).

6 'Take care that you deal one stroke; and if you manage him rightly, I readily believe that you will survive the blow that he is to offer you afterwards' (Tolkien and Gordon, *Sir Gawain and the Green Knight*, p. 86). Arthur may, in fact, be obliquely advising Gawain not to strike a fatal blow (see Sheri Ann Strite, 'Sir Gawain and the Green Knight: To Behead or Not to Behead – That *is* a Question,' *Philological Quarterly* 70 (1991), 1–12).

7 A term suggested to me by Diane Speed in a private communication.

8 On lapses of courteous conduct by the court in this scene, see Nicholls, *The Matter of Courtesy*, p. 124.

9 'The Lists of Knights in *Sir Gawain and the Green Knight*,' *AUMLA* 62 (1984), 171–78.

All þis compayny of court com þe kyng nerre
For to counseyl þe kny3t, with care at her hert.
Þere watz much derue doel driuen in þe sale
Þat so worthé as Wawan schulde wende on þat ernde,
To dry3e a delful dynt, and dele no more
    wyth bronde. (ll. 556–60)

Nonetheless, despite these mournful ministrations, Gawain himself 'mad ay god chere' (l. 562).

The initial failure of Arthur's court to offer the *consilium* which feudal obligation demands in the face of the Green Knight's antics can, perhaps, be charitably put down to astonishment. However, in their disapproval for the undertaking into which Gawain has entered, which they voice only after his departure for the Green Chapel, the court condemn themselves out of their own mouths. Belatedly adjusting their perspective from the ludic to the mundane, that is, from the fantasy world of Christmas games to the grim facts of post-holiday reality, they unanimously, and banally, conclude that it would have been wiser for Arthur to have made Gawain a duke rather than the victim of a supernatural foe (ll. 677–81). Then, freely admitting to their own lack of sound judgment twelve months before, they now abrogate all responsibility by laying the blame for the enterprise squarely with the king and the frivolous circumstances in which the challenge was accepted: 'Who knew euer any kyng such counsel to take/ As kny3tez in cauelaciounz on Crystmasse gomnez!' (ll. 682–83). *Gawain* thus gives us not Chrétien's figurehead monarch, but a problem with more serious implications for the Arthurian world: the case of Arthur the *unrede*.

As a consequence of the Round Table's failure of *consilium*, Gawain is placed in a situation where he must draw on counselling resources outside the court. In circumstances more in accordance with the conventions of French than of insular romance, Gawain embarks on his quest with only his horse and God for company and conversation:

Hade he no fere bot his fole bi frythez and dounez,
Ne no gome bot God bi gate wyth to karp (ll. 695–96).

Given the emphasis on Gawain's faith earlier in Fitt II, and the breakdown of his 'dialogue' with heaven in Fitt III, this reference to God as interlocutor may be more than formulaic. Unlike Guy and Beves at the beginning of their adventures, Gawain explicitly places his trust in divine guidance. 'Bot I am boun to þe bur barely to-morne/ To sech þe gome of þe grene, as God wyl me wysse' (ll. 548–49), he announces, on the eve of his departure. Reinforcing this expressed faith in heavenly direction is the image of the pentangle on the outer side of his shield,

127

which signifies that 'alle his afyaunce vpon folde watz in þe fyue woun-dez' (l. 642), and of Mary on the innner, the sight of which renders his courage infallible: 'Þat quen he blusched þerto his belde neuer payred' (l. 650).

Thus militarily and spiritually armed as he rides in search of the Green Chapel, Gawain perfunctorily demolishes a host of knightly, and mon-strous (dragons, trolls, wild beasts, giants), opponents (ll. 715–23), who might normally have been expected to pose a more substantial threat to the hero. Nevertheless, as the poet reminds us, had he not served God, in addition to being brave and resilient, Gawain would have been dead many times over (ll. 724–25). On Christmas Eve, distressed more by the elements than by any such challengers, he appeals to Mary to 'wysse and rede' him to shelter: 'To Mary made his mone,/ Þat ho hym red to ryde/ And wysse hym to sum wone' (ll. 737–39). As if in answer to his prayer, the miraculous appearance of Bertilak de Hautdesert's magnificent castle provides not only hospitable refuge but also moral testing ground: in accepting an invitation to pass the three days which remain before his appointment at the Green Chapel by sleeping late and staying inside the castle in the company of Lady de Hautdesert, while Bertilak goes hunt-ing, and by swearing 'with trawþe' (l. 1108) to exchange his daily 'win-nings' with his host, Gawain enters the arena for a threefold test of his *cortaysye, trawþe,*[10] and, most critically, his much proclaimed – and so far demonstrably steadfast – faith in divine *red.*

Gawain's own capacity as counsellor is reassigned from the 'feudal' to the 'courtly' in Fitt II: Bertilak's court ostentatiously welcome him as authority and counsellor on the subject of *cortaysye,* sent to them by God's grace. Gawain has, they say, the reputation for being the model of courtesy, and they expect to learn something from him in the way of elegant speech and manners:

> Now schal we semlych se sleȝtez of þewes
> And þe teccheles termes of talkyng noble,
> Wich spede is in speche vnspurd may we lerne,
> Syn we haf fonged þat fyne fader of nurture.
> God hatz geuen vus his grace godly for soþe,
> Þat such a gest as Gawan grauntez vus to haue (ll. 916–21).

Despite their professed desire to benefit from his wisdom in matters of courtly etiquette, however, Gawain is never seen to instruct Bertilak's

---

[10] For detailed discussions of the significance of *trawþe* in *Gawain,* see J.A. Burrow, *A Reading of Sir Gawain and the Green Knight* (London, 1965); W.R.J. Barron, *"Trawthe" and Treason: The Sin of Gawain Reconsidered. A Thematic Study of "Sir Gawain and the Green Knight"* (Manchester, 1980).

court, who are themselves presented as models of *cortaysye*. His designated role as 'courtly counsellor' is, on the other hand, questioned and
exploited by Lady de Hautdesert, his hostess and would-be seducer,
who playfully demands from him a demonstration of, and tuition in,
'sum tokenez of trweluf craftes' (l. 1527). Welcomed as language instructor in the art of 'talkyng noble' (l. 917) and *luf-talkyng* (l. 927), Gawain is
subjected by his hostess to an overt oral test of his knowledge and
practice of the art of *cortaysye* and, simultaneously, to a covert test of his
trawþe.

Their three-day verbal duel is both debate[11] and travesty of instructive
dialogue. On the second day, Lady de Hautdesert flirtatiously plays
courtly instructor to Gawain's slow-witted student:

> 'Þou hatz forȝeten ȝederly þat ȝisterday I taȝtte
> Bi alder-truest token of talk þat I cowþe.
> 'What is þat?' quoþ þe wyghe, 'Iwysse I wot neuer;
> If hit be sothe þat ȝe breue, þe blame is myn awen.'
> ȝet I kende you of kyssyng,' quoþ þe clere þenne'
>
> (ll. 1485–89)

and eager pupil ('Dos, techez me of your wytte,' l. 1533) to Gawain as
courtly maestro. Until the end of the third day, Gawain successfully
employs verbal *gyn* to parry the lady's attack, upholding chivalric honour but, at the same time, maintaining his reputation for elegant banter.[12]
Having lost the verbal battle of seduction, however, the lady makes a
final and successful assault upon Gawain's integrity with the pressing
offer of a keepsake, in the form of a girdle alleged to confer invulnera-
bility upon the wearer. What Gawain takes to be a fortuitious piece of
concrete *gyn* for himself – 'þe sleȝt were noble' (l. 1858), he thinks – is
actually a metaphorical engine of war, wrought by the lady herself (l.
2359), to which he readily falls victim.

The many ambiguities of *Gawain*, and its overt and covert elements of
'game' or 'play',[13] testify to the narrative's all-pervasive presence of *gyn*:

---

11 On the rhetoric of debate in these scenes, see Myra Stokes, '*Sir Gawain and the Green
Knight*: Fitt III as Debate,' *Nottingham Medieval Studies* 25 (1981), 35–51.
12 See Stokes, '*Sir Gawain and the Green Knight*,' pp. 47–48. See also Kim Sydow Campbell, 'A Lesson in Polite Non-Compliance: Gawain's Conversational Strategies in Fitt
3 of *Sir Gawain and the Green Knight*,' *Language Quarterly* 28 (1990), 53–62.
13 On game and ambiguity in *Gawain* see, for example, Charles Muscatine, *Poetry and
Crisis in the Age of Chaucer* (Notre Dame, 1972), pp. 61–65; Robert G. Cook, 'The Play
Element in *Sir Gawain and the Green Knight*,' *Tulane Studies in English* 13 (1963), 5–31;
Martin Stevens, 'Laughter and Game in *Sir Gawain and the Green Knight*,' *Speculum* 47
(1972), 65–78; Robert J. Blanch, 'Games Poets Play: The Ambiguous Use of Color
Symbolism in *Sir Gawain and the Green Knight*,' *Nottingham Medieval Studies* 20 (1976),
64–85; Tony Hunt, 'Irony and Ambiguity in *Sir Gawain and the Green Knight*,' *Forum*

from the machinations of Morgan and the geometric *gyn* of the pentangle, Gawain's symbol of perfection, to that which he comes to view as his symbol of imperfection (ll. 2485–88): the lady's girdle. From the moment when the Green Knight makes his spectacularly theatrical appearance at Camelot, the poem engages in a conflict between illusion and reality, largely contrived through Morgan's *gyn*: Arthur's court first take this uninvited guest for 'fantoum and fayry3e' (l. 240); Bertilak's castle is an imposing piece of architectural *gyn*, described in technical detail (ll. 768–72; 781–801), which simultaneously gives the impression of being a paper cutout (l. 802); the Green Chapel, of course, turns out not to be a chapel at all; and, as for Bertilak, the instrument of Morgan le Fay, it only *'semed* as he mo3t/ Be prynce withouten pere' (ll. 872–73).

The concept of *gyn* appears in the opening lines of the poem, with its references to the 'trammes of tresoun' (l. 3) and *tricherie* (l. 4) associated with the fall of Troy. Troy may, as the poem and the medieval topos have it, be the cradle of that chivalric civilization, founded by Aeneas after his exile for plotting with the Greeks, from which Camelot traces its descent, but Troy is also the scene and victim of one of the most famous pieces of *gyn* in legend and literature: the Trojan horse, the ultimate engine of war. Bertilak's 'explanation' to Gawain in Fitt IV tacitly implies that the Green Knight is to Arthur's court what the Greeks' horse was to Troy: the *gyn* of Morgan le Fay to undermine the Arthurian world.

The Green Knight's origins lie in folktale and vegetation myth,[14] and his antics in the beheading scene mimic the ritual of seasonal mummers' plays,[15] but he has a direct literary ancestor in Merlin, with whom he shares his possibly demonic associations,[16] and whose skills as trickster and shape-shifter are acquired through the medium of Morgan le Fay, Merlin's lover and Bertilak's house guest (ll. 2446–51).[17] On one occasion,

---

for *Modern Language Studies* 12 (1976), 1–16; P.M. Kean, 'Christmas Games: Verbal Ironies and Ambiguities in *Sir Gawain and the Green Knight,' Poetica* (Tokyo) 11 (1979), 9–27.

[14] See, for example, E.K. Chambers, *The Mediaeval Stage* (London, 1903), I, 185–86; cf. Enid Welsford, *The Court Masque*, pp. 3–5, 6 (n. 3); *eadem, The Fool*, pp. 70–71; John Speirs, 'Sir Gawain and the Green Knight,' *Scrutiny* 16 (1949), 274–300 (rpr. in *idem, Medieval English Poetry: The Non-Chaucerian Tradition* [London, 1957], pp. 215–51); William A. Nitze, 'Is the Green Knight Story a Vegetation Myth?,' *Modern Philology* 33 (1935–36), 351–66. See also Francis Lee Utley, 'Folklore, Myth, and Ritual,' in *Critical Approaches to Medieval Literature*, ed. Dorothy Bethurum (New York, 1960), 86–92.

[15] See p. 62, n. 7, above.

[16] Gawain considers the Green Chapel to be a place where the devil might say his matins (ll. 2187–88). On the Green Knight as demon see, for example, Dale B.J. Randall, 'Was the Green Knight a Fiend?,' *Studies in Philology* 57 (1960), 479–91; and, as demon-jester, T. McAlindon, 'Comedy and Terror in Middle English Literature: The Diabolical Game,' *Modern Language Review* 60 (1965), 330–31.

[17] On the mythic origins and role of Morgan le Fay in *Gawain* and elsewhere in medieval narrative, see Margaret Jennings, C.S.J., ' "Heavens defend me from that Welsh

the poet calls the Green Knight *mayster* (l. 136), a title which Merlin confers upon himself in *Of Arthour and of Merlin* (l. 1180). The Green Knight/Bertilak plays the Merlinesque roles of Fool-Trickster in Fitt I and Trickster-Judge in Fitt IV. Merlin is, however, the Arthurian counsellor *par excellence*, and although the Green Knight/Bertilak judges Gawain in the capacity of older and wiser knight,[18] he offers no direct counsel to the Round Table. Instead, his dealings with Gawain recall the pattern in twelfth-century French chivalric romance, as described by R.W. Hanning, of *engigneor* versus the one upon whom the *engin* is practised. The result is this: 'When recognition finally comes to those on whom *engin* has been practiced, the result can be salutary – or the reverse. *Engin*, that is, can deceive, improve, or educate, depending on the intent of the *engigneor*.'[19]

The disclosure of Morgan's *gyn*, the climax of the poem, takes the form of a dialogue between Gawain and Bertilak, who reveals that he himself is the Green Knight and that Gawain and the Round Table have been the targets of an elaborate and sinister *gyn* devised by this *goddes* (l. 2452) herself. The immediate effect of Gawain's realization that he has been duped is a mixed bag of responses, ranging from a blustering attempt to shift the blame elsewhere for his failure of *trawþe* in holding back Lady de Hautdesert's girdle – first to Bertilak ('In yow is vylany and vyse þat vertue disstrye3,' l. 2375) and later to the lady herself (ll. 2414–28) – to an excess of self-mortification (ll. 2378–88). The intention of the *gyn* itself is obscure, the so-called 'facts' of Bertilak's explanation – that its purpose was to test the *surquidré* (l. 2457) ('pride') and glorious reputation (l. 2458) of the Round Table, to deprive them of their wits, and to frighten Guinevere to death (ll. 2459–60) – amounting, by and large, to a trail of red herrings.[20] Gawain's mettle as Arthurian champion is indeed tested,

---

Fairy" (*Merry Wives of Windsor*, V,5,85): the Metamorphosis of Morgain le Fee in the Romances,' in *Court and Poet*, ed. Burgess, pp. 197–205; Edith Whitehurst Williams, 'Morgan le Fee as Trickster in *Sir Gawain and the Green Knight*,' *Folklore* 96 (1985), 38–56.

18 As opposed to the members of Arthur's court, who are in their 'first age' (l. 54). Mary Dove considers that '*hyghe eldee* . . . carries with it the twin ideas of full manhood and old age – but if old age, not withered decrepitude; rather, an old age of "undiminished vigour", like Philosophia's' (*The Perfect Age of Man's Life* [Cambridge, 1986], p. 139). J.A. Burrow considers Bertilak to be 'a powerful image of the middle age' and refers to his 'somewhat paternal teasing of Gawain' at the Green Chapel (*The Ages of Man. A Study in Medieval Writing and Thought* [Oxford, 1986], p. 175). On the treatment of age and ageing in the poem, see further Dove, *The Perfect Age*, pp. 134–40; Burrow, *The Ages of Man*, pp. 173–75.

19 R.W. Hanning, *The Individual*, p. 111.

20 On the general subject of 'red herrings' in *Gawain*, see R.W. Hanning, 'Sir Gawain and the Red Herring: The Perils of Interpretation,' in *Acts of Interpretation. The Text in its Contexts 700–1600. Essays on Medieval and Renaissance Literature In Honor of E. Talbot Donaldson*, ed. Mary J. Carruthers and Elizabeth D. Kirk (Norman, Okla., 1982), 5–23.

but at no point does the Round Table show any sign of mental collapse, and Guinevere's reaction, if any, to the events of Fitt I is never mentioned. Whether the intention of the *gyn* in which Gawain has been entangled at Bertilak's castle is to deceive, improve, or educate, or some combination of all three, is not revealed. The facts are that the hero has been tested by *gyn* and found wanting.

From the *engyneful* optical confusion of the beheading of the Green Knight beheading in Fitt I and the impression of optical illusion projected by Bertilak's castle in Fitt II, Fitts III and IV take up the issue of Gawain's, and the Round Table's, moral blindness. In losing sight of the moral reality of his 'exchange of winnings' agreement with Bertilak, through the illusion of security induced by three days of easy living at Hautdesert, Gawain is led into the sin of breaking his *trawþe* through his own ill-considered attempt at *gyn*. Like many other heroes of English and French romance, he accepts a token from a lady, but, in this instance, that gift is the instrument and symbol of knightly failure: in retaining the girdle, Gawain breaks his *trawþe* with Bertilak; in accepting it, he breaks his *trawþe* with Mary by putting his trust in earthly, or otherworldly, *gyn* at the expense of divine *red*.

The fundamental failure of Arthur's court collectively, and of Gawain individually, is a deficiency of counsel and judgment at every turn. The court fails in its conciliar duty in Fitt I, and Gawain himself makes a serious error of judgment in Fitt II in agreeing to Bertilak's proposal that, during his sojourn, he sleep late and remain indoors with Lady de Hautdesert. It is, after all, well-established in chivalric romance that knights who stay in bed, like Erec and Yvain, and spend their time inside in the company of ladies are asking for trouble.[21] In so doing here, Gawain ignores the spirit of the counsel which he himself gives to the newly married Ywain in *Ywain and Gawain* (*YG* ll. 1457–60), and which Ywain faithfully repeats later in that narrative: 'Þat knyght þat idil lies/ Oft siþes winnes ful litel pries' (ll. 2923–24).

But Gawain's real failure of judgment – to retain the lady's girdle and omit it from the third day's tally of winnings – entails not only the breaking of his *trawþe* with Bertilak but also with heaven: that is, a loss of faith in divine *red*. Although, at the beginning of his quest, Gawain has 'no gome bot God bi gate wyth to karp' (l. 696) and appeals directly to Mary in his prayers on Christmas Eve to *rede* and *wysse* him to shelter:

> Þe kny3t wel þat tyde
> To Mary made is mone,

---

[21] V.J. Scattergood examines the moral question of Gawain's idleness and the sin of sloth in 'Sir Gawain and the Green Knight and the Sins of the Flesh,' *Traditio* 37 (1981), 347–71.

Þat ho hym red to ryde
And wysse hym to sum wone   (ll. 736–39)

where he might hear Mass (l. 755), and then prays that 'Cros Kryst me spede!' (l. 762), he fails to sustain that 'consultative dialogue' with heaven on the eve of his greatest test of faith.

That Gawain has kept faith with Mary throughout the three days of the lady's sexual temptation is signalled by the poet's statement on the last day, just before the fatal offer of the girdle, that it is only she who has saved him from sin: 'Gret perile bitwene hem stod,/ Nif Maré of hir kny3t mynne' (ll. 1768–69).[22] But, despite this reminder that Gawain is, in 'a special sense . . . Mary's knight,'[23] the only further references to her in the poem are mild oaths on the lips of Bertilak (l. 1942) and the guide (l. 2140) respectively. Given the wide currency of the medieval legend that the Virgin let her sash fall into the arms of Doubting Thomas as evidence of her Assumption, Gawain's acceptance of Lady de Hautdesert's may be a symbolic indication of his spiritual infidelity.[24]

The most damning further evidence of Gawain's abandonment of heavenly *red* is not so much that he makes a possibly invalid confession immediately following this scene,[25] a confession perhaps pointedly distanced from the audience by being reported in indirect speech (ll. 1877–84), but that he makes no further plea for guidance to God, Christ, or Mary. On the contrary, having put his trust solely in God to find the Green Knight when he sets out from Camelot, Gawain now invokes the promise which Bertilak made on his arrival at Hautdesert to provide directions to the nearby Green Chapel:

22 On the problems of syntax and interpretation in these lines, see Tolkien and Gordon, *Sir Gawain and the Green Knight*, p. 121. See also Lawton, 'The Unity of Alliterative Poetry,' p. 91.
23 Lawton, 'The Unity of Alliterative Poetry,' p. 91
24 There is pictorial record of the legend in England in the first half of the fourteenth century (see Marina Warner, *Alone of All Her Sex. The Myth and the Cult of the Virgin Mary* [New York, 1976], pp. 90, 278–79). Richard Firth Green cites evidence in literature and drama of its probable familiarity to the *Gawain*-poet and his audience, and suggests that an association of the lady's sash with that of the Virgin sharpens the irony of Gawain's acceptance of it ('Sir Gawain and the *Sacra Cintola*,' *English Studies in Canada* 11 [1985], 1–11).
25 On the validity, or otherwise, of Gawain's confession see J.A. Burrow, *A Reading of Sir Gawain and the Green Knight*, 104–10; W.R.J. Barron, *"Trawthe" and Treason*, ch. 3; Tony Hunt, 'Gawain's Fault and the Moral Perspectives of *Sir Gawain and the Green Knight*,' *Trivium* 10 (1975), 6; P.J.C. Field, 'A Reading of *Sir Gawain and the Green Knight*,' *Studies in Philology* 68 (1971), 255–69; Nicolas Jacobs, 'Gawain's False Confession,' *English Studies* 51 (1970), 433–35; Gerald Morgan, 'The Validity of Gawain's Confession in *Sir Gawain and the Green Knight*,' *Review of English Studies* n.s. 36 (1985), 1–18; J.R.R. Tolkien, 'Sir Gawain and the Green Knight,' in J.R.R. Tolkien, *The Monsters and the Critics and Other Essays*, ed. Christopher Tolkien (London, 1983), pp. 87–89, 101–04.

For I schal teche yow to þat terme by þe tymez ende

(l. 1069)

Mon schal yow sette in waye,
Hit is not two myle henne   (ll. 1077–78)

and asks him to provide 'sum tolke' (l. 1966) for the purpose. In practical terms, as Paul Delany notes, the guide is superfluous:

Gawain has won his way to the castle by his own efforts, overcoming great hardships in the course of his journey, and he could easily go the mere two miles to the Green Chapel alone.[26]

Gawain was not, however, entirely alone on that perilous journey: he had God as guide, companion and protector (ll. 548–49, 696, 724–25). His forsaking of heavenly direction now is further underlined by the wording of his request to Bertilak: whereas, in his parting words to Arthur, he described his mission as 'To sech þe gome of þe grene, *as God wyl me wysse*' (l. 549), now he tells Bertilak that he needs directions to 'Þe gate to þe grene chapel, *as God wyl me suffer*' (l. 1967). Even in formulaic terms, it seems, God has been displaced as Gawain's chosen guide.

In what may also be a syntactic sleight of formula, Gawain's direct address to God in his declaration to the lady on the second day that he will always be 'seruaunt to yourseluen, so saue me Dry3tyn' (l. 1548) is echoed in his self-righteous words to the guide, who duly directs him to the Green Chapel but tries to deflect him from the last stage of his journey with a terrifying account of its reputation: 'Com 3e þere, 3e be kylled, may þe kny3t rede' (l. 2111), he 'advises'.[27] 'Ful wel con Dry3tyn schape/ His seruauntez for to saue' (ll. 2138–39), replies Gawain, the switch from first-person invocation to third-person reference syntactically suggestive of the extent of his own distancing from heaven since his departure from Camelot. In view of the shift of trust evidenced by his words and conduct at the end of his stay at Bertilak's castle, Gawain's parting words to the guide ('To Goddez wylle I am ful bayn,/ And to hym I haf me tone,' ll. 2158–59) ring hollow.

[26] 'The Role of the Guide in *Sir Gawain and the Green Knight*,' in *Critical Studies of Sir Gawain and the Green Knight*, ed. Howard and Zacher, p. 230.

[27] For 'may þe kny3t rede,' Tolkien and Gordon consider that: 'Sisam's interpretation, "(I) may þe, kny3t, rede", "I can advise you, sir knight", has much to commend it (*Fourteenth Century Verse and Prose* [Oxford, 1921], V. 43 n.)' (*Sir Gawain and the Green Knight*, p. 125). In their edition of Cotton Nero A.x, Malcolm Andrew and Ronald Waldron agree that Sisam's reading '[i]n some ways . . . is to be preferred' (*The Poems of the Pearl Manuscript* [London, 1978], 284).

Confronted with Bertilak's knowledge of his failure to abide by the terms of their 'exchange of winnings' agreement, Gawain's reaction is to judge himself guilty of the corruption of the ideals of chivalry. Bertilak, on the other hand, who, seems to endorse a more pragmatic code of behaviour, considers Gawain's conduct to be no more than a mild infringement of the terms of a hard bargain and reproves him for being only a little bit lacking in *trawþe*. Bertilak gives the appearance of subscribing to the values of the 'real' world, from whose perspective Arthurian ideals are beyond human capability, and Gawain's own failure of *trawþe* a minor and fully understandable infraction of the rules, for which the nick in the neck which he receives at the Green Chapel is little more than the equivalent of a robust slap on the wrist. Nevertheless, it is Bertilak who comes closest to the truth of Gawain's error, when he points out that it constitutes a failure of *lewté* (l. 2366) or 'faith'. Bertilak's role in the narrative ends here. Although, as judge, confessor, and knight 'of hyghe eldee' (l. 844), he is ideally placed to proffer Gawain moral counsel at this point, he offers further hospitality and reconciliation with Lady Bertilak (ll. 2400–06) instead.

When Gawain returns to Arthur's court, his neck wound healed but the girdle in full view, and recounts the details of the 'chaunce of þe chapel' (l. 2496), their delighted reaction is to laugh and decide that all shall wear a similar sash for his sake. The poem thus offers three views of Gawain's fault: Gawain's own, as measured by the standards of Arthurian chivalry; Bertilak's, based on a less idealistic view of the world; and that of Arthur's court, which lacks any clear direction. The poet makes no overt attempt to slant our perspective towards any one of these views. There is no partisan narrator of the type found in *Havelok or Athelston*, or non-omniscient, opinionated commentator of the Chrétien variety.[28] None of Gawain's judges, including himself, however, sees his fault for what it really is: a serious lapse of religious faith.[29] Although he accuses himself before Bertilak (ll. 2379–83) and Arthur's court (ll. 2506–09) of cowardice, covetousness, dishonesty, treachery, and a lack of *trawþe*, Gawain's inability to recognize that his real error is the failure to trust in that spiritual *red* which he invoked at the outset of his quest is underlined by the fact that his speech of self-accusation to Bertilak, in which he appears to be getting to the heart of the matter, is trivialized by its

---

28 See, for example, Peter F. Dembowski, 'Monologue, Author's Monologue and Related Problems in the Romances of Chrétien de Troyes,' *Yale French Studies* 51 (1974), 102–14; John L. Grigsby, 'Narrative Voices in Chrétien de Troyes – A Prolegomenon to Dissection,' *Romance Philology* 32 (1978–79), 261–73.

29 As D.A. Lawton expresses it: 'Gawain's failure, as Burrow suggests, is in "trawþe"; or, as Bertilak puts it, in a word of great religious significance in *Piers Plowman*, "lewté" (2366). It is a failure not just in perfection, but in faith' ('The Unity of Alliterative Poetry,' *Speculum* 58 [1983], 90).

juxtaposition to his largely irrelevant and unchivalrous hypocritical denunciation of women's wiles (ll. 2414–28).[30]

Whereas both Gawain and Bertilak give reasons for their response to
the revelation of his broken *trawþe*, the court are apparently bereft of a
code of ethics by which to judge the conduct of its members. The king,
says the poet, offers comfort, while the court laughs at Gawain's tale of
humiliation and shame; Arthur, however, apparently concurs with the
rest of the Round Table in their determination to remain *unrede* and to
ignore the lesson that 'sin will out' – a salutary reminder, but one erro-
neously understood by Gawain to be the lesson of his quest:

> 'For mon may hyden his harme, bot vnhap ne may hit,
> For þer hit onez is tachched twynne wil hit neuer.'
> Þe kyng comfortez þe kny3t, and alle þe court als
> La3en loude þerat . . . (ll. 2511–12).

Just as the court condemned Gawain's feudal counsel to Arthur in Fitt I,
so they ignore the moral counsel which he offers them now.

The audience of *Gawain* are therefore left to ask the question: what, if
any, are the ethical standards by which this apparently *redeless* Round
Table operates? At the beginning and the end of the poem, Arthur's court
give an impression of careless youth, living in a private world of fantasy
and game. Only Gawain, whose involvement in one particular *game* (l.
365) has forced him to venture out into the world beyond Camelot,
whence he returns slightly wiser, but physically, mentally, and morally
scarred, has any glimmer of awareness of the true significance of his
fault.

That which *Gawain* finally rejects is all forms of human counsel. Its
underlying message is that the only *red* on which one can and should
rely is heavenly, and that that *red* can be obtained only through faith, that
is, through keeping *trawþe* with God. The lesson for the audience, and for
Gawain, in Morgan le Fay's elaborate *gyn* is to show the illusory and
transitory nature of this world. Whereas romance in general celebrates
human potential, *Gawain* demonstrates human limitation. The poem's
opening and closing references to Troy not only foreshadow the pivotal
role of *gyn* in the poem, but also serve as reminders of the fragility of
worldly civilization. Arthur is introduced as only one of a number of
'Bretaygne kynges' (l. 25); his world is subject to a seasonal cycle and
enclosed within an historical framework antithetical to the amaranthine
springtime of Camelot in Chrétien's *romans courtoirs*.

Gawain gives us a much sterner reminder of the historical process than

---

[30] John Eadie argues that the speech is intended ironically, in 'Sir Gawain and the
Ladies of Ill Repute,' *Annuale Medievale* 20 (1980), 52–66.

any other Middle English romance. Unlike Gawain, Havelok, Beves, and Guy marry, beget, and die, but they do not force us to confront mortality in the compelling fashion of *Gawain*. Although Arthur and his court are said to be 'in her first age' (l. 54), the text surrounds them with reminders of the transience of earthly life. Such intimations of mortality are not sufficiently lugubrious to detract from what can, on one level, be interpreted as a witty exposé of the inadequacies of Arthurian chivalry.[31] *Gawain* is, however, a profoundly religious poem, which demonstrates the fundamental truth that, although the cycle of the seasons may be constant, the course of human events is not:

> A ȝere ȝernes ful ȝerne, and ȝeldez neuer lyke,
> Þe forme to þe fynisment foldez ful selden   (ll. 498–99)

and the only sure anchor for humankind is divine *red*.

In its focus on counsel and strategy, *Gawain* is the quintessential Middle English romance, but the ultimate failure of its hero on both counts is unique. *Gawain*'s implicit rejection of worldly chivalry, counsel, and strategy, puts it in step with the penitential spirit of Middle English alliterative poetry,[32] but, as chivalric romance, it looks forward to the decline of the Round Table in Malory's Arthuriad rather than back to the Arthurian Eden of Chrétien de Troyes.

---

[31] Or, on the other hand, as Andrew and Waldron suggest: 'The poet's aim may be specified as a loving critique of courtesy' (*The Poems of the Pearl Manuscript*, p. 43).

[32] See Lawton, 'The Unity of Middle English Alliterative Poetry,' pp. 87–94. On the penitential aspects of *Gawain*, and for a review of scholarship on the subject, see Hopkins, *The Sinful Knights*, pp. 204–18.

Bibliography

Primary sources

(listed alphabetically by title, or by author, if known; collections and articles listed by editor)

Ælfric, *De XII abusivis*, ed. Richard Morris, *Old English Homilies*, Part II, *EETS* 34 (London, 1868), pp. 101–18.

Andrew, Malcolm, and Ronald Waldron. *The Poems of the Pearl Manuscript: Pearl, Cleanness, Patience, Sir Gawain and the Green Knight* (London, 1978).

The Anglo-Norman Alexander (Le roman de toute chevalerie) by Thomas of Kent, ed. Brian Foster, assisted by Ian Short, 2 vols, *Anglo-Norman Text Society* 29–31, 32–33 (London, 1976–77).

The Anonimalle Chronicle, 1331–1381, ed. V.H. Galbraith (London, 1927; rpr. 1970).

Of Arthour and of Merlin, ed. O.D. Macrae-Gibson, *EETS* 268, 279 (London, 1973, 1979).

Aspin, Isabel S.T. *Anglo-Norman Political Songs* (Oxford, 1953).

Athelston. A Middle English Romance, ed. A. McI. Trounce, *EETS* 224 (London, 1951).

The Auchinleck Manuscript. National Library of Scotland Advocates' MS. 19.2.1, introd. by Derek Pearsall and I.C. Cunningham (London, 1977).

Beowulf and the Fight at Finnsburg, ed. Fr. Klaeber (3rd.edn., Boston, 1950).

The Romance of Sir Beues of Hamtoun. Edited from Six Manuscripts and the Old Printed Copy, with Introduction, Notes, and Glossary, ed. Eugen Kölbing, *EETS*, e.s. 46, 47, 48 (London, 1885, 1886, 1894).

The Book of the Knight of La Tour-Landry, ed. Thomas Wright, *EETS* 33 (London, 1906; revised edn., New York, 1969).

Bracton de Legibus et Consuetudinibus Angliæ, ed. George E. Woodbine; *Bracton on the Laws and Customs of England*, trans. Samuel E. Thorne, 4 vols. (New Haven, 1922; rpr. Cambridge, Mass., 1968–77).

The Works of Geoffrey Chaucer, ed. F.N. Robinson, 2nd. edn. (London, 1957).

Chrétien de Troyes. *Cligés*, ed. André Micha (Paris, 1957).

——— *Der Percevalroman (Li Contes del graal) von Christian von Troyes*, ed. Alfons Hilka (Halle, 1932).

——— *Yvain (Le Chevalier au lion), the critical text of Wendelin Foerster with introduction, notes and glossary*, ed. T.B.W. Reid (Manchester, 1942; rpr. 1967).

Chronicon Angliæ ab anno domini 1328 usque ad annum 1388, ed. Edward Maunde Thompson (London, 1874).

The Romance of Sir Degrevant. A parallel-text edition from MSS Lincoln Cathedral A.5.2. and Cambridge University FF I.6, ed. L.F. Casson, *EETS* 221 (London, New York, Toronto, 1949; rpr. 1970).

Dobson, R.B. and J. Taylor. *Rymes of Robyn Hood. An Introduction to the English Outlaw* (London, 1976).

English Historical Documents III, 1189–1327, ed. Harry Rothwell (London, 1974).

English Historical Documents IV, 1327–1485, ed. A.R. Myers (London, 1969).

Floire et Blancheflor: édition du MS. 1447 du fonds français avec notes, variantes et glossaire, ed. Margaret Pelan, 2nd edn. (Paris, 1956).

Le Conte de Floire et Blancheflor, ed. Jean-Luc Leclanche (Paris, 1980).

Floris and Blancheflour: a Middle-English Romance, ed. A.B. Taylor (Oxford, 1927).

Floris and Blauncheflur: a Middle English Romance edited with introduction, notes and glossary, ed. F.C. de Vries (Groningen, 1966).

Foedera, Conventiones, Literæ, et cujuscunque generis acta publia, inter reges Angliæ, ed. Thomas Rymer, 3rd edn. (The Hague, 1739).

Fragments of an Early Fourteenth-Century Guy of Warwick, ed. Maldwyn Mills and Daniel Huws, *Medium Ævum* Monographs, n.s. IV (Oxford, 1974).

French, Walter Hoyt, and Charles Brockway Hale, ed. *Middle English Metrical Romances*, 2 vols. (New York, 1930; reissued 1964).

The Tale of Gamelyn, from the Harleian MS. No. 7334, collated with six other MSS, ed. Walter W. Skeat, 2nd. edn., revised (Oxford, 1893).

Sir Gawain and the Green Knight, ed. J.R.R. Tolkien and E.V. Gordon, 2nd edn., revised by Norman Davis (Oxford, 1968).

The Complete Works of John Gower, edited from the manuscripts, with introductions, notes, and glossaries, 4 vols. (Oxford, 1899–1902; republ. Grosse Pointe, Mich. , 1968).

The Major Latin Works of John Gower: The Voice of One Crying and the Tripartite Chronicle, trans. Eric W. Stockton (Seattle, 1962).

Gui de Warewic, roman du XIIIe siècle, ed. Alfred Ewert, 2 vols. (Paris, 1933),

The Romance of Guy of Warwick. Edited from the Auchinleck MS. in the Advocates' Library, Edinburgh, and from MS.107 in Caius College, Cambridge, ed. Julius Zupitza, *EETS*, e.s. 42, 49, 59 (1883, 1887, 1891; rpr. as one volume, London, New York, Toronto, 1966).

Le Lai d'Haveloc and Gaimar's Haveloc Episode, ed. Alexander Bell (Manchester, 1925).

Havelok, ed. G.V. Smithers (Oxford, 1987).

Herrtage, Sidney J.H., ed. *The English Charlemagne Romances, Part VI, The Taill of Rauf Coilyear, with the fragments of Roland and Vernagu and Otuel. Re-edited from the originals, with Introduction, Notes, and Glossary, EETS*, e.s. 39 (London, 1882).

Horn Childe and Maiden Rimnild, ed. from the Auchinleck MS, National Library of Scotland, Advocates' MS 19.2.1, ed. Maldwyn Mills (Heidelberg, 1988).

Ipomedon. Ein Französischer Abenteuerroman des 12 Jahrhunderts, ed. Eugen Kölbing (Breslau, 1889; rpr. Geneva, 1975).

Joannis Saresberiensis Episcopi Carnotensis Policratici, ed. Clemens C.I. Webb, 2 vols. (London, 1909; rpr. Frankfurt am Main, 1965).

The Statesman's Book of John of Salisbury, ed. and trans. John Dickinson (New York, 1963).

Kyng Alisaunder, ed. G.V. Smithers, 2 vols., *EETS* 227, 237 (London, 1952, 1957).

King Horn, ed. Joseph B. Hall (Oxford, 1901).

King Horn: An Edition Based on Cambridge University Library MS Gg.4.27(2), ed. Rosamund Allen (New York, 1984).

The King of Tars ed. from the Auchinleck MS. Advocates 19.2.1, ed. Judith Perryman (Heidelberg, 1980).

Kölbing, Eugen. 'Kleine Publicationen aus der Auchinleck-HS. III. Zwei fragmente von King Richard,' *Englische Studien* 8 (1885), 115–19.

Konungs Skuggsjá, ed. Ludvig Holm-Olsen, 2nd edn. (Oslo, 1983).

Leges Henrici Primi, edited, with translation and commentary, by L.J. Downer (Oxford, 1972).

Llull, Ramón, ed. José Ramón de Luanco, *Libro de la Orden de Caballería del B. Raimundo Lulio* (Barcelona, 1901).

Malory: Works, ed. Eugène Vinaver, 2nd. edn. (London, New York, Toronto, 1971).

Mossé, Fernand, trans James A. Walker. *A Handbook of Middle English* (Baltimore, 1952; rpr. 1961).

Mum and the Sothsegger, ed. Mabel Day and Robert Steele, *EETS* 199 (London, 1936).

Brennu-Njáls saga, ed. Einar Ól. Sveinsson, *Íslenzk Fornrit* 12 (Reykjavík, 1954).

Sir Orfeo, ed. A.J. Bliss, 2nd. edn. (Oxford, 1966).

The Owl and the Nightingale, ed. Eric Gerald Stanley (London, 1960).

Parsons, H. Rosamond, ed. 'Anglo-Norman Books of Courtesy and Nurture,' *Publications of the Modern Language Association* 44 (1929), 383–455.

Piers Plowman, by William Langland. An Edition of the C-text, ed. Derek Pearsall (London, 1978).

Pronay, Nicholas and John Taylor. *Parliamentary Texts of the Later Middle Ages* (Oxford, 1980).

Der mittelenglische Versroman Über Richard Löwenherz. Kritische Ausgabe nach allen Handschriften mit Einleitung, Anmerkungen und Deutscher Übersetzung, ed. Karl Brunner, *Wiener Beitrage zur Englischen Philologie* 42 (Vienna and Leipzig, 1913).

Robbins, Rossell Hope, ed. *Historical Poems of the XIVth and XVth Centuries* (New York, 1959).

Rotuli parliamentorum; ut et petitiones et placita in parliamento, tempore Edward r. I, collated with original rolls by Philip Morant, John Tiopham, and Thomas Astle; ed. John Strachey, 6 vols. (London, 1767–77).

Rotuli Parliamentorum Anglie Hactenus Inediti MCCLXXIX–MCCCLXXII, ed. H.G. Richardson and George Sayles (London, 1935).

Schmidt, A.V.C., and Nicolas Jacobs, ed. *Medieval English Romances*, 2 vols. (London, 1980).

Le Roman des Sept Sages de Rome. A Critical Edition of the Two Verse Redactions of a Twelfth-Century Romance, ed. Mary B. Speer (Lexington, Ky., 1989).

The Seven Sages of Rome, edited from the manuscripts, with introduction, notes, and glossary, ed. Killis Campbell (Boston, New York, Chicago, London, 1907).

The Seven Sages of Rome (Southern Version), ed. Karl Brunner, *EETS* 191 (london, 1933).

The Buke of the Seven Sages, ed. Catherine van Buren (Leiden, 1982).

Smithers, G.V. 'Two newly-discovered fragments from the Auchinleck Manuscript,' *Medium Ævum* 18 (1949), 1–11.

—— 'Another Fragment of the Auchinleck MS,' in Pearsall and Waldron, ed., *Medieval Literature and Civilization*, pp. 192–210.

Speculum Guidonis de Warwyk, ed. G.L. Morrill, *EETS*, e.s. 75 (London, 1898).

Die englische Version der Tristan-Sage. Sir Tristrem, ed. Eugen Kölbing (Heilbronn, 1882; rpr. Hildesheim, Zürich, New York, 1985).

Sir Tristrem, edited from photostats of the MS collated with previous editions and provided with introduction and notes, ed. Charles Edward Long, Jr. unpubl. University of Arkansas Ph.D diss. (1963).

The Squyr of Lowe Degre. A Middle English Metrical Romance, ed. William Edward Mead (Boston, 1904).

Thomas. Les fragments du Roman de Tristan, poème du XIIe siècle, édités avec un commentaire par Bartina H. Wind (Paris and Geneva, 1960).

Two of the Saxon Chronicles Parallel with supplementary extracts from the others, ed. Charles Plummer (on the basis of an edition by John Earle), 2 vols. (Oxford, 1892; reissued in 1952 with a bibliographical note by Dorothy Whitelock; rpr. 1972).

Speed, Diane, ed. *Medieval English Romances*, 2 vols. 2nd edn. (Sydney, 1989).

Stubbs, William, ed. *Select Charters and Other Illustrations of English Constitutional History from the earliest times to the reign of Edward the First*, 7th edn. (London, 1890).

The Thornton Manuscript (Lincoln Cathedral MS.91), introd. D.S. Brewer and A.E.B. Owen (London, 1975).

141

Treharne, R.E., ed., I.J. Sanders. *Documents of the Baronial Movement of Reform and Rebellion 1258–1267* (Oxford, 1973).

Wright, Thomas, ed. and trans. *The Political Songs of England, from the reign of John to that of Edward II* (London, 1839; rpr. Hildesheim, 1968).

Ywain and Gawain, ed. Albert B. Friedman and Norman T. Harrington, *EETS* 254 (London, New York, Toronto, 1964).

Secondary sources: critical and historical works

Aers, David. *Community, Gender, and Individual identity. English writing 1360–1430* (London and New York, 1988).

Aerts, W.J., Jos. M.M. Hermans, and Elizabeth Visser. *Alexander the Great in the Middle Ages. Ten Studies on the Last Days of Alexander in Literary and Historical Writing* (Nijmegen, 1978).

Allen, Rosamund. 'The Date and Provenance of *King Horn*: Some Interim Reassessments,' in *Medieval English Studies Presented to George Kane*, ed. Edward Donald Kennedy, Ronald Waldron, and Joseph S. Wittig (Cambridge, 1985), pp. 99–125.

Anderson, Andrew Runni. *Alexander's Gate, Gog and Magog, and the Inclosed Nations* (Cambridge, Mass., 1932).

Anderson, J.J. 'The Three Judgments and the Ethos of Chivalry in *Sir Gawain and the Green Knight*,' *Chaucer Review* 24 (1989–90), 337–55.

Arrathoon, Leigh A., ed. *The Craft of Fiction: Essays in Medieval Poetics* (Rochester, Mich. 1984).

—————— 'Jacques de Vitry, the Tale of Calogrenant, *La Chastelaine de Vergi*, and the Genres of Medieval Narrative Fiction,' in Arrathoon, ed., *The Craft of Fiction*, pp. 281–368.

Astill, G.G. 'Social Advancement through Seignorial Service? The case of Simon Pakeman,' *Transactions of the Leicestershire Archaeological and Historical Society* 54 (1978–79), 14–25.

Auerbach, Erich, trans. Willard Trask. *Mimesis: The Representation of Reality in Western Literature* (Princeton, 1953).

Baldwin, Anna P. *The Theme of Government in Piers Plowman* (Cambridge, 1981).

Baldwin, James Fosdick. *The King's Council in England During the Middle Ages* (Oxford, 1913).

Baldwin, Dean R. '*Amis and Amiloun*: The Testing of *Treupe*,' *Papers on Language and Literature* 16 (1980), 353–65.

Barber, Richard. *The Knight and Chivalry* (Ipswich, 1970).

Barnes, Geraldine. 'Some observations on *Flóres saga ok Blankiflúr*,' *Scandinavian Studies* 46 (1977), 48–66.

—————— 'Deception and Game in *The Earl of Toulouse*,' *Poetica* (Tokyo) 17 (1984), 31–42.

—————— 'Cunning and Ingenuity in the Middle English *Floris and Blauncheflur*,' *Medium Ævum* 53 (1984), 10–25.

—————— 'On the ending of *Flóres saga ok Blankiflúr*,' *Saga-Book of the Viking Society* 22 (1986), 69–73.

Barron, W.R.J. 'French romance and the structure of *Sir Gawain and the Green Knight*,' in Rothwell, Barron, Blamires, Thorpe, ed., *Studies in Medieval Literature and Languages in memory of Frederick Whitehead*, pp. 7–25.

—————— "*Trawthe*" *and Treason: The Sin of Gawain Reconsidered. A Thematic Study of "Sir Gawain and the Green Knight"* (Manchester, 1980).

—————— 'The Ambivalence of Adventure: Verbal Ambiguity in *Sir Gawain and the Green Knight*, Fitt I,' in *The Legend of Arthur in the Middle Ages. Studies presented to A.H. Diverres by colleagues, pupils and friends*, ed. P.B. Grout, R.A. Lodge, C.E. Pickford and E.K.C. Varty (Cambridge, 1983), pp. 28–40.

—————— *English Medieval Romance* (London and New York, 1987).

—————— 'Chrétien and the *Gawain*-poet: Master and Pupil or Twin Temperaments?,' in Lacy, Kelly, Busby, ed., *The Legacy of Chrétien de Troyes*, II, 255–84.

Baugh, Albert C. 'The Authorship of the Middle English Romances,' *Annual Bulletin of the Modern Humanities Association* 22 (1950), 13–2

—————— *A History of the English Language*, 2nd. edn. (New York, 1957).

—————— 'Improvisation in the Middle English Romance,' *Proceedings of the American Philosophical Society* 103 (1959), 418–54.

—————— 'The Middle English romance: some questions of creation, presentation, and preservation,' *Speculum* 42 (1967), 1–31.

—————— 'Convention and Individuality in the Middle English Romance,' in *Medieval Literature and Folklore Studies. Essays in Honor of Francis Lee Utley*, ed. Jerome Mandel and Bruce A. Rosenberg (New Brunswick, N.J., 1970), 123–46.

Bellamy, J.G. *Crime and Public Order in England in the later Middle Ages* (Oxford, 1973).

Bennett, J.A.W., ed. and completed by Douglas Gray. *Middle English Literature* (Oxford, 1986).

Bennett, Michael J. '*Sir Gawain and the Green Knight* and the Literary Achievementof the North-West Midlands: the Historical Background,' *Journal of Medieval History* 5 (1979), 63–88.

—————— 'Courtly Literature and Northwest England in the Later Middle Ages,' in Burgess, ed., *Court and Poet*, pp. 69–78.

—————— *Community, Class and Careerism: Cheshire and Lancashire Society in the Age of Sir Gawain and the Green Knight* (Cambridge, 1983).

Benson, Larry D. *Art and Tradition in Sir Gawain and the Green Knight* (New Brunswick, N.J., 1965).

Bercovitch, Sacvan. 'Romance and Anti-Romance in *Sir Gawain and the Green Knight*,' *Philological Quarterly* 44 (1965), 30–37; rpr. in Howard and Zacher, *Critical Studies of Sir Gawain and the Green Knight*, pp. 257–66.

Bergner, H. 'The Two Courts. Two Modes of Existence in "Sir Gawain and the Green Knight",' *English Studies* 67 (1986), 401–46.

Billings, Anna Hunt. *A Guide to the Middle English Metrical Romances, dealing with English and Germanic Legends, and with the Cycles of Charlemagne and of Arthur* (New York, 1901).

Billington, Sandra. '"Suffer Fools Gladly": the fool in medieval England the play Mankind,' in Williams, ed., *The Fool and the Trickster*, pp. 36–54.

—————— *A Social History of the Fool* (Brighton and New York, 1984).

Blakeslee, Merritt R. *Love's Masks. Identity, Intertextuality, and Meaning in the Old French Tristan Poems* (Cambridge, 1989).

Blanch, R.J. 'Games Poets Play: The Ambiguous Use of Color Symbolism in *Sir Gawain and the Green Knight*,' *Nottingham Medieval Studies* 20 (1976), 64–85.

Blanch, R.J., and Julian N. Wasserman. 'The Medieval Court and the *Gawain* Manuscript,' in Haymes, ed., *The Medieval Court in Europe*, pp. 176–88.

Blanchfield, Lynne S. 'The romances in MS Ashmole 61: an idiosyncratic scribe,' in Mills, Fellows, Meale, ed., *Romance in Medieval England*, pp. 65–87.

Bliss, A.J. 'Notes on the Auchinleck Manuscript,' *Speculum* 26 (1951), 652–58.

Bloch, R. Howard. *Medieval French Literature and Law* (Berkeley, Los Angeles, London, 1977).

Bloomfield, Morton W. '*Sir Gawain and the Green Knight*: An Appraisal,' *Publications of the Modern Language Association* 76 (1961), 7–19.

Bloomfield, Morton and Charles W. Dunn, *The Role of the Poet in Early Societies* (Cambridge, 1989).

Boitani, Piero, trans. Joan Krakover Hall. *English Medieval Narrative in the thirteenth and fourteenth centuries* (Cambridge, 1982).

Boone, Lalia Phipps. 'Criminal Law and the Matter of England,' *Boston University Studies in English* 2 (1956), 2–16.

Bordman, Gerald. *Motif-Index of the English Metrical Romances* (Helsinki, 1963).

Borroff, Marie. '*Sir Gawain and the Green Knight*: The Passing of Judgment,' in *The Passing of Arthur. New Essays in Arthurian Tradition*, ed. Christopher Baswell and William Sharpe (New York and London, 1988), 105–28.

Bradstock, Margaret. '*Roberd of Cisyle* and the Amalgamation of Forms,' *Parergon*, n.s.5 (1987), 103–16.

Brewer, Derek. 'The Nature of Romance,' *Poetica* (Tokyo) 9 (1978), 9–48.

—— *Symbolic Stories. Traditional narratives of the family drama in English literature* (London and New York, 1980).

—— ed., *Studies in Medieval English Romances. Some New Approaches* (Cambridge, 1988).

Broughton, Bradford B. *The Legends of King Richard I Cœur de Lion. A Study of Sources and Variations to the year 1600* (The Hague and Paris, 1966).

Brown, R. Allen. *The Normans and the Norman Conquest* (Woodbridge, 1962; 2nd edn., 1985).

Brunner, Karl. 'Middle English Romances and their Audience,' in *Studies in Medieval Literature in Honor of Albert Croll Baugh*, ed. MacEdward Leach (Philadelphia, 1961), pp. 219–26.

Bühler, Curt F. 'Wirk Alle Thyng By Conseil,' *Speculum* 24 (1949), 410–12.

Bunt, G.H.V. 'Alexander's Last Days in the Middle English *Kyng Alisaunder*,' in *Alexander the Great in the Middle Ages*, pp. 202–25.

Burgess, Glyn, ed. *Court and Poet. Selected Proceedings of the Third Congress of the International Courtly Literature Society (Liverpool, 1980)* (Liverpool, 1981).

Burgess, Glyn S. and Robert A. Taylor, ed. *The Spirit of the Court. Selected proceedings of the Fourth Congress of the International Courtly Literature Society (Toronto 1983)* (Woodbridge and Dover, N.H., 1985).

Burrow, J.A. *A Reading of Sir Gawain and the Green Knight* (London, 1965).

—— *Ricardian Poetry* (London, 1971).

—— *Medieval Writers and Their Work. Middle English Literature and its Background 1100–1500* (Oxford, 1982).

—— *The Ages of Man. A Study in Medieval Writing and Thought* (Oxford, 1986).

Burrows, Jean Harpham. *The Auchinleck Manuscript: Contexts, Texts and Audience*, unpubl. Washington University PhD. diss. (1984).

Busby, Keith. 'Chrétien de Troyes English'd,' *Neophilologus* 71 (1987), 596–613.

Busby, Keith and Erik Kooper, *Courtly Literature: Culture and Context. Selected papers from the 5th Triennial Congress of the International Courtly Literature Society, Dalfsen, The Netherlands, 9–16 August, 1986* (Amsterdam and Philadelphia, 1990).

Butt, Ronald. *A History of Parliament. The Middle Ages* (London, 1989).

Calin, William. 'Flower imagery in *Floire et Blancheflor*,' *French Studies* 18 (1964), 103–11.

—— 'Rapports entre chanson de geste et romans courtois au XIIe siècle,' in *Essor et Fortune de la Chanson de geste*, pp. 407–24.

—— '*Gui de Warewic* and the Nature of Late Anglo-Norman Romance,' *Fifteenth-Century Studies* 17 (1990), 23–32.

Cam, Helen M. 'From Witness of the Shire to Full Parliament,' in *eadem, Law-Finders and Law-Makers in Medieval England. Collected Studies in Legal and Constitutional History* (London, 1962), pp. 106–31.
———— 'The relation of English Members of Parliament to their constituencies in the Fourteenth Century: a neglected text,' in *eadem, Liberties & Communities in Medieval England. Collected Studies in Local Administration and Topography* (London, 1963), pp. 223–35
———— 'The Theory and Practice of Representation in Medieval England,' *History* 1 (1953), 11–26 (substantially rpr. in Fryde and Miller, ed., *Historical Studies of the English Parliament, Volume I: Origins to 1399*, pp. 262–78).
Camargo, Martin. 'The Metamorphosis of Candace and the Earliest English Love Epistle,' in Burgess, ed., *Court and Poet.*, pp. 101–11.
Campbell, Killis. *A Study of the Romance of The Seven Sages with special reference to the Middle English Versions* (Baltimore, 1898).
Campbell, Kim Sydow. 'A Lesson in Polite Non-Compliance: Gawain's Conversational Strategies in Fitt 3 of *Sir Gawain and the Green Knight,' Language Quarterly* 28 (1990), 53–62.
Carpenter, D.A. *The Minority of Henry III* (Berkeley and Los Angeles, 1990).
Cary, George, ed. D.J.A. Ross. *The Medieval Alexander* (Cambridge, 1956).
Chadwick, H. Munro and N. Kershaw Chadwick. *The Growth of Literature*, Vol. I, *The Ancient Literatures of Europe* (Cambridge, 1932; rpr. 1968).
Chambers, E..K. *The English Folk-Play* (Oxford, 1933).
———— *The Medieval Stage*, 2 vols. (Oxford, 1903; rpr. 1967).
Chesnutt, Michael. 'Minstrel Reciters and the Enigma of the Middle English Romance,' *Culture and History* 2 (1987), 48–67.
Clanchy, M.T. *England and its Rulers 1066–1272. Foreign Lordship and National Identity* (Oxford, 1983).
Clark, Cecily. '*Sir Gawain and the Green Knight*: Its Artistry and Audience,' *Medium Ævum* 40 (1971), 10–20.
Clarke, M.V. *Medieval Representation and Consent* (New York, 1964).
Clein, Wendy. *Concepts of Chivalry in Sir Gawain and the Green Knight* (Norman, Okla., 1987).
Coleman, Janet. *English Literature in History 1350–1400. Medieval Readers and Writers* (London, 1981).
Combarieu du Grès, Micheline de. *L'idéal humain et l'expérience morale chez les héros des chansons de geste, des origines à 1250*, 2 vols (Paris, 1979).
Cook, Robert G. 'The Play Element in *Sir Gawain and the Green Knight,' Tulane Studies in English* 13 (1963), 5–31.
Cooper, Helen. 'Magic that Does Not Work,' *Medievalia et Humanistica*, n.s.7 (1976), 131–46.
Cosman, Madeleine Pelner. *The Education of the Hero in Arthurian Romance* (Chapel Hill, 1966).
Coss, P.R. 'Aspects of Cultural Diffusion in Medieval England: The Early Romances, Local Society and Robin Hood,' *Past and Present* 108 (1985), 35–79.
Crane, Susan. *Insular Romance. Politics, Faith, and Culture in Anglo-Norman and Middle English Literature* (Berkeley, Los Angeles, London, 1986).
Crosby, Ruth. 'Oral delivery in the Middle Ages,' *Speculum* 11 (1936), 88–110.
Cunningham, I.C. and J.E.C. Mordkoff. 'New Light on the signatures of the Auchinleck manuscript (Edinburgh, National Library of Scotland Adv. MS. 19.2.1),' *Scriptorium* 36 (1982), 280–92.
Curtius, Ernst Robert, trans. Willard R. Trask. *European Literature and the Latin Middle Ages* (New York and Evanston, 1963).

Daniel, Niel. 'A Metrical and Stylistic Study of "The Tale of Gamelyn",' *Studies in Medieval, Renaissance, American Literature*, ed. Betsy F. Colquitt (Fort Worth, Texas), pp. 19–32.

Dannenbaum (Crane), Susan. 'Anglo-Norman Romances of English Heroes: "Ancestral Romance"?,' *Romance Philology* 35 (1982), 601–08.

—— 'Insular Tradition in the Story of Amis and Amiloun,' *Neophilologus* 67 (1983), 611–22.

Dannenbaum, Susan Crane. 'Guy of Warwick and the Question of Exemplary Romance,' *Genre* 17 (1984–85), 351–74.

Davenport, W.A. *The Art of the Gawain-Poet* (London, 1978).

—— 'Patterns in Middle English Dialogues,' in *Medieval English Studies Presented to George Kane*, ed. Edward Donald Kennedy, Ronald Waldron, and Joseph S. Wittig (Woodbridge, 1988), pp. 127–45.

Davies, James Conway. *The Baronial Opposition to Edward II, its Character and Policy. A Study in Admininstrative History* (Cambridge, 1918).

Davies, R. G., and J. H. Denton, ed. *The English Parliament in the Middle Ages* (Manchester, 1981).

De Weever, Jacqueline. 'Candace in the Alexander Romances: Variations on the Portrait Theme,' *Romance Philology* 43 (1990), 527–46.

Dean, Christopher. *Arthur of England. English Attitudes to King Arthur and the Knights of the Round Table in the Middle Ages and the Renaissance* (Toronto, 1987).

Delany, Paul, 'The Role of the Guide in *Sir Gawain and the Green Knight*,' in Howard and Zacher, ed., *Critical Studies of Sir Gawain and the Green Knight*, pp. 227–35.

Delany, Sheila, and Vahan Ishkanian. 'Theocratic and Contractual Kingship in *Havelok the Dane*,' *Zeitschrift für Anglistik und Amerikanistik*, 1974, 290–302; (rpr. as 'The romance of kingship: *Havelok the Dane*,' in Sheila Delany, *Medieval literary politics: shapes of ideology* [Manchester, 1990], pp. 61–73).

Dembowski, Peter F. 'Monologue, Author's Monologue and Related Problems in the Romances of Chrétien de Troyes,' *Yale French Studies* 51 (1974), 102–14.

Denholm-Young, N. *Seignorial Administration in England* (London, 1937; rpr. 1963).

—— 'The Tournament in the Thirteenth Century,' in *Studies in Medieval History Presented to Frederick Maurice Powicke*, ed. R.W. Hunt, W.A. Pantin, R.W. Southern (Oxford, 1948), pp. 240–68.

—— *The Country Gentry in the Fourteenth Century, with special reference to the heraldic rolls of arms* (Oxford, 1969).

Detienne, Marcel, and Jean-Pierre Vernant, trans. Janet Lloyd. *Cunning Intelligence in Greek Culture and Society* (Hassocks, Sussex, and Atlantic Highlands, N.J., 1978).

Deyermond, Alan. 'The *Libro de los engaños*: its Social and Literary Context,' in Burgess and Taylor, ed., *The Spirit of the Court*, pp. 158–67.

Dicey, Albert Venn. *The Privy Council. The Arnold Prize Essay 1860* (London and New York, 1887).

Dickerson, A. Inskip. 'The Subplot of the Messenger in *Athelston*,' *Papers on Language and Literature* 12 (1976), 115–24.

Doob, Penelope B.R. *Nebuchadnezzar's Children. Conventions of Madness in Middle English Literature* (New Haven and London, 1974).

Dove, Mary. 'Gawain and the *Blasme des femmes* tradition,' *Medium Ævum* 41 (1972), 20–26.

—— *The Perfect Age of Man's Life* (Cambridge, 1986).

Doyle, A.I. 'English Books in and out of Court from Edward III to Henry VII,' in Scattergood and Sherborne, ed., *English Court Culture in the Later Middle Ages*, pp. 163–81.

Doyle, A.I., and M.B. Parkes, 'The Production of Copies of the *Canterbury Tales and the Confessio Amantis* in the Early Fifteenth Century,' in *Medieval Scribes, Manuscripts and Libraries: Essays Presented to N.R. Ker*, ed. M.B. Parkes and Andrew G. Watson (London, 1978), pp. 163–210.

Du Fresne, Charles (Seigneur Du Cange). *Glossarium ad scriptores mediæ et infimæ Latinitatis*, ed. Leopold Favre, 10 vols. (Niort, 1882–87).

Duby, Georges, ed., Arthur Goldhammer, trans., *Revelations of the Medieval World* (Vol. II of Philippe Ariès and Georges Duby, ed., *A History of Private Life*) (Cambridge, Mass., and London, 1988).

Eadie, John. 'Sir Gawain and the Ladies of Ill Repute,' *Annuale Medievale* 20 (1980), 52–66.

Eberle, Patricia J. 'The Politics of Courtly Style at the Court of Richard II,' in Burgess, ed., *The Spirit of the Court*, pp. 168–78.

Eckhardt, Caroline D. 'Woman as Mediator in the Middle English Romances,' *Journal of Popular Culture* 14 (1980), 94–107.

Edwards, A.S.G. 'Marriage, Harping and Kingship: The Unity of *Sir Orfeo*,' *American Benedictine Review* 32 (1981), 282–91.

Edwards, Goronwy (J.G.) 'The Personnel of the Commons in Parliament under Edward I and Edward II,' in *Essays in Medieval History presented to Thomas Frederick Tout*, ed. A.G. Little and F.M. Powicke (Manchester, 1925), pp. 197–214 (rpr. in Fryde and Miller, ed., *Historical Studies of the English Parliament, Volume I*, pp. 150–67).

—— *The Second Century of the English Parliament. The Ford Lectures Delivered in the University of Oxford 1960–1* (Oxford, 1979).

Ellis, George. *Specimens of Early English Metrical Romances, to which is prefixed an Historical Introduction on the Rise and Progress of Romantic Composition in France and England*, new edn., revised by J.C. Halliwell (London, 1848).

Ellis Davidson, H.R. 'Loki and Saxo's Hamlet,' in Williams, ed., *The Fool and the Trickster*, pp. 3–17.

Embree, Dan. ' "The King's Ignorance": A Topos for Evil Times,' *Medium Ævum* 54 (1984), 121–26.

Essor et Fortune de la Chanson de geste dans l'Europe et l'Orient latin (Actes du XIe Congrès International de la Société Rencesvals pour l'Etude des Epopées Romanes, Padoue-Venise, 29 août – 4 september 1982 (Modena, 1984).

Evans, W.O. ' "Cortaysye" in Middle English,' *Mediaeval Studies* 29 (1967), 143–57.

Everett, Dorothy, ed. Patricia Kean, 'A Characterization of the English Medieval Romances,' in *eadem, Essays on Middle English Literature* (Oxford, 1955), pp. 1–22.

Farrell, Anthony J. 'A Late Spanish Survival of the Seven Sages: *Historia de los siete sabios De Roma*, Madrid, 1859,' in Niedzielski, Runte, Hendrickson, ed., *Studies on the Seven Sages of Rome*, pp. 92–103.

Fellows, Jennifer. 'Editing Middle English romances,' in Mills, Fellows, Meale, ed., *Romance in Medieval England*, pp. 5–16.

Ferguson, Arthur B. 'The Problem of Counsel in *Mum and the Sothsegger*,' *Studies in the Renaissance* 2 (1955), 67–83.

—— *The Articulate Citizen and the English Renaissance* (Durham, N.C., 1965).

Ferris, Sumner. 'Chronicle, Chivalric Biography, and Family Tradition in Fourteenth-Century England,' in *Chivalric Literature. Essays on relations between literature and life in the later Middle Ages*, ed. Larry D. Benson and John Leyerle (Kalamazoo, Mich., 1980), pp. 25–38.

Fewster, Carol. *Traditionality and Genre in Middle English Romance* (Cambridge, 1987).

Fichte, Jörg O. 'The Middle English Arthurian Romance: the Popular Tradition in the Fourteenth Century,' in *Literature in Fourteenth-Century England. The J. A. W.*

Bennett Memorial Lectures, Perugia, 1981–82, ed. Piero Boitani and Anna Torti (Cambridge, 1983), 137–53.

Field, P.J.C. 'A Reading of *Sir Gawain and the Green Knight,*' *Studies in Philology* 68 (1971), 225–69.

Field, Rosalind. 'The Anglo-Norman Background to Alliterative Romance,' in David Lawton, ed., *Middle English Alliterative Poetry,* pp. 54–69.

———— 'Romance as history, history as romance,' in Mills, Fellows, Meale, ed., *Medieval Romance in England,* pp. 163–73.

Finlayson, John. '*Ywain and Gawain* and the Meaning of Adventure,' *Anglia* 87 (1969), 312–37.

———— 'The Expectations of Romance in *Sir Gawain and the Green Knight,*' *Genre* 12 (1979), 1–24.

———— 'Definitions of Middle English Romance,' *Chaucer Review* 15 (1980), 44–62, 168–81.

———— '*Richard, Coer de Lyon*: Romance, History or Something in Between?,' *Studies in Philology* 87 (1990), 156–80.

Fisher, John H. *John Gower, Moral Philosopher and Friend of Chaucer* (London, 1965).

———— 'Chancery and the Emergence of Standard Written English in the Thirteenth Century,' *Speculum* 52 (1977), 870–99.

Foley, Michael. 'Gawain's Two Confessions Reconsidered,' *Chaucer Review* 9 (1974), 73–79.

Friedman, John Block. *The Monstrous Races in medieval Art and Thought* (Cambridge, Mass., 1981).

Fryde, E.B. and Edward Miller, ed. *Historical Studies of the English Parliament, Volume I: Origins to 1399* (Cambridge, 1970).

Fryde, Natalie. *The Tyranny and Fall of Edward II 1321–1326* (Cambridge, 1979).

Gadomski, Kenneth E. 'Narrative Style in *King Horn* and *Havelok the Dane,*' *Journal of Narrative Technique* 15 (1985), 133–45.

Ganim, John M. 'History and Consciousness in Middle English Romance,' *The Literary Review* 23 (1979–80), 481–96.

———— *Style and Consciousness in Middle English Narrative* (Princeton,1983).

Ganshof, F.L., trans. Philip Grierson. *Feudalism* (London, New York, and Toronto, 1952).

Gee, Elizabeth. 'The Lists of Knights in *Sir Gawain and The Green Knight,*' *AUMLA* 62 (1984), 171–78.

Gifford, D.J. 'Iconographical notes towards a definition of the medieval fool,' in Williams, ed., *The Fool and the Trickster,* pp. 18–35.

Gimpel, Jean. *The Medieval Machine. The Industrial Revolution of the Middle Ages* (London, 1977).

Gist, Margaret Adlum. *Love and War in the Middle English Romances* (Philadelphia, 1947).

Godefroy, Frédéric. *Dictionnaire de l'ancienne langue française* (Paris, 1884; rpr. Vaduz, 1965).

Gold, Penny Schine. *The Lady and the Virgin: Image, Attitude, and Experience in Twelfth-Century France* (Chicago and London, 1985).

Green, D.H. 'The Pathway to Adventure,' *Viator* 8 (1977), 145–88.

———— *Irony in Medieval Romance* (Cambridge, 1979).

Green, Richard Firth. *Poets and Princepleasers. Literature and the English Court in the Late Middle Ages* (Toronto, Buffalo, London, 1980).

———— 'Sir Gawain and the *Sacra Cintola,*' *English Studies in Canada* 11 (1985), 1–11.

Grigsby, John L. 'Narrative Voices in Chrétien de Troyes – A Prolegomenon to Dissection,' *Romance Philology* 32 (1978–79), 261–73.

Guddat-Figge, Gisela. *Catalogue of manuscripts containing Middle English romances* (München, 1976).

Halverson, John. '*Havelok the Dane* and Society,' *Chaucer Review* 6 (1971), 142–51.

Hamilton, Gayle K. 'The Breaking of the Troth in *Ywain and Gawain*,' *Mediaevalia* 2 (1976), 111–35.

Hamilton, J.S. *Piers Gaveston, Earl of Cornwall 1307–1312. Politics and Patronage in the Reign of Edward II* (Detroit and London, 1988).

Hanning, Robert W. '*Havelok the Dane*: Structure, Symbols, Meaning,' *Studies in Philology* 64 (1967), 586–605.

—————— *The Individual in Twelfth-Century Romance* (New Haven and London, 1977).

—————— '*Engin* in Twelfth Century Romance: an Examination of the *Roman d'Enéas* and Hue de Rotelande's *Ipomedon*,' *Yale French Studies* 51 (1974), 82–101.

—————— 'Sir Gawain and the Red Herring: The Perils of Interpretation,' in *Acts of Interpretation: The Text in its Contexts 700–1600. Essays on Medieval and Renaissance Literature In Honor of E. Talbot Donaldson*, ed. Mary J. Carruthers and Elizabeth D. Kirk (Norman, Okla., 1982), pp. 5–23.

Hansen, Elaine Tuttle. 'Hrothgar's 'sermon' in *Beowulf* as parental wisdom,' *Anglo-Saxon England* 10, ed. Peter Clemoes (Cambridge, 1982), 53–67.

Harding, Carol E. *Merlin and Legendary Romance* (New York and London, 1988).

Harrington, Norman T. 'The Problem of the Lacunae in *Ywain and Gawain*,' *Journal of English and Germanic Philology* 69 (1970), 659–65.

Harriss, G.L. 'The Formation of Parliament, 1272–1377,' in Davies and Denton, ed., *The English Parliament in the Middle Ages*, pp. 29–60.

Haskins, George L. *The Growth of English Representative Government* (Philadelphia and London, 1948).

Hauer, Stanley R. 'Richard Cœur de Lion: Cavalier or Cannibal?,' *Mississippi Folklore Register* 14 (1980), 88–95.

Haymes, Edward R, ed. *The Medieval Court in Europe*, Houston German Studies 6 (München, 1986).

Heffernan, Thomas J. ed. *The Popular Literature of Medieval England*, Tennessee Studies in Literature 28 (Knoxville, 1985).

Hibbard Laura A. (Mrs. Laura Hibbard Loomis). *Mediæval Romance in England. A Study of the sources and analogues of the non-cyclic metrical romances. New Edition with Supplementary Bibliographical Index* (1926–1959) (New York, 1963).

Hill, Thomas D. 'Gawain's Jesting Lie: Towards an Interpretation of the Confessional Scene in *Sir Gawain and the Green Knight*,' *Studia Neophilogica* 52 (1980), 279–86.

Hoffman, Dean A. ' "After Bale Cometh Boote": Narrative Symmetry in the *Tale of Gamelyn*,' *Studia Neophilologica* 60 (1988), 159–66.

Holland, William E. 'Formulaic Diction and the Descent of a Middle English Romance,' *Speculum* 48 (1973), 89–109.

Holmes, George. *The Good Parliament* (Oxford, 1975).

Holt, J.C. 'The Prehistory of Parliament,' in Davies and Denton, ed., *The English Parliament in the Middle Ages*, pp. 1–28.

Holthausen, F. 'Zur erklärung und textkritik der me. romanze "Sir Tristrem",' *Anglia* 39 (1916), 373–83.

Hopkins, Andrea. *The Sinful Knights. A Study of Middle English Penitential Romance* (Oxford, 1990).

Hornstein, Lillian Herlands. 'Middle English Romances,' in Severs, ed., *Recent Middle English Scholarship and Criticism*, pp. 55–95.

Hosington, Brenda. 'The Englishing of the Comic Technique in Hue de Rotelande's

Ipomedon,' in *Medieval Translators and Their Craft,* ed. Jeanette Beer, (Kalamazoo, Mich. , 1989), pp. 247–63.

Howard, Donald R. '*Sir Gawain and the Green Knight,*' in Severs, ed., *Recent Middle English Scholarship and Criticism,* pp. 29–54.

Howard, Donald R., and Christian K. Zacher, ed. *Critical Studies of Sir Gawain and the Green Knight* (Notre Dame and London, 1968).

Hughes, Derek W. 'The Problem of Reality in *Sir Gawain and the Green Knight,*' *University of Toronto Quarterly* 40 (1971), 217–35.

Hudson, Harriet. 'Middle English Popular Romances: The Manuscript Evidence,' *Manuscripta* 28 (1984), 67–78.

—— 'Toward a Theory of Popular Literature: The Case of the Middle English Romances,' *Journal of Popular Culture* 23 (1989), 31–50.

Hume, Kathryn. 'Middle English Romance: a perdurable pattern,' *College English* 36 (1974), 129–46.

—— 'The Formal Nature of Middle English Romance,' *Philological Quarterly* 53 (1974), 158–60.

Hunt, Tony. 'Gawain's Fault and the Moral Perspectives of *Sir Gawain and the Green Knight,*' *Trivium* 10 (1975), 1–18.

—— 'Irony and Ambiguity in *Sir Gawain and the Green Knight,*' *Forum for Modern Language Studies* 12 (1976), 1–16.

—— 'Chrestien de Troyes: The Textual Problem,' *French Studies* 33 (1979), 257–71.

—— 'The Emergence of the Knight in France and England 1000–1200,' *Forum for Modern Language Studies* 17 (1981), 93–114.

—— 'Beginnings, Middles, and Ends: Some Interpretative Problems in Chrétien's *Yvain* and Its Medieval Adaptations,' in Arrathoon, ed., *The Craft of Fiction,* pp. 83–117.

Hynes-Berry, Mary. 'Cohesion in *King Horn* and *Sir Orfeo,*' *Speculum* 50 (1975), 652–70.

Ihle, Sandra, 'The English *Partonope of Blois* as Exemplum,' in Busby and Kooper, ed., *Courtly Literature: Culture and Context,* pp. 301–11.

Jack, George B. 'The Date of *Havelok,*' *Anglia* 95 (1977), 20–33.

Jacobs, Nicolas. 'Gawain's False Confession,' *English Studies* 51 (1970), 433–45.

—— '*Sir Degarré, Lay le Freine, Beves of Hamtoun* and the "Auchinleck Bookshop",' *Notes and Queries* 227 (1982), 294–301.

—— 'The Lost Conclusion of the Auchinleck *Sir Degarre,*' *Notes and Queries* 235 (1990), 154–58.

Jaeger, G. Stephen. *The Origins of Courtliness: civilizing trends and the formation of courtly ideals, 939–1210* (Philadelphia, 1985).

Jaunzems, John. 'Structure and Meaning in the *Seven Sages of Rome,*' in Niedzielski, Runte, Hendrickson, ed., *Studies on the Seven Sages of Rome,* pp. 43–62.

Jennings, Margaret, C.S.J. ' "Heavens defend me from that Welsh Fairy" (*Merry Wives of Windsor,* V,5,85): the Metamorphosis of Morgain le Fee in the Romances,' in Burgess, ed., *Court and Poet,* pp. 197–205.

Jensen, Sonya, 'Merlin: Ambrosius and Silvester,' in *Words and Wordsmiths: a volume for H.L. Rogers,* ed. Geraldine Barnes, John Gunn, Sonya Jensen, Lee Jobling (Sydney, 1989), pp. 45–48.

Jewell, Helen M. 'The cultural interests and achievements of the secular personnel of the local administration,' in *Profession, Vocation, and Culture. Essays dedicated to the memory of A. R. Myers* ed. Cecil H. Clough (Liverpool, 1982), pp. 130–54.

Johnson, Lynn Staley. *The Voice of the Gawain-Poet* (Madison, Wis., and London, 1984).

────── 'Inverse Counsel: Contexts for the *Melibee*,' *Studies in Philology* 87 (1990), 137–55.

Jonassen, Frederick B. 'Elements from the Traditional Drama of England in *Sir Gawain and the Green Knight*,' *Viator* 17 (1986), 221–54.

Jones, Richard H. *The Royal Policy of Richard II: Absolutism in the Middle Ages* (Oxford, 1968).

Jonin, Pierre. *Prolégomènes à une édition d'Yvain* (Aix-en-Provence, 1958).

Kaeuper, Richard W. 'Law and Order in Fourteenth-Century England: The Evidence of Special Commissions of Oyer and Terminer,' *Speculum* 54 (1979), 734–84.

────── 'An Historian's Reading of *The Tale of Gamelyn*,' *Medium Ævum* 52 (1983), 51–62.

────── *War, Justice, and Public Order. England and France in the Later Middle Ages* (Oxford, 1988).

Kane, George. *Middle English Literature. A Critical Study of the Romances, the Religious Lyrics, Piers Plowman* (London, 1951).

Kaske, R.E. 'Sapientia et Fortitudo as the Controlling Theme of *Beowulf*,' *Studies in Philology* 55 (1958), 423–56; (rpr. in Nicholson, ed., *An Anthology of Beowulf Criticism*, pp. 269–316).

Kean, P.M. 'Christmas Games: Verbal Ironies and Ambiguities in *Sir Gawain and the Green Knight*,' *Poetica* (Tokyo) 11 (1979), 9–27.

Keen, Maurice. *The Outlaws of Medieval Legend* (London, 1961; rev. edn., 1977).

────── *Chivalry* (New Haven and London, 1984).

────── *English Society in the Later Middle Ages 1348–1500* (London, 1990).

Kelly, Douglas. 'Fortune and Narrative Proliferation in the *Berinus*,' *Speculum* 51 (1976), 6–22.

────── 'Motif and Structure as Amplification of Topoi in the *Sept Sages de Rome* Prose Cycle,' in Niedzielski, Runte, Hendrickson, ed., *Studies on the Seven Sages of Rome*, pp. 133–54.

Kelly, Henry Ansgar. 'The Varieties of Love in Medieval Literature According to Gaston Paris,' *Romance Philology* 40 (1986–87), 301–27.

Kennedy, Edward D. 'Sir Orfeo as *Rex Inutilis*,' *Annuale Medievale* 17 (1976), 88–110.

Keynes, Simon. 'The declining reputation of King Æthelred the Unready,' in David Hill, ed., *Ethelred the Unready: papers from the Millenary Conference* (Oxford, 1978), pp. 227–53.

Kieckhefer, Richard. *Magic in the Middle Ages* (Cambridge, 1989; rpr. 1990).

Kindrick, Robert L. 'Gawain's Ethics: Shame and Guilt in *Sir Gawain and the Green Knight*,' *Annuale Medievale* 20 (1980), 5–32.

King, R.W. 'A Note on 'Sir Gawayn and the Green Knight', 2414 ff.,' *Modern Language Review* 29 (1934), 435–46.

Klausner, David N. 'Didacticism and Drama in *Guy of Warwick*,' *Medievalia et Humanistica*, n.s.6 (1975), 103–19.

Knight, Stephen. 'The Social Function of the Middle English Romances,' in *Medieval Literature. Criticism, Ideology & History*, ed. David Aers (Brighton, 1986), pp. 99–122.

Koff, Leonard Michael. *Chaucer and the Art of Storytelling* (Berkeley and Los Angeles, 1988).

Köhler, Erich. *L'aventure chevaleresque. Idéal et réalité dans le roman courtois. Études sur la forme des plus anciens poèmes d'Arthur et du Graal*, translated from the German by Eliane Kaufholz (Paris, 1974).

Kratins, Ojars. 'Treason in Middle English Metrical Romances,' *Philological Quarterly* 45 (1966), 668–87.

Krueger, Roberta L. 'The Author's Voice: Narrators, Audiences, and the Problem of Interpretation,' in Lacy, Douglas, and Busby, ed., *The Legacy of Chrétien de Troyes*, I, 115–40.

—— 'Misogyny, Manipulation, and the Female Reader in Hue de Rotelande's *Ipomedon*,' in Busby and Kooper, ed., *Courtly Literature: Culture and Context*, pp. 395–409.

Labarge, Margaret Wade. *A Baronial Household of the Thirteenth Century* (New York, 1965).

Lacy, Norris J. *The Craft of Chrétien de Troyes. An Essay in Narrative Art* (Leiden, 1980).

—— 'The Typology of Arthurian Romance,' in Lacy, Kelly, Busby, ed., *The Legacy of Chrétien de Troyes*, I, 33–56.

Lacy, Norris J., Douglas Kelly, and Keith Busby, ed. *The Legacy of Chrétien de Troyes*, 2 vols. (Amsterdam, 1987–88).

Lane, Roland. 'A critical review of the major studies of the relationship betwen the Old French *Floire et Blancheflor* and its Germanic adaptations,' *Nottingham Medieval Studies* 30 (1986), 1–19.

Lapsley, Gaillard. 'Archbishop Stratford and the Parliamentary Crisis of 1341,' *English Historical Review* 30 (1915), 6–18; 193–215.

Lattimore, Richmond. 'The Wise Adviser in Herodotus,' *Classical Philology* 34 (1939), 24–35.

Lawton, David A. 'The Unity of Middle English Alliterative Poetry,' *Speculum* 58 (1983), 72–94.

—— ed., *Middle English Alliterative Poetry and Its Literary Background. Seven Essays* (Cambridge, 1982).

Legge, M. Dominica. *Anglo-Norman Literature and Its Background* (Oxford, 1963).

Lepow, Lauren. 'The Contrasted Courts in *Sir Gawain and the Green Knight*,' in Haymes, ed., *The Medieval Court in Europe*, pp. 200–08.

Lerer, Seth. 'Artifice and Artistry in *Sir Orfeo*,' *Speculum* 60 (1985), 92–109.

Lewis, N.B. 'Re-election to Parliament in the Reign of Richard II,' *English Historical Review* 48 (1933), 364–94.

Leyerle, John. 'The Game and Play of Hero,' in *Concepts of the Hero in the Middle Ages and Early Renaissance*, ed. Norman Burns and Christopher Reagan (Albany, N.Y., 1975), pp. 49–82.

Loomis, Laura Hibbard. 'Chaucer and Auchinleck Manuscript: *Thopas* and *Guy of Warwick*,' in *Essays and Studies in Honor of Carleton Brown* (New York, 1940), pp. 111–28.

—— 'Chaucer and the Breton Lays of the Auchinleck Manuscript,' *Studies in Philology* 38 (1941), 14–33.

—— 'The Auchinleck Manuscript and a Possible London Bookshop of 1330–1340,' *Publications of the Modern Language Association* 57 (1942), 595–627.

—— '*Gawain and the Green Knight*,' in *Arthurian Literature in the Middle Ages: A Collaborative History*, ed. Roger Sherman Loomis (Oxford, 1959), pp. 528–40 (rpr. in Howard and Zacher, ed., *Critical Studies of Sir Gawain and the Green Knight*, pp. 3–23).

Lot-Borodine, Myrrha. *Le Roman idyllique au moyen âge* (Paris, 1913; rpr. Geneva, 1972).

Lumiansky, R.M. 'Thematic Antifeminism in the Middle English *Seven Sages of Rome*,' *Tulane Studies in English* 7 (1957), 5–16.

Lynch, Andrew. ' "Now, fye on youre wepynge!": tears in medieval English romance,' *Parergon*, n.s.9, 1 (1991), 43–62.

McAlindon, T. 'Comedy and Terror in Middle English Literature: The Diabolical Game,' *Modern Language Review* 60 (1965), 323–32.

——— 'The Emergence of a Comic Type in Middle English Narrative: the Devil and Giant as Buffoon,' *Anglia* 81 (1963), 365–71.

McGillivray, Murray. *Memorization in the Transmission of the Middle English Romances* (New York and London, 1990).

McKisack, May. *The Fourteenth Century, 1307–1399* (Oxford, 1959).

——— *The Parliamentary Representation of the English Boroughs During the Middle Ages* (Oxford, 1932; rpr. 1962).

Maddicott, J.R. 'Parliament and the Constituencies 1272–1377,' in Davies and Denton, ed., *The English Parliament in the Middle Ages*, pp. 61–87.

——— 'The County Community and the Making of Public Opinion in Fourteenth-Century England,' *Transactions of the Royal Historical Society*, 5th series, 28 (1978), 27–43.

——— *Thomas of Lancaster 1307–1322. A Study in the Reign of Edward II 1321–1326* (Cambridge, 1979).

Marchalonis, Shirley. 'Above Rubies: Popular Views of Medieval Women,' *Journal of Popular Culture* 14 (1980), 87–93.

Margeson, Robert W. 'Structure and Meaning in *Sir Gawain and the Green Knight*,' *Papers on Language and Literature* 13 (1977), 16–24.

Meale, Carol. 'The Middle English Romance of *Ipomedon*: A Late Medieval 'Mirror' for Princes and Merchants,' *Reading Medieval Studies* 10 (1984), 136–91.

Mehl, Dieter. *The Middle English Romances of the Thirteenth and Fourteenth Centuries* (London, 1968).

Metlitzki, Dorothee. *The Matter of Araby in Medieval England* (New Haven and London, 1977).

Ménard, Philippe. 'Les fous dans la société médiévale. Le témoignage de la littérature au XIIe et au XIIe siècle,' *Romania* 98 (1977), 433–59.

Menkin, Edward Z. 'Comic Irony and the Sense of Two Audiences in the *Tale of Gamelyn*,' *Thoth* (Winter 1969), pp. 41–53.

Mertes, Kate. *The English Noble Household 1250–1600. Good Governance and Politic Rule* (Oxford, 1988).

Middle English Dictionary. ed. Hans Kurath, *et al.* (Ann Arbor, 1956–).

Middleton, Anne. 'The Idea of Public Poetry in the Reign of Richard II,' *Speculum* 53 (1978), 94–114.

Miller, Edward. *The Origins of Parliament* (London, 1960).

Miller, William Ian, *Bloodtaking and Peacemaking. Feud, Law, and Society in Saga Iceland* (Chicago and London, 1990).

Mills, Maldwyn. 'Havelok's Return,' *Medium Ævum* 45 (1976), 20–35.

——— 'Havelok and the Brutal Fisherman,' *Medium Ævum* 36 (1967), 219–30.

Mills, Maldwyn, Jennifer Fellows and Carol M. Meale, ed. *Romance in Medieval England* (Cambridge, 1991).

Mohl, Ruth. 'Theories of Monarchy in *Mum and the Sothsegger*,' *Publications of the Modern Language Association* 59 (1944), 26–44.

Moores, Elizabeth. 'MS Milan Ambrosianus I. 64 and medieval perceptions of similitude,' *Parergon*, n.s.7 (1989), 77–89.

Morgan, Gerald. 'The Validity of Gawain's Confession in *Sir Gawain and the Green Knight*,' *Review of English Studies*, n.s. 36 (1985), 1–18.

Muscatine, Charles. 'The Emergence of Psychological Allegory in the Old French Romance,' *Publications of the Modern Language Association* 68 (1953), 1160–82.

——— *Poetry and Crisis in the Age of Chaucer* (Notre Dame, 1972).

Nicholls, J.W. *The Matter of Courtesy. A Study of Medieval Courtesy Books and the Gawain-Poet* (Woodbridge and Dover, N.H., 1985).

Nicholson, Lewis E., ed. *An Anthology of Beowulf Criticism* (Notre Dame, 1963).

Nicholson, R.H. 'Sir Orfeo: a "Kynges noote",' Review of English Studies 36 (1985), 161–79.

Niedzielski, H., H.R. Runte and W.L. Hendrickson, ed. Studies on the Seven Sages of Rome and Other Essays in Medieval Literature: Dedicated to the Memory of Jean Misrahi (Honolulu, 1978).

Nitze, William A. 'Is the Green Knight Story a Vegetation Myth?,' Modern Philology 33 (1935–36), 351–66.

Nykrog, Per. 'The Rise of Literary Fiction,' in Renaissance and Renewal in the Twelfth Century, ed. Robert L. Benson and Giles Constable, (Cambridge, Mass., 1982), pp. 593–611.

Oleson, Tryggvi J. The Witenagemot in the Reign of Edward the Confessor. A Study in the Constitutional History of Eleventh-Century England (London, 1955).

Owen, D.D.R. 'Burlesque Tradition and Sir Gawain and the Green Knight,' Forum for Modern Language Studies 4 (1968), 125–45.

Packe, Michael, ed. L.C.B. Seaman, Edward III (London and Boston, 1983).

Patterson, Lee. Negotiating the Past. The Historical Understanding of Medieval Literature (Madison, Wis., 1987).

————— ' "What Man Artow"? Authorial Self-Definition in The Tale of Sir Thopas and The Tale of Melibee,' Studies in the Age of Chaucer 11 (1989), 117–75.

Pearsall, Derek. 'The Development of Middle English Romance,' Mediaeval Studies 27 (1965), 91–116 (rpr. in Brewer, ed., Studies in Medieval English Romances, pp. 11–35).

————— 'The English romance in the fifteenth century,' Essays and Studies 29 (1976), 56–83.

————— 'Middle English Romance and its Audiences,' in Historical & Editorial Studies in Medieval and Early Modern English for Johan Gerritsen, ed. Mary-Jo Arn and Hanneke Wirtjes, with Hans Jansen (Groningen, 1985), pp. 37–47.

Pearsall, D.A., and R.A. Waldron, ed., Medieval Literature and Civilization. Studies in Memory of G.N. Garmonsway (London, 1969).

Perryman, Judith. 'Decapitating Drama in Sir Gawain and the Green Knight,' The Dutch Quarterly Review of Anglo-American Letters 8 (1978), 283–300.

Pickford, Cedric E. 'Sir Tristrem, Sir Walter Scott and Thomas,' in Rothwell, Barron, Blamires, Thorpe, ed., Studies in Medieval Literature and Languages in memory of Frederick Whitehead, pp. 219–28.

Platt, Colin. The English Medieval Town (London, 1976).

Plucknett, Theodore F.T., 'Parliament', in The English Government at Work, 1327–1336, ed. J.F. Willard and W.A. Morris, I (Cambridge, Mass., 1940), pp. 82–128; (rpr. in Fryde and Miller, ed., Historical Studies of the English Parliament, Volume I: Origins to 1399, pp. 195–241).

Powicke, M.R. 'Distraint of Knighthood and Military Obligation under Henry III,' Speculum 25 (1950), 547–70.

Pratt, Karen. 'The Rhetoric of Adapatation: The Middle Dutch and Middle High German Versions of Floire et Blancheflor,' in Busby and Kooper, ed., Courtly Literature, Culture and Context, pp. 483–97.

Prestwich, Michael. The Three Edwards. War and State in England 1272–1377 (New York, 1980).

————— Edward I (Berkeley and Los Angeles, 1988).

Price (Wogan-Browne), Jocelyn. 'Floire et Blancheflor: the Magic and Mechanics of Love,' Reading Medieval Studies 8 (1982), 12–33.

Quinn, William A., and Audley S. Hall, Jongleur. A Modified Theory of Oral Improvisation and Its Effects on the Performance and Transmission of Middle English Romance (Washington, D.C., 1982).

Ramsey, Lee C. *Chivalric Romance. Popular Literature in Medieval England* (Blooming-ton, 1983).

Randall, Dale B.J. 'Was the Green Knight a Fiend?,' *Studies in Philology* 57 (1960), 479–91.

Rawcliffe, Carole. 'Baronial Councils in the Later Middle Ages,' in *Patronage, Pedigree and Power in Later Medieval England*, ed. Charles Ross (Gloucester and Totowa, N.J., 1979), 87–108.

Reed, Thomas L., Jr. ' "Bothe blysse and blunder": *Sir Gawain and the Green Knight* and the Debate Tradition,' *Chaucer Review* 23 (1988), 140–61.

Reid, Wendy M. 'The Drama of *Sir Gawain and the Green Knight*,' *Parergon* 20 (1978), 11–23.

Reinhold, Joachim. *Floire et Blancheflor: étude de littérature comparée* (Paris, 1906; rpr. Geneva, 1970).

Reiss, Edmund. 'Romance,' in Heffernan, ed., *The Popular Literature of Medieval England*, pp. 108–30.

Rice, Joanne A. *Middle English Romance: An Annotated Bibliography 1955–85* (New York, 1986).

Richardson, H.G., and G.O. Sayles. *The Governance of Medieval England from the Conquest to Magna Carta* (Edinburgh, 1963).

Richmond, Velma Bourgeois. '*Guy of Warwick*: A Medieval Thriller,' *South Atlantic Quarterly* 73 (1974), 554–63.

——— *The Popularity of Middle English Romance* (Bowling Green, Ohio, 1975).

Rickert, Edith. 'King Richard II's Books,' *The Library (Transactions of the Bibliographical Society)* 13 (1932–33), 144–47.

Rider, Jeff. 'The Fictional Margin: The Merlin of the *Brut*,' *Modern Philology* 87 (1989), 1–12.

Robertson, D.W., Jr. 'Who Were "The People"?,' in Heffernan, ed., *The Popular Literature of Medieval England*, pp. 3–29.

Rogers, Katharine. *The Troublesome Helpmate. A History of Misogyny in Literature* (Seattle and London, 1966).

Roskell, J.S. *Parliament and Politics in Late Medieval England*, 3 Vols. (London, 1981–85).

Rosenberg, Bruce A. 'The Morphology of the Middle English Metrical Romance,' *Journal of Popular Culture* 1 (1967), 63–77.

Rothwell, W., W.R.J. Barron, David Blamires, Lewis Thorpe, ed., *Studies in Medieval Literature and Languages in memory of Frederick Whitehead* (Manchester, 1973).

Rumble, Thomas C. 'The Middle English *Sir Tristrem*: Toward a Reappraisal,' *Comparative Literature* 11 (1959), 221–28.

Runte, Hans R., J. Keith Wikeley, Anthony J. Farrell. *The Seven Sages of Rome and the Book of Sindbad. An Analytical Bibliography* (New York and London, 1984).

Ruthrof, Horst J. 'The Dialectic of Aggression and Reconciliation in the *Tale of Gamelyn*, Thomas Lodge's *Rosalynde* and Shakespeare's *As You Like It*,' *University of Cape Town Studies in English* 4 (1973), 1–15.

Saenger, Paul. 'Silent Reading: Its Impact on Late Medieval Script and Society,' *Viator* 13 (1982), 367–414.

Saul, Nigel. *Scenes from Provincial Life: Knightly Families in Sussex, 1280–1400* (Oxford, 1986).

——— *Knights and Esquires. The Gloucestershire Gentry in the Fourteenth Century* (Oxford, 1981).

Sayles, G. O. *The Functions of the Medieval Parliament of England* (London and Ronceverte, 1988).

Scattergood, V.J. 'Sir Gawain and the Green Knight and the Sins of the Flesh,' Traditio 37 (1981), 347–71.

——— 'Literary Culture at the Court of Richard II,' in Scattergood and Sherborne, ed., English Court Culture in the Later Middle Ages, pp. 29–43.

Scattergood, V.J. and J.W. Sherborne, ed., English Court Culture in the Later Middle Ages (London, 1983).

Schelp, Hanspeter. Exemplarische Romanzen im Mittelenglischen (Göttingen, 1967).

Schücking, Levin L. 'Das Königsideal im Beowulf,' Englische Studien 67 (1932), 1–14 (rpr. in English translation in Nicholson, ed., An Anthology of Beowulf Criticism, pp. 35–49).

Scott, Anne. 'Plans, Predictions, and Promises: Traditional Story Techniques and the Configuration of Word and Deed in King Horn,' in Brewer, ed., Studies in Medieval English Romances, pp. 37–68.

Severs, J. Burke, ed. A Manual of the Writings in Middle English 1050–1500, I, (New Haven, 1967).

——— ed. Recent Middle English Scholarship and Criticism: Survey and Desiderata (Pittsburgh, 1971).

Shannon, Edgar F., Jr. 'Mediaeval Law in The Tale of Gamelyn,' Speculum 26 (1951), 458–64.

Sherborne, J.W. 'Aspects of English Court Culture in the Later Fourteenth Century,' in Scattergood and Sherborne, ed., English Court Culture in the Later Middle Ages, pp. 1–27.

Sherwood, Merriam. 'Magic and Mechanics in Medieval Fiction,' Studies in Philology 44 (1947), 567–92.

Shonk, Timothy A. 'A Study of the Auchinleck Manuscript: Bookmen and Bookmaking in the Early Fourteenth Century,' Speculum 60 (1985), 71–91.

Silverstein, Theodore. 'Sir Gawain, Dear Brutus, and Britain's Fortunate Founding: A Study in Comedy and Convention,' Modern Philology 62 (1965), 189–206.

Simons, John. 'Northern Octavian and the question of class,' in Mills, Fellows, Meale, ed., Medieval Romance in England, pp. 105–11.

Sklar, Elizabeth S. 'Arthour and Merlin: The Englishing of Arthur,' Michigan Academician 8 (1975), 49–57.

Sklute, Larry. 'The Ambiguity of Ethical Norms in Courtly Romance,' Genre 11 (1978), 315–32.

Smith, J.B. 'Konrad Fleck's Floire und Blanschesflûr and the Old Norse Flóres saga ok Blankiflúr,' unpubl. Univ. of Manchester M.A. thesis (1955).

Smithers, G.V. 'The Style of Hauelok,' Medium Ævum 57 (1988), 190–218.

Southern, R.W. The Making of the Middle Ages (London, 1953).

Southworth, John. The English Medieval Minstrel (Woodbridge and Wolfeboro, N.H., 1989).

Spearing, A.C. The Gawain-Poet. A Critical Study (Cambridge, 1970).

——— 'Central and Displaced Sovereignty in Three Medieval Poems,' Review of English Studies n.s. 131 (1982), 247–61.

——— Readings in Medieval Poetry (Cambridge, 1987).

——— 'Secrecy, listening, and telling in The Squyr of Lowe Degre,' Journal of Medieval and Renaissance Studies 20 (1990), 273–92.

Speed, Diane. Gower's Narrative Technique as revealed by his adaptations of source material in the tales of 'Confessio Amantis', unpubl. Univ. of London PhD. thesis (1970).

——— 'The Saracens of King Horn,' Speculum 65 (1990), 564–95.

Speirs, John. 'Sir Gawain and the Green Knight,' Scrutiny 16 (1949), 274–300 (rpr. in *idem, Medieval English Poetry: The Non-Chaucerian Tradition* [London, 1957], pp. 215–51).

Spiegel, Gabrielle M. 'History, Historicism, and the Social Logic of the Text in the Middle Ages,' *Speculum* 65 (1990), 59–86.

Staines, David. '*Havelok the Dane*: A Thirteenth-Century Handbook for Princes,' *Speculum* 51 (1976), 601–23.

Starkey, David. 'The age of the household: politics, society and the arts in *c.*1350–*c.*1550,' in *The Later Middle Ages*, ed Stephen Medcalf (New York, 1981), pp. 225–90.

Steel, Anthony. *Richard II* (Cambridge, 1941).

Stevens, John. *Medieval Romance. Themes and Approaches* (New York, 1973).

Stevens, Martin. 'Laughter and Game in *Sir Gawain and the Green Knight*,' *Speculum* 47 (1972), 65–78.

——— 'The Performing Self in Twelfth-Century Culture,' *Viator* 9 (1978), 193–212.

Stillwell, Gardiner, 'The Political Meaning of Chaucer's *Tale of Melibee*,' *Speculum* 19 (1944), 433–44.

Stokes, Myra. '*Sir Gawain and the Green Knight*: Fitt III as Debate,' *Nottingham Medieval Studies* 25 (1981), 35–51.

Strite, Sheri Ann. '*Sir Gawain and the Green Knight*: To Behead or Not to Behead – That *is* a Question,' *Philological Quarterly* 70 (1991), 1–12.

Strohm, Paul. 'The Origin and Meaning of Middle English *Romaunce*,' *Genre* 10 (1977), 1–28.

——— *Social Chaucer* (Cambridge, Mass., and London, 1989).

Sturm-Maddox, Sara. 'King Arthur's prophetic fool: prospection in the *Conte du Graal*,' *Marche Romane* 29 (1979), 103–08.

Swain, Barbara. *Fools and Folly during the Middle Ages and the Renaissance* (New York, 1932).

Taylor, Andrew. 'The Myth of the Minstrel Manuscript,' *Speculum* 66 (1991), 43–73.

Taylor, John. *English Historical Literature in the Fourteenth Century* (Oxford, 1987).

Thompson, John J. 'The Compiler in Action: Robert Thornton and the 'Thornton Romances' in Lincoln Cathedral MS 91,' in Derek Pearsall, ed., *Manuscripts and Readers in Fifteenth-Century England: The Literary Implications of Manuscript Study. Essays from the 1981 Conference at the University of York* (Cambridge, 1983), pp. 113–24.

——— 'Collecting Middle English romances and some related book-production activities in the later Middle Ages,' in Mills, Fellows, Meale, ed., *Romance in Medieval England*, pp. 17–38.

Thrupp, Sylvia L. *The Merchant Class of Medieval London [1300–1500]* (Chicago, 1948).

Tolstoy, Nikolai. *The Quest for Merlin* (London, 1985).

Tolkien, J.R.R. 'Sir Gawain and the Green Knight,' in J.R.R. Tolkien, *The Monsters and the Critics and Other Essays*, ed. Christopher Tolkien (London, 1983), pp. 72–108.

Treharne, R.F. *The Baronial Plan of Reform, 1258–1263* (Manchester, 1932; rpr. with additonal material, 1971).

Turville-Petre, Thorlac. *The Alliterative Revival* (Cambridge, 1977).

Tuve, Rosamund. *Allegorical Imagery: Some Medieval Books and Their Posterity* (Princeton, 1966).

Vale, Juliet. *Edward III and Chivalry: Chivalric Society and Its Context 1270–1350* (Bury St Edmunds, 1982).

Vance, Eugene. *From Topic to Tale. Logic and Narrativity in the Middle Ages* (Minneapolis, 1987).

Vaneman, Karen Haslanger. *Interpreting the Middle English Romance: The Audience in Of Arthour and of Merlin,* unpubl. Wayne State University PhD. diss. (1986).

Veldhoen, N.H.G.E. and H. Aertsen, ed. *Companion to Early Middle English Literature* (Amsterdam, 1988).

Warner, Marina. *Alone of All Her Sex. The Myth and The Cult of the Virgin Mary* (New York, 1976).

Warren, W.L. *The Governance of Norman and Angevin England 1086–1272* (Stanford, 1987).

Watts, J.L. 'The Counsels of King Henry VI, c. 1435–1445,' *The English Historical Review* 106 (1991), 279–98.

Waugh, S.L. 'The Profits of Violence: The Minor Gentry in the Rebellion of 1321–1322 in Gloucestershire and Herefordshire,' *Speculum* 52 (1977), 843–69.

—— *England in the reign of Edward III* (Cambridge, 1991).

Weiss, Judith. 'Structure and Characterisation in *Havelok the Dane*,' *Speculum* 44 (1969), 247–57.

—— 'The Auchinleck MS and the Edwardes MSS,' *Notes and Queries* 214 (1969), 444–46.

—— 'The Major Interpolations in *Sir Beues of Hamtoun*,' *Medium Ævum* 48 (1979), 71–76.

—— 'The Date of the Anglo-Norman *Boeve de Haumtone*,' *Medium Ævum* 55 (1986), 237–40.

—— 'The wooing woman in Anglo-Norman romance,' in Mills, Fellows, Meale, ed., *Medieval Romance in England*, pp. 149–61.

Weiss, Victoria L. 'The "laykyng of enterludez" at King Arthur's Court: The Beheading Scene in *Sir Gawain and the Green Knight*,' in Haymes, ed., *The Medieval Court in Europe*, pp. 189–99.

Welsford, Enid. *The Court Masque. A Study in the Relationship Between Poetry and the Revels* (Cambridge, 1927).

—— *The Fool. His Social and Literary History* (New York, 1961).

West, C.B. *Courtoisie in Anglo-Norman Literature* (Oxford, 1938).

Wilkinson, B. *Studies in the Constitutional History of the Thirteenth and Fourteenth Centuries* (Manchester, 1937; 2nd edn., 1952).

Willeford, William. *The Fool and His Scepter: A Study in Clowns and Jesters and Their Audience* (Evanston, Ill. , 1969).

Williams, Edith Whitehurst. 'Morgan La Fee as Trickster in *Sir Gawain and the Green Knight*,' *Folklore* 96 (1985), 38–56.

Williams, Paul V.A. *The Fool and the Trickster. Studies in honour of Enid Welsford* (Cambridge and Totowa, N.J., 1979).

Wilson, R.M. *The Lost Literature of Medieval England*, 2nd revised edn. (London, 1970).

Wimsatt, W.J. *Allegory and Mirror: Tradition and Structure in Middle English Literature* (New York, 1970).

Wittig, Susan. *Stylistic and narrative structures in the Middle English Romances* (Austin and London, 1978).

Wood-Legh, K.L. 'The Knights' Attendance in the Parliaments of Edward III,' *English Historical Review* 47 (1932), 398–413.

Young, Charles R. *The Royal Forests of Medieval England* (Philadelphia, 1979).

INDEX

Ælfric, Abbot of Eynsham x
  De XII abusivis x
Æthelred, the Unready 6, 58
Against the king's taxes 5, 9
Alexander, the Great 99, 100, 103, 104,
  105
Alexis, Saint 68
Alisaunder, King (in *Kyng Alisaunder*)
  15, 17, 99–104, 108, 111, 113, 124
Allen, Rosamund 22, 26, 27n
Amis and Amiloun 20n, 52n, 60
'ancestral romance' xii
Andrew, Malcolm 134n, 137n
Anglo-Saxon Chronicle 6
Anglo-Norman romance (*See also* insular
  romance) xii, 17, 26
Anonimalle Chronicle 4
Aristotle 15, 99, 103
Arthour and of Merlin, Of xii, 14, 20n, 60,
  61, 62–67, 90, 94n
Arthur, King 49, 99, 100, 104; (in *Ywain
  and Gawain:*) 34, 36, 39; (in *Of Arthour
  and of Merlin*) 62–63, 65–67; (in *Sir
  Gawain and the Green Knight*) 95n,
  124–27, 135–36
Aspin, Isabel 56n
Astill, G.G. 26n
Athelston xi, 13, 14, 15, 16, 17, 24, 29, 30,
  32, 52–59, 61, 86–87, 90, 92, 95, 120, 135
Athelston, King (in *Athelston*) 14, 53–59,
  87, 90
Athelwold, King (in *Havelok*) 14, 41–42,
  46, 80
Auchinleck MS (National Library of Scotland Advocates' MS 19.2.1.) xi, 13, 19,
  20, 27, 60–61, 63n, 73n, 91, 97n, 105,
  108, 113, 116, 120, 122n
aventure 48, 49
Baldwin, James Fosdick 1, 2n, 52n
Bannockburn, Battle of 7
Baronial reform movement (1258–67) 3, 7
barons (magnates of England) xi, 1–2, 5–
  8
Barron, W.R.J. 74n
Bateman, William, Bishop of Norwich
  56n
Bedwynd, John 12

Bellamy, John 48n
Bennett, Michael 125n
Beowulf x
Beowulf 31
Beves (in *Beves of Hamtoun*) 15, 17, 18,
  30, 50, 82–90, 97, 98, 104, 137
Beves of Hamtoun xii, 13, 14, 16, 17, 18,
  20, 24, 27, 32n, 49, 58–59, 60, 61, 67, 81–
  90, 93, 95, 100, 105, 106, 108, 111, 122
blasme des femmes tradition 17
Blanchefleur (in *Floire et Blancheflor*) 112
Blauncheflur (in *Floris and Blauncheflur*)
  113–15
Bloch, R. Howard 31n
Boeve d'Hamtoune xii, 18n, 81, 86, 88n
Boitani, Piero 117n
Book of the Knight of La Tour Landry ix
Bracton, Henry of xi n, 41n
  De Legibus et Consuetudinis Angliae
  xi n, 41n
Broughton, Bradford B. 105n, 109n
Brown, R. Allen 7n
Brunner, Karl 22n, 105n
burgesses xii, 4–5, 11, 24
Burrow, J.A. 10n, 131n
Burrows, Jean Harpham 61n, 75n
Butt, Ronald 1, 4, 8
Calin, William 77n, 88n
Cam, Helen 24, 55
Camargo, Martin 100–101n
Canterbury Tales. See Chaucer, Geoffrey
Cary, George 99n, 103n
chanson de geste xii, 29, 30, 85n, 86, 106
Charlemagne 31, 105
'Charlemagne romances' xii, 106
Chaucer, Geoffrey 10, 11, 19, 27, 46
  Canterbury Tales 46, 99
  'Cook's Prologue' 46
  'Tale of Melibee' 11, 14n
  'Tale of Sir Thopas' 27
  The Book of the Duchess 19
chivalric romance 11, 13, 136, 30, 137; (*ro-
  mans courtois*) 14, 27, 31, 136
Chrétien de Troyes ix, 14, 18, 31, 33, 34,
  36, 38n, 40, 66, 70n, 95, 96, 127, 136, 137
  Erec et Enide 31n, 96
  Li Contes del Graal x, 18n, 31n, 70n

159